Kateřina Mildn

From Where Does the Bad Wind Blow?

To professor Baker

Kateřina Mildn

ETHNOLOGIE ANTHROPOLOGY

Band / Volume 49

LIT

Kateřina Mildnerová

From Where Does the Bad Wind Blow?

Spiritual Healing and Witchcraft in Lusaka, Zambia

LIT

Cover image: © Kateřina Mildnerová, 2009.
Photo of a traditional healer, Lusaka.

This publication was made possible by a grant
from the University of Ss. Cyril and Methodius,
Faculty of Philosophy.

Academic review: Doc. PaedDr. Hana Horáková, Ph. D

**Bibliographic information published by the Deutsche
Nationalbibliothek**
The Deutsche Nationalbibliothek lists this publication in the Deutsche
Nationalbibliografie; detailed bibliographic data are available in the
Internet at http://dnb.d-nb.de.

ISBN 978-3-643-90273-3

A catalogue record for this book is available from the British Library

© **LIT VERLAG GmbH & Co. KG Wien,**
Zweigniederlassung Zürich 2015
Klosbachstr. 107
CH-8032 Zürich
Tel. +41 (0) 44-251 75 05   Fax +41 (0) 44-251 75 06
E-Mail: zuerich@lit-verlag.ch   http://www.lit-verlag.ch
Distribution:
In the UK: Global Book Marketing, e-mail: mo@centralbooks.com
In North America: International Specialized Book Services, e-mail: orders@isbs.com
In Germany: LIT Verlag Fresnostr. 2, D-48159 Münster
Tel. +49 (0) 2 51-620 32 22, Fax +49 (0) 2 51-922 60 99, E-Mail: vertrieb@lit-verlag.de

In Austria: Medienlogistik Pichler-ÖBZ, e-mail: mlo@medien-logistik.at
e-books are available at www.litwebshop.de

Acknowledgement

This book would not have been possible without the essential and gracious support of many individuals. I am most grateful to my family, especially to my mother Alena Mildnerová for providing me moral and financial support throughout my research and text production.

I would like to thank the Department of Ethnology at the University of Saint Cyril and Methodius in Trnava for funding this book. At the same time my thanks belong to the Department of Anthropology at the University of West Bohemia that enabled me to carry out my Ph.D. fieldwork in Zambia. I would like to express my deepest appreciation to Doctor Jitka Kotalová for tutoring, reading conscientiously and commenting on my drafts. Her useful advice and intellectually stimulating conversations contributed largely to the production of this monograph.

Many people from Lusaka contributed significantly to my research and greatly enhanced my pleasure in this research by providing hospitality and companionship. I am particularly obliged to my main research assistants Sikalinda Musanje, Mark Chilundo, and Samuel Musonda, who helped me with the translations from the chiNyanja; language and accompanied me throughout my rsearch. I appreciate their companionship and willingness to give me assistance whenever I asked them.

I wish to express my thanks to all my informants who were willing to share their experiences and ideas with an inquisitive stranger, who were concerned about my safety, well-being and who introduced me to their friends and colleagues and therefore enriched my research experience. I am grateful to all healers and members of the Traditional Health Practitioners Association of Zambia (THAPAZ) namely to Doctor Kadansa Sansakuwa, Doctor Joseph Mudenda, Doctor Kashita Solo, Doctor Mwale, Doctor Vongo, Doctor Sato and Irene Mwembe. Furthermore, to the healers and members of the Zambian National Council of Ng'angas (ZNCN) namely to Doctor Samson Lukwesa, Conrad Kaingu, Doctor Banda Lekani, Doctor Chembe and Doctor Aron. My appreciation belongs also to all the patients who willingly shared their experiences and patiently endured my interviews.

My deep thanks belong to all members of the New Jesus Disciples Church in the Chawama/Kuku compound, namely to Pastor J. Sinfukwe and Bishop Hector Sivimba, to prophets Lameck Phiri, Joyce Kazembe, Loveness Mbemwe and Mister Daka, for their warm welcome and helpful attitude to my research.

I apologize to all of my informants that their names were changed in the book as I had to acquit a claim of the ethics of research.

Dedicated to Otto Mildner
(1951–2008)

Table of Contents

Acknowledgement v
List of Schemas xi

Introduction 1
Book Outline 3
Notes on Research 5

1. Lusaka's Socio-Urban Context 13
Urban and Demographic Development 13
Social Structure of Compounds 19
Household and Livelihood in Compounds 22

2. Medical Culture in Lusaka 27
Medical Pluralism and "Therapy Shopping" 33
The Conceptualisation of Health and Illness 40
The Conceptualisation of Body 52
Illness Aetiology 64
Typology of Healing and Afflicting Spirits 68

3. The Figure of a Healer 73
Categories of Healers 73
The Characteristics and Role of Urban Healers 79
Biographies of Healers 83
The Relationship between Healers and Patients 95

4. Indigenous Spiritual Healing 99
Divination (Illness Diagnosis) 100
Interpretations of Dreams 108
Healing (Therapy and Prophylaxis) 114

5. Christian Spiritual Healing 129
The History of African Independent Churches in Zambia 131
Spiritual Healing in the Mutumwa Church (The Case Study of the New Jesus Disciples Church) 137
Sermon-Prayer Service 142

Healing Service *145*
Prophesying (Illness Diagnosis) *149*
Healing (Therapy and Prophylaxis) *152*

6. Spirit Possession 157
Anthropological Studies on Spirit Possession *157*
Mashabe Possession *159*
Holy Spirit Possession versus Demon Possession *165*
Possession as a Social Construction of a Healers Identity *167*

7. Witchcraft 173
Historical Context *173*
Cosmological Context *177*
Anthropological Studies on Witchcraft *178*
Local Conceptualisation of Witchcraft in Lusaka *189*
Symbolism of Witch Helpmates *198*
Witchcraft as a Theory, System and Practice *220*

Conclusion – Summary 239

Bibliography 249

Appendix I: Additional Illustrative Witchcraft Cases 271
Witchcraft case 5: Anna, Iris and Catherine *271*
Witchcraft case 6: Rebecca and Hope *274*
Witchcraft case 7: Irene *276*
Witchcraft case 8: Alice *279*

Appendix II: Witchcraft Act 283

Appendix III: Zambia Statistical Figures and Maps 289
Statistical Figures about Zambia (In the time of the research 2008–2009) *289*
List of Coumpounds in Lusaka *290*
Geographical Map of Zambia *291*
Map of Lusaka *292*

Appendix IV: Languages Spoken in Zambia 293
Language of Communication in Lusaka (in percentage) 293
ChiNyanja Language 293
Bemba Language 294
Language Map of Zambia 295
ChiNynanja (Bemba) – English Glossary 296

Appendix V: Photos and Images 299

List of Schemas

Schema 1: Population of Lusaka 1963 – 2000 15
Schema 2: Medical Pluralism And "Therapy Shopping" in Lusaka 34
Schema 3: Medical Case 1 – Integrated Theory of Illness 50
Schema 4: Dreams Associated with Mashabe Spirits 111
Schema 5: Dreams Associated with Witchcraft 112
Schema 6: Illustration of the Use of Chizimba 118
Schema 7: History of the New Jesus Disciples Church 140
Schema 8: The Most Common Field of Afflictions Linked to Witchcraft 230
Schema 9: Psycho-physiological Aspects of Illnesses linked to Witchcraft 232

Note on terminology
The term "Doctor" in front of the name of traditional healers does not refer to an academic title but to a title of honour.

All respondents' names are pseudonyms.

Introduction

The monograph deals with the phenomenon of spiritual healing and witchcraft both within the field of indigenous medicine and African Independent Churches in the contemporary urban setting of Lusaka, the capital of Zambia. Grounded in theoretical concepts of medical and symbolical anthropology, the book draws on data from ethnographic fieldwork carried out between 2008 and 2009.[1] The book deals with the pluralistic and syncretic character of medical culture in Lusaka, a special attention is paid to the local conceptualization of health, illness and body, cultural aetiology, the analysis of the phenomenon of spirit possession, the description and interpretation of different diagnostic and therapeutic praxis of traditional and Christian healers. A substantial part of the book is dedicated to the interpretation of witchcraft.

The topic as such has not yet been systematically elaborated by anthropologists[2]. As for Zambia, we can only find brief selective studies of traditional medicine from the seventies and eighties dealing with the issue from the perspective of ethnomedicine. Instead of endeavouring to understand local cultural beliefs and practices linked to traditional healing, authors (such as Frankenberg 1969; Frankenberg, Leeson 1976, 1977; Jules-Rosette 1981; Last, Chavunduka 1986) paid attention to distribution of medical services in Lusaka, patients' priorities and the potentiality of traditional herbal *materia medica* for biomedical use. More valuable sources of information about spiritual healing in Zambia comes from authors such as Dillon-Malone (1983a; 1983b 1988) or Jules-Rosette (1981) who focused mainly on the healing praxis of the new arising African Independent Churches in Lusaka. Older, but no less useful are the anthropological studies of anthropologists from the Manchester school (Marwick 1950, 1965; Mitchell 1965; Colson 1969) concerning primarily the social aspects of the witchcraft belief in a fast changing urban

---

[1] Fieldwork lasted in total 11 months.
[2] The only exceptions are the articles of Sugishita 2009 and Gewald 2011.

Copperbelt during the colonial era. Although in the nineties several thematically different pornographies and essay's about the religious situation in Zambia appeared (Binsbergen 1981, 2006; Bond 2001; Hudson 1999; Jonker 2000; Sembreka 1996; Willis 1999), comments about spiritual healing and witchcraft still remain scant and very fragmentary. This book endeavours to fulfil the vacuum in academic literature.

The theoretical framework is rather eclectic. The study of spiritual healing and witchcraft is primarily grounded in theoretical concepts of medical anthropology[3] as well as symbolic anthropology[4]. In order to grasp the issue in its wholeness, i.e. not generalized and abstract but deep and in detail, I analyse and interpret the rich corpus of empiric data from the *emic* perspective while focusing primarily on the micro-level. I am interested in exploring face-to-face social relations, social networks within the relatively small social groups such as household, family, neighbourhood or church community that play an important role in the process of healing, witchcraft accusations as well as in the social construction of illness.

In my interpretation I have diverged from the abundant current anthropological studies on witchcraft and healing dominated by the discourse of power relations either modern, or that issuing from colonial history, which over-emphasize the significance of the political and economic processes. Approaching the problem of suffering from the macro perspective, i.e. searching for the causes of poverty, violence and the health crisis in the ravages of colonialism, post-colonial exploitation, or poor political governance,[5] might not, in my opinion, sufficiently uncover the essence of suffering as experienced by Lusaka dwellers today. My intention here is not to challenge the statements of my colleagues that the healing and witchcraft discourse is inevitably grounded in the political and economic structure of colonial and post-colonial domination. It undoubtedly has its significant weight of evidence, at least in the field of witchcraft imagery as I will demonstrate in the last chapter. But as my

---

[3] Augé, Zémpleni 1989; Kleinman 1980; Young 1982.
[4] Symbolical anthropology: Douglas 1966, 1970; Turner 1968, 1970. French structuralism: Héritier 1979, 1985.
[5] Chabal 1999.

data from fieldwork did not conspicuously disclose any power connotations on the studied issue overlapping the context of given social group, I thus had no reason to tackle the problems from this perspective.

Rather, I focused on the micro-level, studying everyday social life and question how human suffering caused by different kinds of afflictions is reflected in local witchcraft and healing discourse, how is it interpreted by social actors themselves, and the society in which they live. How is the individual suffering linked to the tensions and animosities within the family and society and what are its psycho-physiological consequences?

Book Outline

In the brief introduction, theoretical background, research aims and the question as well as employed methodology are outlined. The first chapter gives a short history of the urban and demographical development of Lusaka city. The low-income settlements known as compounds and its social structure is depicted from the perspective of the main social integrative components – ethnicity, kinship and religion.

The second chapter deals with the issue of health/illness from the perspective of medical anthropology. After defining the key notions such as "medical culture", "medical system" and "medical pluralism" I proceed to the analysis of the phenomenon of "therapy shopping", thus patients strategic medical behaviour consisted of circulating among different medical options in the expectation of finding an optimal solution for their problems. At the background of medico-anthropological theories, the local conceptualisation of illness, health, body and cultural aetiology is explored with the help of examples from fieldwork. When dealing with the issue of the local conceptualisation of illness, body and healing I focused on two crucial questions: "How is the notion and meaning of illness, health, body and healing conceptualised by the local population?" and "how is illness/health constructed, negotiated and maintained in the context of 'therapy shopping' and in the process of diagnosis and what is the role of dreams in this respect?"

The third chapter outlines different types of traditional healers (*ng'angas*) and Christian healers operating in Lusaka in relation to their specific distinguishing features and strategic competitive behaviour stimulated by a rapidly changing urban setting. Drawing on the biographies of healers, I analyse the spiritual calling and crises of possession as a typical basis of a healer's career. Topics such as the relationship between healers and patients and the role of the patient's significant Other within the therapy are also discussed in this section.

The fourth chapter describes and interprets, different ways of diagnosis, therapy and prophylaxis used by traditional healers. I closely investigate the process of divination through "magic mirrors" used by witch-finders and analyse the role of dreams. As for therapeutic practices, attention is paid to rituals of cleansing the body and the patient's house, detection and destruction of magical objects, the *Ngoma* medico-religious ceremony and diverse surgery methods such as *ndembo* incisions, *mulumiko* cupping horn and many others.

The fifth chapter deals with Christian spiritual healing within the syncretic African Independent Churches, in particular prophet-healing churches. As there are plenty of them in Lusaka, I decided to centre my attention on one of the prophet-healing churches of the Mutumwa type situated in the Chawama/Kuku compound. I carried out an in-depth case study of this church community while focusing on roles of individual social actors (prophets, patients, and other church members), instrumental properties and symbols involved in the process of the spiritual healing. The aim was to show what types of afflictions are most often treated in the church, what are the methods of diagnosis and therapy.

As spirit possession plays a crucial role in spiritual healing, an individual chapter is dedicated to this phenomenon. After outlining the brief theoretical background, I proceed to the interpretation of spirit possession from the point of view of the traditional medicine and prophet-healing churches by means of a comparative analysis. My aim is to show what social and economic implications of spirit possessions are and how is this phenomenon linked to the social construction of the charismatic identity of healers, in particular Christian prophets.

The most voluminous part of the book, chapter seven, focuses on the contemporary phenomenon of witchcraft. My aim is to offer a comprehensible explanation of witchcraft from the point of view of theory, system and practice (Augé 1982), while paying special attention to the symbolic conceptualisation of witchcraft among Lusaka dwellers today.

The comprehensive approach to the study of witchcraft necessitated an in-depth examination of particular social events, roles, contexts and relations. For this purpose I analysed eight different multi episodic medical cases linked to witchcraft. I attempted to inter-relate the cultural, social and medical components of the afflictions while paying special attention to the symbolic meanings of witchcraft narratives playing an important role in the process of diagnosis and healing. The case studies were used to support some of the theoretical assumptions of the recent anthropologic discourse on witchcraft. The last section of the book was aimed at four main questions: 1. How does the process of witchcraft accusation reflect the problems in the social structure and how does it enhance the normative system based on shared collective reciprocity? 2. What kind of social, political and economic problems does the current witchcraft symbolic imaginary reflect? 3. What are the specific conditions and circumstances in which witchcraft accusations appear? 4. How is witchcraft diagnosed and treated by local traditional healers?

Notes on Research

During my long term ethnographic fieldwork (2008–2009) in Lusaka I employed different methods of data collection such as structured and biographical interviews, questionnaires, participant and non-participant observations, collection of primary written data – the biomedical files of patients, the Constitution of Traditional Healers and Practitioners Association of Zambia (THAPAZ), personal documents (diary of healers, founders of the church) and Media outputs (radio broadcasting and newspapers). In order to study in detail the phenomenon of witchcraft and spiritual healing, I decided to employ the case study method.

The structured and semi-structured interviews were conducted with different traditional and Christian prophetic healers, their patients and the patient's relatives. In total 45 people were interviewed during my fieldwork, the majority of them repeatedly. The structured interviews were employed either as an additional support for participant observations, or aimed at the reconstruction of a particular problem that emerged in the past. Additionally, I used narrative interviews in order to collect biographical data about healers and patient's life episodes. Some biographic episodes concerning dreams or kinship relations were subsequently reinvestigated by means of structured interviews.

To my surprise most patients were not inhibited in talking about their health and social problems and did not consider my questions to be over intimate. Personal health was not regarded as a private matter on the contrary it was a common topic of everyday conversation at home, in the neighbourhood, church, or at other public places such as waiting areas or bus stops.

When conducting narrative interviews with informants I noticed that they do not keep a chronological structure even if it is requested. To eliminate the discontinuity which made the informant's statements unclear, I had to carry out the interviews repeatedly. However, even the answers on the same repeated questions proved to be ambiguous, or even contradictory in many cases. These "logical" discrepancies might be explained either by my respondents' vague idea about the problem concerned, issuing from their lay medical knowledge or by the specific way of their thinking that is much more synthetic then analytic.[6] Let me give an example. Grace, one of the patients I interviewed, claimed to have fled to Lusaka to avoid the alleged witches from her family living in Kitwe who continued afflicting her in her dreams. However, during another interview, she affirmed that the witches use a "magical aeroplane" able to overcome big distances in short time in order to bewitch her. The logical contradiction in Grace's statements that appeared evident to me was however not evident to her. She simply considered both statements as complementary.

The inconsistencies, discrepancies and contradictions in the informant's statements appear to be the most explicit when dealing with the issue of medical knowledge. In a pluralistic medical culture such as in Lusaka, medical knowledge is basically eclectic, syncretic and subject to continuous innovations penetrating from outside. Unlike healers who are well acquainted with medical knowledge, patients do not really understand the medical terms and ideas they use, but take them for granted. Moreover, in diverse medical settings the boundaries between medical knowledge and other kinds of knowledge often overlap. Murray

---

[6] See the notion *bricolage* of Lévi-Strauss (1966).

Last (1976) who analysed the medical culture among the Hausa of northern Nigeria employed the term "non system" to emphasize the inconsistencies included in Hausa traditional medicine. I fully agree with his opinion that popular medical knowledge is characterised by the lack of sharp boundaries between ideas and experiences. It is thus especially difficult, to analyse the patient's vague, incoherent and ever changing narratives.

The participant and non-participant observations, as the essential methods of qualitative research, were repeatedly employed during my fieldwork. Participant observation in combination with interviews was used during several social events such as traditional divination séances, therapeutic consultations, the collection and preparation of medical herbs, church healing services and participation in special medico-religious rituals.

In order to obtain a larger amount of comparative data concerning the "therapy shopping" phenomenon in Lusaka I decided to employ structured questionnaires amongst the patients. The questionnaire, written in the chiNyanja language, was structured on the basis of both closed-ended and open-ended questions that concerned the general information about a patient and his medical history. The questions were drawn up in a way to investigate the factors involved in the respondent's decision making process, their motivations and strategies in the health seeking process within "therapy shopping". The inquiry through questionnaires covered a total sample of 57 respondents.[7]

The application of this method faced several difficulties. Firstly, as the majority of respondents were illiterate, my research assistants had to help them to fill out the questionnaires. This procedure was on the one hand time consuming, on the other some of respondents expressed their mistrust as they felt not to have control over what was being written down and did not know the research assistants personally. Secondly, the patients had difficulties in expressing their own personal opinion as they were used to discussing and solving their problems collectively, thus within the family or with other church members.

---

[7] 37 patients of the Mutumwa church and 20 respondents who used traditional healers.

In order to provide the systematic analysis of the above mentioned research topic I draw also on documents and the physical data of several governmental and non-governmental institutions such as: 1. The Constitution of Traditional Health Practitioners Association of Zambia (THAPAZ); and the Constitution of the New Jesus Disciple Church; 2. The study of physical objects in Lusaka National Museum and Livingstone Museum at the Department of Ethnography and Art putting on the witchcraft exhibition[8]; 3. The biomedical files of certain patients admitted at the Chainama psychiatric hospital[9]; 4. The personal diaries of traditional healers and founders of the Mutumwa church.

To support my arguments concerning witchcraft I employed the method of instrumental case study (Stake 1995) which focused on the exploration of eight patients multi-episodic medical cases in Lusaka. By the presentation of particular medical cases I attempt to inter-relate the cultural, social and medical components of witchcraft afflictions which have changed over time. The medical case studies focused on the detailed history of affliction in the background of a patient's life history and social relations, on the nature of the interconnections between the available therapeutic options and the shifting nature of a patient's decision-making process. In spite of this ambition, some of the illustrative cases were not completed and remained fragmented. The limited time of my fieldwork prevented me from following the whole case from beginning to end in the majority of cases. Moreover, as I found out the medical cases are in principle multi-episodic and respective medical treatment can lasts several years. As a result, I could examine only one or two episodes in its entirety, whereas other episodes were reconstructed a posteriori on the basis of structured interview with patients. Some cases also had to be abandoned during the fieldwork because of the unwillingness of patients to participate.[10]

---

[8] Exhibition "Witchcraft in Zambia" in the Lusaka National Museum. Permanent exhibition "Ethnography and Art" in the Livingstone Museum.

[9] I gained the permission to see patient's medical files after having shown documents drawn by THAPAZ proving my research intentions.

[10] The reasons for abandoning the research of a particular medical case were for instance – patient's business occupation, my refusal to pay for his

... footnote continues on next page

For the purpose of demonstration Christian healing, I decided to employ the method of "community case study" of the church congregation of The New Jesus Disciple Church located in the Chawama/Kuku compound. I focused primarily on the nature of the diverse social relationships within the community (prophets, preachers, patients, church members) linked to healing and spirit possession. My "strategic group of informants" consisted on the one hand of patients (sample of fifteen informants), their close relatives, friends and neighbours and on the other, different types of *ng'angas* mainly witch-finders (five key informants)[11] and spiritual healers (four key informants)[12]. The choice of informants followed the method of "combined focused sampling" (Patton 1990:169), and "complex triangulation" (Sardan 1995) i.e. a combination of several kinds of informants and several points of view. This method helped me to see the contrasting discourses and to discover the significant discrepancies of the examined issue forming the basis of the social reality under investigation. In the initial phase of the fieldwork I contacted the THAPAZ association in order to get in touch with prominent traditional healers (*ng'angas*) and their patients. They consequently introduced me to their colleges in their environs. This "snowball sampling" (Goodman 1961) enabled me to reach a wide variety of informants and enlarge the field of my inquiry.

However, the rivalry and animosity between traditional and Christian healers prevented me from employing the method of sampling in all of the cases. In order to maintain the complexity of my research, i.e. to respect the method of triangulation, I could not rely solely on one information flow within the network of informants acquired on the recommendation of my key informants. It was precisely this animosity issuing from different attitudes and contradictory opinions that I was interested in as it constituted a valuable material for later comparison. By enlarging the group of informants engaged in different social networks I avoided,

---

treatment, or the patients mistrust issuing from a suspicion that I belong to the group of witches.

[11] Doctor Mukanda, Doctor Kasanda Sakukuwa, Doctor Lukesha, Doctor Sushita Kalolo, Doctor Kunda Kaleni.

[12] Doctor Chembe, Doctor Sato, Doctor Aron, Doctor Irene.

what Jean-Pierre Olivier de Sardan (1995) calls, the "risk of enclicage", that is the situation when an anthropologist might get entrapped, "socially encapsulated" in the social network of his strategic group of informants.

During my fieldwork I adopted the reflexive approach[13] that inherently raised the question about my status given to me by people I studied. The implications of my objective social status – that of a woman, white, and a student – were not clear at the beginning of my research. As a single childless young woman who came alone to Africa I represented someone who might potentially get married there, especially when proved to be interested in the local culture and language. As I soon realised, dealing with male informants necessitated being introduced to their wife and family in order to avoid any doubts of my relationship with them and dispel gossip in their vicinity. My status as a white person (*muzungu*) was even more complicated. In the local culture *muzungu* is highly valued for his economic, social and symbolic capital (Bourdieu 1992).[14] When dealing with me the motivation and strategies of people

---

[13] Since the 1980s postmodernism has fully penetrated anthropology and ignited the debate centred on the critique of ethnographic inquiry and writing. This led to an emphasis on self-critical reflexivity Adopting the reflexive strategy means to problematise the role of ethnography in the construction of ethnographic subjects. Current post-modern scholars stress the subjective, the experiential, empathy and ethic during fieldwork. In this perspective, the anthropologist is considered to be a social actor as he influences the social reality in the same way as his informants.

[14] Economic and social capital of a white person does not always play a primary role in attributing him high social status. Of more importance is his symbolical capital. A Zambian man may consider an aged, low-income woman of European origin (who cannot provide him either with children, or economic or social capital) as more attractive than a young rich African woman. I witnessed several couples of young African men married to older European women. When I asked one of them (a 25 year old man who worked as a guide in the national park in Livingstone) whose wife was a middle-aged German woman who lost in drink all her property and did not work, why he had just married her, he answered „*because she was white*". After this

... footnote continues on next page

were in many ways driven by their deep-rooted idea about a white person as "someone who helps". My presence in the compound initiated many misunderstandings that had to be cleared up every day. My attempt to explain the objective of my stay was not always well apprehended by people. Some of them suspected that I wanted to enrich myself at their expense and therefore asked money for interviews as a sort of "self-serving reciprocity". Others contented themselves with an idea that establishing a relationship with me might raise their social prestige in the compound. When I visited my informants at their home, they often asked me to *zunguluka compound* – to promenade with them around the compound – in order to introduce me to their neighbours and relatives as *musanga uanga wa bwino* "my very good friend". Another time, they just accompanied me on the way to the bus, whilst holding my hand[15] and greeting their friends.

My position as a European student, similarly as that of *muzungu*, had to be negotiated many times during my fieldwork. Unlike the sponsored researchers from the U.S.A. and Sweden whom the local people were used to meeting, my financial budget for research was rather limited. I could not afford to pay assistants, translators, to rent a car, or pay the expenses related to the organisation of several day long healing rituals. My status as a European student "who eats *nshima* and walks" was generally perceived as ambivalent. When confronted with people's permanent requests for helping them with procuring money or food, my African friends defended me by arguing, "*she is a student, she does not work (...) she is like us eating nshima and walking. Look at her she can even speak our language*". The informants who knew me thus used my position of a student of anthropology to dispel the widespread prejudice about *muzungu* commonly viewed by local people as rich, never walking but

---

experience, I finally realised that the high social status of a white woman in the eyes of an African man is primarily based on her symbolic capital which is appreciated by his fellows and whose judgment conditions significantly his prestige.

[15] Holding hands between friends of the same sex (both men and women) is a common habit. As I observed, people also like to touch each other as a sign of approval when talking.

using a big luxurious car, never eating *nshima* and do not speak the local language. However, even those who understood that I could not provide them with money, tried to take advantage. I was asked to get their children into a school in Europe, to write a book about traditional healing for them, to find a job or a white fiancé in Zambia, or Europe, or even to teach them anthropology.[16]

---

[16] Some of my informants were fascinated by anthropology which they often called "study of traditions". One of them claimed that he would be an excellent anthropologist as he understood his own culture better than me.

1. Lusaka's Socio-Urban Context

When you run alone, you run fast.
When you run together, you run far.
—Zambian proverb

Urban and Demographic Development

The history of Lusaka city stretches back to 1905 when the railway line was constructed for the purpose to connecting the copper mines in the Katanga region located in former Belgian Congo to the seaports of South Africa. As with other cities in Zambia, Lusaka also emerged along this railway line. The development of the copper mine industry in the early years of British colonial rule resulted in rapid urbanisation, especially around the copper mines situated in the northern part of the country known as Copperbelt. The development of Lusaka city however began in 1931 when it was designated as the new capital, the principle administrative centre of Northern Rhodesia, for its strategic central location as a transport junction. The original urban plan elaborated by professor Adshead conceived Lusaka city as only a government administrative centre. Industrial activities and a large population of Africans were not anticipated to form part of the city of Lusaka (Collins 1969; Williams 1984).

During the late thirties[1] and the Second World War when Northern Rhodesia[2] experienced an economic boom due to the high demand for

---

[1] The value of export copper increased five-fold between 1930 and 1933 and the contribution of copper rose from 30 percent to 90 percent. During the Second World War the Allies made heavy demands on the Copperbelt mines and by 1945 Northern Rhodesia was firmly established as one of the world's major copper producers (Roberts 1976: 186).

copper on the international markets the massive work migration begun. Work migration in Zambia in general has always been influenced by copper production, as the economy of both the colonial and post-colonial period has been primarily oriented on the export of this commodity. The huge work migration of this period had a significant impact on Lusaka, even if it was not a copper mining town.[3] As a result, Lusaka started growing demographically which led to a housing shortage. The reluctance of local authorities and employers to provide accommodation for African immigrants resulted in the proliferation of unauthorised settlements beyond the limits of the original Lusaka urban plan (Hansen 1982). In the quest for a solution, the local authorities passed the Urban African Housing Ordinance (1948) which aimed to make employers provide low cost housing for their employees and their families.[4] The passing of the Ordinance led to the construction of the African housing areas called "townships"[5], and "private compounds"[6] in particular in the postwar period. However, neither the new housing areas were able to accommodate the new massive wave of immigrants, in particular workers' relatives. As a result, the built up area known as "unauthorised

---

[2] Northern Rhodesia was administered under charter by the British South Africa Company and formed by it in 1911. From 1924 it was administered by the United Kingdom government as an official British protectorate. Northern Rhodesia became independent in 1964 as Zambia.

[3] Although Lusaka benefited from this economic boom its main economic activities were: manufacturing (food, textile and chemical processing enterprises), construction, commerce and finance, agriculture and administration.

[4] Before the African Housing Ordinance Africans in Lusaka were treated as temporary residents with short-term employment contracts. The wives and children were not allowed to accompany their husbands and fathers to urban centres.

[5] Municipal African townships in 1963: Matero, Chilenje, Kabwata, Chibolya, Chinika, Kambala, Balovale (Kay 1967: 125).

[6] Private compounds in 1963: Zambia Regiment's barrack, Wardroper police camp, Prison camp, Hospital compound, Howard compound (Kay 1967: 125).

compounds"[7], or "squatters" (Hansen 1982) emerged in high numbers on the privately owned agricultural land on the periphery of the city. "The unauthorised urban settlements however lacked essential social and physical infrastructure such as schools, health facilities, water supply, electricity, access roads and security services" (Mulenga 2003: 8).

Lusaka experienced an unprecedented demographical growth after independence (1964) when its population doubled (from 123 000 in 1963 to 263 000 in 1968). This was due to huge rural–urban migration of the chiNyanja–speaking people from the Eastern province in the 1960s and 1970s followed by migrants from the Northern and Southern Province (Mulenga 2003). As these were predominantly young people, Lusaka also recorded a considerable natural population increase. As shown in the schema below, the population also doubled between years 1969 and 1980. The focus on mining during the 1970s made Zambia one of the most urbanised countries in Africa. During the 1980s about 40 percent of the total population lived in urban centres (Mulenga, Campenhout 2003).

Schema 1: Population of Lusaka 1963 – 2000

Year	Population	Annual Growth Rate	Population	Percentage of Total Urban Population	Percentage of Large Urban Areas
1963	123,146	—	3.5	17.2	18
1969	262,425	13.4	6.5	22.0	23.5
1974	421,000	9.9	9.0	25.3	27.2
1980	535,830	4.1	9.4	21.9	28.2
1990	769,353	3.7	10.4	26.5	—
2000	1,103,413	4.0	10.7	—	—

Sources: Wood et al (1986) and Central Statistics Office (1994; 2001)

---

[7] Unauthorised compounds in 1963: Kalingalinga, Kanyama, Marripodi, Mandevu, Antonio, Mtengo (Kay 1967: 125).

Since the 1980s the economic crisis in the country due to the fall in the price of copper on the world market led to the collective redundancies of mine workers in the Copperbelt. These, mostly of the Bemba origin, migrated to Lusaka during this period in large numbers. Whereas before 1980 the migration in Zambia was primarily between rural and urban areas, since the 1980s up to 85% of migration has been between urban centres while only 15% between villages and towns.[8]

Today, Lusaka is one of the most demographically growing towns in Africa with a total number of 1.460.566 inhabitants.[9] In 2008, at the time of my research, approximately 80% of Lusaka's residents lived in townships known as "compounds"[10], i.e. low-income housing and squatter settlements and 40% of them were officially unemployed (Hansen 2008; Mulenga 2003). According to the United Nation's Human Development Report from 2007, 64.2% the Zambian population lived in multidimensional poverty[11], thus below the international poverty line which was 1.25 dollars per day, while an additional 17.2 percent were vulnerable to multiple deprivations.[12] Among the major causes of actual poverty, the counterproductive policies of Kenneth Kaunda's regime (1964–1991), the high population growth, a one sided oriented economy and the negative

---

[8] Central Statistical Office, 1994.

[9] Estimations from 2010 available at www.populationmondiale.com. The total number of Lusaka inhabitants in 2000 was 1.084.703.

[10] The term derives from the urban-control apparatus that during the colonial period invoked race to segregate housing, labour, health, and domestic arrangements. Compound, a term common throughout the southern African region, first came into use for the housing institution adopted on the gold and diamond mines in South Africa in the late 1980s. In postcolonial Zambia, the semantic field of the term has come to encompass all low-income areas (Hansen 2005).

[11] *The 2010 Human Development Reports* introduced the Multidimensional Poverty Index (MPI), which identifies multiple deprivations in the same households in education, health and standard of living.

[12] Available at: http://hdr.undp.org/en/country-reports (retrieved 2013)

impact of the IMF/World Bank initiated Structural Adjustment Program (SAP) in the 1990's[13] are often cited.

Since the late 1980's the Zambians experienced what James Ferguson (1999a, 1999b) calls a failure of modernity. The proclaimed development that Zambians desired failed to deliver the promised economic progress. Modernisation and development became a myth, in some respects a trap and tragedy for those whose hopes and expectations have been shattered (Ferguson 1999b: 43). The end of modernity the most visible in the urbanised Copperbelt province has manifested itself in its disconnection with the world community. Zambia has been excluded from the mainstream global economy which was accompanied by a feeling of disillusion, abjection and betrayal. Zambians became again the "citizens of a second class", poor Africans. The development myth brought the new forms of economic and social inequalities, an increase in unemployment, a difficult access to education and health care and the deterioration of urban infrastructure. The privatisation of the Zambian economy has also pushed many adults into the informal economy (Hansen 2009).

Since the 1980s when the rate of unemployment in Lusaka has significantly increased, the rank of "self-employed" people emerged. This new socio-economic class composed of young men and women is characterised by the ability at economic improvisation and social negotiation, they employ diverse strategies to survive and safeguard their livelihoods. This class has become a symbol of new ways of conceptualisation of urban life pitfalls that according to Ferguson "value multiplicity, variation, improvisation, and opportunism and distrust to fixed, unitary modes of practice" (Ferguson 1999b: 44).

Poverty as the most burning problem of modern Zambia has increased from 49% in 1991 to 53% in 2006[14] whilst the largest incidence of

---

[13] The increasing economic crisis of the late 1980s led to the implementation of the Structural Adjustment Programme (SAP) in the 1990s comprising reforms such as the privatisation of the copper industry, exchange rate liberalization, tax reforms, removal of subsidies, control of agriculture prices, privatization of agriculture, introduction of user fees for health and education. These reforms however sparked violent protest in the Copperbelt and Lusaka (Mulenga, Campenhout 2003).

poverty was recorded in the period 1991–1998.[15] In 2008 and 2009 at the time of my research, Zambia occupied a low position on the scale of Countries Human Development Index, namely 164th out of 187 countries. In comparison with its position today (141/187 in 2013), we can conclude that national economic and living conditions of Zambians have significantly improved. At least in Lusaka, economic growth can be seen practically on every corner. Many new commercial buildings, shopping malls, banks, hotels, petrol stations are mushrooming in downtown, the quality of bus transport and infrastructure among the cities has visibly improved, even the living conditions in compounds have enhanced significantly.[16] The development of national economics has meant that the formerly one sided economy which was oriented to the export of copper, has been advanced within the last five years by close trading partnerships with China, Brazil and India.

Since 2008 also the health sector has recorded progress in most of the key areas of healthcare service. The high HIV/AIDS prevalence estimated at 16.5% of the total population in 2007 has decreased by more than 2 % within the last five years. The development of the health sector contributed to a rise in the average life expectancy at birth from 47 years (in 2008) to 52 years (in 2012).[17]

As results from the outline of the urban and demographical development of Lusaka city Lusaka's dwellers represent a complex composed of different ethnic groups which have immigrated there in recent history. These are mostly Nyanja, Chewa, Nsenga and Ngoni from the Eastern and Central Province, Bemba from the Luampula Province, Central Province, Copperbelt and Northern Province, Tonga from the Southern Province, and Lenje and Soli from the Central Province. The ethnic composition of the majority of compounds in Lusaka is thus heterogeneous. Hansen however assumes that in the past, there was a tendency for an

---

[14] The headcount poverty uses the national poverty line of Zambian Kwacha 46.2 (US 24.89) per month in 1998 prices.

[15] Central Statistical Office 2009b.

[16] According to my observation after having returned to Lusaka in March 2014.

[17] UNDP 2010.

ethnic clustering in Lusaka "The geographical location of squatter areas tended to reflect the ethnic geography – settlements on the southern side of town had more people from the southern ethnic groups than those on the eastern fringe where several eastern ethnic groups were represented. This relative ethnic clustering was reinforced to some extent by church associations that tended to reflect the regional basis of the mission churches" (Hansen 1982: 124).

Although the official language of the country is English, the majority of Lusaka dwellers speak chiNyanja that serves as a *lingua franca*. ChiNyanja is a Bantu language based largely on Chewa (spoken in Malawi) and Nsenga containing loan words from Bemba and English. Other languages commonly spoken in Lusaka are Bemba (15.5%), English (6.6%) and Tonga (4.6%).[18] The majority of the Lusaka's dwellers speak three or more local languages fluently and those who attended school master English at the basic communicative level. Although the statistics show that more than 80% of the population is literate and thus should master English, from my own experience I can say that it is not so.

Social Structure of Compounds

The well known fact that in Africa, the communal and local dimensions prevail over that of the individual is closely linked to the problem of a person's identity. This is inseparable from the collective identity based on a belonging to the community. "The individuals conceive of themselves in terms of the multiple and multifaceted relations which link them with others within ever expanding and overlapping concentric spheres of identity" (Chabal 2009: 43).

Habitually, anthropologists tend to describe the social structure of the communities from the perspective of ethnicity, kinship and religion. These factors are considered to be the main structural principles

---

[18] At national level, there are 72 ethnic groups officially recognised with each of them speaking a dialect of the seven language cluster groups. The majority of Zambian population belongs to the Bemba group (33.6%), the second largest is the Eastern Province group (18.2 %) and the Tonga ethnic group is the third (16.8%).

cementing a society. It has often been supposed that in towns where different ethnic traditions intermingle, the people become acutely aware of their differentness. Mitchell who studied tribalism in Northern Rhodesian towns in the 1950s assumed that, "belonging to the tribe therefore provides the initial means whereby Africans in town can express their need for social relationship and common supports" (Mitchell 1956b: 117). With respect to Lusaka, he claimed that the "tribal composition" of unauthorised settlements reflects the pattern of cohabitation of fellow-tribesmen and inter-tribal marriages. However, according to my observations, the principle of ethnicity did not play any such essential role in the "politics of belonging" in today´s Lusaka. Rather the principle of kinship and "religious social networking" contributes to a sense of socially meaningful belonging.

What is the most important element about kinship as a structuring principle of communities in Lusaka is the way in which it integrates, sustains or excludes one's position in its network of belonging. To be a member of a kinship group means to respect the system of obligations and values. "In day to day socio-economic and political life, kinship obligations translate into the structures of expected reciprocity which govern interpersonal and intra-communal relations" (Chabal 2009: 47). The reciprocity – both material and symbolic – is especially important, not only for its instrumental value, but in particular because it sustains identity, maintains social cohesion and assures social security. This is inherently linked to the value system based on the collective sharing of economic and social capital (Bourdieu 1992).

The reciprocity within the nuclear and extended family is expected especially in the situations when economically or socially disadvantaged kinsmen search for financial help or ask for preferential education, medical treatment, work opportunities from a relative of higher socio-economical status. People in compounds in order to bear the high costs of medication that may vastly exceed their earnings tend to activate several local and distant solidarity networks, in particular family, church community they belong to, or if needed they do not hesitate to travel large distances to visit a distant family member about whom they know would be able to assist them.

Lusaka dwellers rely on activating different solidarity networks not only in the situation of economic hardship, but also as a strategy of economic interdependence and cooperation. Clearly, this leads either to nepotism, or to clientelism. The imperative of shared reciprocity based on the notion of "limited good"[19] that prevails in the symbolism of witchcraft, implies that those who have access to financial resources, political power or social contacts should share this capital with those disadvantaged family members. On the contrary, someone who violates the expected system of reciprocity may thus become a target and be accused of witchcraft. Any wellbeing such as success in work, business, school or even politics is publicly suspected and conceptualised in terms of individualism and selfishness. As will further analysis of witchcraft accusation show, it functions as a levelling moral agency.

Diverse church associations represent another important socio-structural component of Lusaka's compounds. As the majority of Zambians are strong believers, belonging to a church community is a fundamental part of their social life. Christianity which came to Zambia, former Northern Rhodesia through European missionary activities at the beginning of the 20th century has flexibly adapted to the African world view, as well as to urban living conditions and offered a meaningful substitute for "old values" by providing new moral frameworks for living.

The most popular and much frequented are African Independent Churches of the Pentecostal type abundantly located in every compound. A typical feature of these churches is an emphasis on spiritual healing and building the strong sense of communality, a "common conscience" which is periodically reinforced during the regular church services charged with the "collective effervescence" (Durkheim 1965).[20]

---

[19] See Foster 1965.

[20] "Collective effervescence" is the term of Emile Durkheim (1965) referring to emotional collective experience during the sacred rites which enable to overcome the division among individuals and subgroups and thus reinforces social cohesion. The church members in Lusaka who experience spirit possession (trance) feel the loss of their individuality and the unity with God whom Durkheim equals to a social group). Such an experience of collective effervescence forges collective identity that sustains members of society during periods of dispersion into routine, i.e. profane activities that

… footnote continues on next page

In particular Sunday church meetings represent one of the most important social events in the week. It is not only the worship of God that makes people gather in the church, but their concern for maintaining social solidarity in the sense of Durkheim's term. Meeting kin, neighbours and friends, strengthening old and establishing new contacts[21], exchanging information with church fellows helps to extend the social networks and gain social capital. As will be shown later, the church community as the social body also significantly influences the process of individual healing.

The growing popularity of African Independent Churches mushrooming in urban compounds since Independence (1964) is based on their endeavour to solve the problems that contemporary urban dwellers encounter. As the state had failed to fulfil the needs of its citizens and did not provide more certainties and assistance to them, the expectation of a better future is laid on the Christian churches that promise salvation in this life. Pentecostal and prophet-healing churches are particularly popular amongst the low-income population as they can find relief from their economical and social insecurity there. Church associations represent an alternative solidarity network substituting for the nowadays fragmented traditional kinsfolk's networks as well as an alternative medical institution. In the sense of belonging they significantly contribute to the construction of individual and collective identity.

Household and Livelihood in Compounds

The compounds represent a spectrum of ethnic and socio-economical groupings, made up of disparate population segments. The basic structural unit of the compound is a household. An average household consists of five to six persons living in only one or two rented rooms.[22] The

---

follow. This force is experienced both mentally and bodily and binds people to the ideals valued by their social group.

[21] For instance, I observed that during the Sunday church service a man can easily take his chance to meet his female partner or future bride.

[22] Central Statistics Office 2001. In 1950s average size of family type household was 3.38 persons. For comparison see Betisson 1959.

most common pattern is a male headed household composed of a nuclear family. However, we can also find unconventional household arrangements due to the socio-economic changes underway in the city. For example the domestic group of young unmarried men mostly cousins or brothers who came to town as a work migrants or students sharing a flat, or a household composed of single, divorced or widowed women living together with their children and sometimes even with the children of their dead sister. Due to the huge mortality rate (HIV/AIDS) causing the problem of orphanage, grand-mothers take on the role of care giver and live together with their grand children.

The general assumption that men are in charge of family households having the status of providers pressures the young men (20 – 30 year old) to search for a job and ensure a livelihood. Unlike the young women who depend on their parents until they get married, young men become independent earlier and occasionally get piecework or try their luck as small-scale traders. These men often express their future aspirations by saying *"I want to run a business, buy a house, get married, to have a lot of children"*. However, not many succeed in fulfilling their dreams so quickly and easily, as they often lack the needed education. Moreover, the poor economic situation in the compounds due to the general economical crisis in the country does not enable them to find a waged occupation in the town, as their "parents generation" enjoyed. The majority of men therefore get involved in informal economic skilled and semi-skilled activities to earn their livelihood in fields such as small scale trading[23], quarrying building stones, wood processing carpentry and the fabrication of building materials. These activities change with the seasons, economic conditions and individual circumstances, and therefore do not provide a reliable source of income throughout the whole year. Those semi-skilled who succeeded in getting a waged occupation work most often as security guards, bus or taxi drivers, gardeners or bricklayers. As I noted, the majority of young men in Lusaka resort to any type of work

---

[23] According to Hansen's research of gender and age composition of the urban informal economy in the mid-1990s, the majority of street vendors in Lusaka city centre and Kamwala market were 90% men between 20–30 years old whereby only a minority of them were married (Hansen 2008).

before getting married in order to save money to pay *lobola*.[24] As the *lobola* fee exceeds several fold annual savings of majority of the young men between 20 and 30 years, they usually stay single. Having no obligations, they tend to change sexual partners or get involved in casual sex.[25] It is worth noting, that even if they are married they do not tend to abandon this habit. This risky behaviour then goes hand in hand with alcohol consumption so popular among men of all age brackets. There are many bars in every compound where men drink local beer *chibuku*[26] and discuss diverse topics. The bar is a popular meeting point where many types of social interactions occur ranging from exchanges of news, to sexual encounters, to verbal arguments that time to time lead to fights.

As the role of the majority of Lusaka's women is still connected with the domestic domain, marriage represents a principal means of economic support. In this respect Hansen assumes that "gender roles in the domestic domain were viewed by the state as complementary during the colonial period, and they still are today. This has obscured women's economic dependence on men and legitimized an unequal relationship between the two within the domestic domain, and it continues to curtail women's active labour force participation" (Hansen 1984: 220). Although they depend mainly on their low-income husbands for economic

---

[24] *Lobola* is a general term for the dowry the man pays the family of his fiancée for her hand in marriage. Traditionally the *lobola* payment was in cattle, as cattle were the primary source of wealth in African society. However, modern urban couples have switched to using cash. The process of *lobola* negotiations can be long and complex, and involves many members from both the bride's and the groom's extended families (www.wikipedia.org). Due to the endemic poverty in Lusaka, *lobola* is not always paid. However it always depends on an agreement between families. In the majority of cases, part of *lobola* is asked to be paid in cash in advance (before marriage), the rest remains as a debt that the man should pay off, however he usually does not.

[25] See Kambou, Meera, Gladys 1998.

[26] *Chibuku* is a local low alcoholic sorghum beer sold in a paper box. It is also called "shake shake" because it has to be shaken to mix up the content before drinking. *Chibuku* has an unpalatable acidic flavour therefore people mix it with milk.

support, the majority of women in Lusaka engage in small scale trade activities to earn some money on the side. However, this offers just a little security as the income is fluctuant. The petty trading consists of selling foodstuffs, such as fresh vegetables, dry fish (*capenta*) or caterpillars, oil, prepared food (*nsima*, grilled maize, or boiled peanuts), or selling second-hand clothes or charcoal. Whereas some women have stalls in the Lusaka city market, others trade from their yards or streets. When interviewed about their occupation, many women said that *"they were just sitting"*. This saying does not mean non-doing (actual sitting at home all day long), but the fact that they do not have regular work and occasionally try their luck at petty trading. However, there are also few lucky women who have regular wage labour work the most common as housemaids, or house-cleaners. Lusaka's women, spend most of their time in the street market–selling or shopping food, or at home taking care of children and doing housework. Whereas many men often meet at bars, or during football matches, women meet in particular at the hair dressers and in diverse Christian churches.

Widowed and divorced women with children or those married whose husband does not support them financially remain dependent on petty market trading which leaves them especially vulnerable economically.[27] No wonder therefore, that some of them see no other possibility than to resort to prostitution as a means of obtaining the household support they need as mothers. The vulnerability of economically disadvantaged women and children, in particular orphans whose number due to the AIDS pandemic increases every year, is the most visible within the context of expanding human traffic. The International Labour Organisation (2008) describes Zambia as "hub" for human traffickers operating in southern Africa, whereas big urban centres such as Lusaka are the most afflicted in this respect.[28] Lusaka is the transit point for the regional

---

[27] Although the endemic poverty in Lusaka compounds, only a few people can be seen begging or sleeping in the street.

[28] This is due to the fact that Zambia is in the geographic centre of the region and thus serves as a major battleground in the fight against the illegal movement of people, usually from countries like Mozambique and the D.R. Congo, who are abducted to South Africa and beyond.

trafficking of women and children for the purposes of forced labour and sexual exploitation.

The social exclusion of the majority of low-income women from the economic and political sphere issues from the customary role that a women's rightful place is the home. As Hansen adds, "their chief career is that of housewife and mother, instilling in them the standards of housewifery and the 'house-proud' instinct" (Hansen 1984: 227). This also reflects the fact that woman are generally less educated than men which disadvantages them in the labour market where the knowledge of English is required. As a result, women have fewer occasions to enter diverse social networks and extend their social capital. As we will see further, Lusaka women have no other option to gain economic privileges and achieve their social status than within the medico-religious sector as prophetess or traditional spiritual healers.

As marriage remains the key to women's economic survival, their dependence on husbands makes them feel that they have little control over the relationship. Many women in Lusaka face neglect and infidelity from their husbands. The promiscuity of men represents a serious problem as it threatens not only the marital relationship, the health of couple but in particular women's socio-economic position. Contrary to women, for men promiscuity is not perceived as immoral, as they in fact just reproduce the recurring structural pattern of polygamy. This in turn leads men to the free-from-guilt attitude toward their wives.

In her study of Mazabuka in Zambia, Keller (1978) noticed the increased use of love potions (*muito*) and other charm medicine by urban women. According to her it reflects the marital and financial insecurity. Wives use love potions to improve their sexual attraction in order keep a husband's love and therefore secure his financial support. This argument holds true even for the situation in Lusaka. Nowadays women do not only resort to the use of love medicine to keep their husbands, but get involved in a whole range of magical means to secure their marriage such as *kavundula* or *mukunko*. These charms are believed to be capable of directly attacking the love rival. Women do not only rely on traditional healers in this respect, but also search for help in the prophet-healing churches providing psychosocial counselling for their marital problems.

2. Medical Culture in Lusaka

"The cross must be always carried by someone"
—Doctor Bongo, Lusaka

The phenomenon of spiritual healing is a constituent component of present-day medical culture in Lusaka. By the term "medical culture" I mean the complex of socio-cultural representations of health, illness and body, various patterns of human behaviour that include specific language, ideas, communications, actions, customs, beliefs, values, and institutions linked to a specific medical system in a given space.

It is precisely the history of labour migration, the proliferation of Christianity and biomedicine during the whole 20th century that brought together different medical beliefs and practices in growing urban cities. The coexisting and intermingled traditions have given rise to a pluralistic and syncretic medical culture that today has also been significantly shaped by the process of modernization, and globalization. The new trends in institutional organisation, healing procedures that have developed within the last two decades has led towards a greater bureaucratization and medicalization of indigenous medicine.

By using term "traditional medicine" or "traditional healers" I do not refer to tradition as opposed, inferior category to modernity but as relational category that is flexible, changing and in time developing on the same continuum as modernity. Tradition is understood as an "ongoing historically layered set of conversations and discursive practices and modernity itself as constituted by multiple traditions" (Lambeck 2014: 5). The terms "traditional" or "indigenous" medicine are here interchangeably used in order to distinguish it from other medical systems. However, as we will see later, its concepts and practices encompassing many aspects of modernity are constructed uniquely in relation with other medical system, in particular with biomedicine whose symbols are appropriated, recasted and incorporated by traditional healers.

The contemporary medical culture in Lusaka consists of three main coexisting and intermingling medical systems. These are Christian medico-religious system, indigenous medico-religious system and western biomedicine. I am aware of the fact that there might be other medical systems existing in Lusaka, such as Chinese medicine for example. As these have just a marginal importance for the majority of Lusaka dwellers, they are not comprised in this book. The term "medical system" whether biomedical, traditional or Christian, can be defined as a system encompassing distinctive social behaviour, institutions, socially legitimate statuses, roles and certain interactional settings that changes over time.

As Christian and traditional systems of healing are significantly anchored in the cosmological matrix of both traditional and imported religion I call these systems "medico-religious". It is also for this reason that the domain of the medicine is not clearly differentiated from the domain of religion and the rest of the social life. The sickness may involve the world of ancestral spirit and healing may require the resolution of social conflict (Hahn 1995:4).

Indigenous Medico-Religious System

During the colonial period, traditional medicine was rather denigrated. After independence in 1964, the Zambian Government did not enact legislation to regulate traditional medicine, nor was a clear policy postulated. The change has come in the 1980s when diverse traditional healers' associations were founded and partly supported by the policies of national government. The associations gather, control and register all traditional health practitioners. Indigenous medicine is neither integrated within biomedicine nor into the national health system. However, traditional birth attendants and community health care workers practise at the level of primary health care.[1] According to World Health Organisation's statistics (2001) at least 70% of the Zambian population use traditional medicine and there are more than 35 000 members of the Traditional Health Practitioners' Association of Zambia (THAPAZ) and other thousands of non-members.

---

[1] World Health Organisation 2001.

Indigenous medicine in Zambia represents an amalgam of heterogeneous beliefs, ideas, non-standardised healing and diagnostic practices, procedures, skills and the use of herbal medicine that vary according to different ethnic and even family traditions represented by different types of traditional healers. The THAPAZ officially recognises five categories whereas only two of them – spiritual healers and diviners (or witch finders) are involved in spiritual healing, i.e. healing by means of spirits, medicinal herbs, magic and ritual. The *ng'angas* differ in methods of diagnosis and healing. Their approach is dynamic and eclectic, they freely combine inherited family tradition with new methods of healing or diagnosis learnt from other healers, they invent their own effective combination of herbal medicine by combining old attested herbs with the new ones.

Christian Medico-Religious System

In Lusaka we can find various catholic and protestant churches involved in spiritual healing. These are on the one hand mainstream churches of long tradition (such as the Roman Catholic Church of Zambia, the United church of Zambia, the Methodist church, the Reformed churches, the Adventists of the Seventh Day) and on the other various African Independent Churches (AICs) that have been mushrooming in the urban areas since the 1960s. AICs in Lusaka vary in their religious doctrine, liturgy and ways of spiritual healing due to their different historical roots and the spiritual source they issue from. There are two main streams we can distinguish: "Prophet-healing churches" (Turner 1979), or "spirit type churches" (Deneel 1987) and "African Independent Pentecostal churches" (Anderson 1993; Hollenweger 1972).

In this book I focus primarily on syncretic prophet-healing churches providing the healing through the Holy Spirit combining both the Christian and indigenous methods of healing. The increasing popularity of these churches situated in the poor urban compounds of Lusaka lies in its ability to flexibly respond to the burning problems that the low-income urban population encounter. These are various health and socio-economic afflictions such unemployment, poverty, alcohol abuse, promiscuity, marital and family problems as well as physiological and psychological disorders. The priests and prophets of these new churches put stress on the "rejection of traditions" represented by indigenous medicine, cults of ancestors and diverse cultural customs. They proclaim that poverty, unemployment, diseases are the results of sticking to "traditions" that hinder the progress and modernity. At the core of their doctrine stands the idea that the origin of human suffering lies in the world of invisible powers such as demons, witches and fallen angels. A devotee is thus incited to "be strong in belief and prayers" to overcome devilish wiles. The preaching aimed at demonology is reflected in the arrangement of so called deliverance services focused on the praxis of exorcism.

Whereas the mainstream churches organised in the Churches Health Association of Zambia (CHAZ)[2] rely mostly on the western-type medical care system, provide special HIV, TB and malaria health programs and provide the networks of hospitals and hospices all around the country, AICs have faith in the healing power of the Holy Spirit. These churches shares common elements with indigenous medico-religious systems s such as illness aetiology, healing through spirit possession, using herbal medicine or practice of detection of witches.

Western Biomedical System

Biomedicine is a socio-cultural system, a predominant medical theory and practice of Euro-American societies which was widely disseminated throughout the world. Its primary focus is on human biology or pathophysiology. The health care system which has both its genesis and sustenance in western politic, economic and ideological institutions was imposed in Zambia during the colonial era (1899–1964) and has maintained its existence until today. The National Health Service is represented by a number of state hospitals formerly founded by Christian missionaries and a wide range of private and state clinics located both in the cities and rural districts.[3] It is currently estimated that in urban areas,

---

[2] The Church Health Association of Zambia formed in Lusaka in 1970 is the largest non-government health provider in Zambia.

[3] Core health service delivery facilities fall into five categories, namely: Health Posts (HPs) and Health Centres (HCs) at community level; Level 1 hospitals

... footnote continues on next page

approximately 99% of households are within five kilometres of a health facility, compared to 50% in rural areas.[4]

Since 1992, the Zambian Government has been implementing significant health sector reforms, aimed at strengthening health service delivery in order to improve the health status of Zambians. The reforms have yielded significant results in the form of strengthened medical systems, improved access to health care and improved health outcomes as reported in the 2007 Zambia Demographic Health Survey.[5]

My analysis of the medical culture in Lusaka focuses on the specification of socio-cultural representation of health and illness, norms and values in different medical systems that govern therapy provisions, patient's choice and their evaluation of a respective treatment. Although my main interest leads to patients' and healers' motivations and strategies, we need to take into consideration also other social agents involved in the medical culture such as associations of traditional healers, African independent churches, and finally the Media. Each medical system is socially constructed and ideologically assumed. It legitimizes the social order, reproduces social relationships and determines the social consequences of an illness (Good 1970). In this respect, the role of the sick can

---

at district level; Level 2 general hospitals provincial level; and Level 3 tertiary hospitals at national level.

[4] The Republic of Zambia, Ministry of Health 2009a.

[5] According to the *Zambia Demographic and Health Survey 2007* (Central Statistical Office 2009), Maternal Mortality Ratio (MMR) reduced, from 729 deaths per 100,000 live births in 2002, to 591 in 2007, Under-Five Mortality Rate (U5MR) reduced from 168 per 1000 live births in 2002, to 119 in 2007, and Infant Mortality Rate (IMR) from 95 to 70, respectively. Neonatal Mortality Rate (NMR) reduced from 37 to 34, respectively. During the same period, HIV prevalence in adults, aged 15 to 49 years, reduced from 16.1% to 14.3%. The malaria and TB programme performance reviews conducted in 2010, and other reporting health systems, also reported major improvements in the prevention and control of malaria and TB. Malaria incidence per 1000 population dropped from 412 in 2006, to 246 in 2009. TB treatment success rate improved from 79% in 2005 to 86% in 2008. *National Health Strategic Plan 2011–2015*. The Republic of Zambia, Ministry of Health.

be perceived either as an advantage or disadvantage according to the given circumstances. The ideological background of healing implicates the idea that a symbol of healing appears to represent the symbols of power as they express ambivalent motives, seeking at once to contest and affirm aspects of the dominant social and normative order (Comaroff and Comaroff 1989). According to current medical anthropologists healing discourse in Africa interfaces closely with the discourse of power and thus embodies "contested realities" issuing from the interaction between global forces of modernisation and local contingencies (Comaroff 1993; Geschiere 1997; Ciekawy and Geschiere 1998; Niehaus 2001).

As mentioned above, the praxis of African healing is closely linked to the domain of African traditional religion. Victor Turner showed, with the example of the Ndembu of Zambia, that "healing procedures are governed by the same principle and mode of classification as their religious rites and moral concepts" (Turner 1967: 300). The interconnection between the spiritual and biological domains becomes the most apparent at the aetiological level, drawing on a religious cosmology based on a belief in the interrelation of "visible" and "invisible" worlds in everyday life. The classical anthropological ethnographies from the 1930s to the 1960s treated indigenous healing from the perspective of traditional religions and cosmology. Since the 1960s medical anthropology has been established and traditional healing has become a study subject in its own right. The ongoing process of the medicalization of African religion has been characterised as a transformation of the previously religious terminology (Last, Chavunduka 1986). This means that what was analysed before at the system of cosmology as a sacred ritual, has been now articulated as a therapy. The term magician has been replaced by the term traditional healer, or traditional practitioner as designated by the World Health Organisation and divination has been perceived as a practise of the diagnosis. Although the majority of Lusaka dwellers today believe in Jesus and attend a Christian church they all without exception share the belief in the power of traditional spiritual agents such as witches, ancestral spirits, errant spirits and in the efficiency of magic.

Medical Pluralism and "Therapy Shopping"

The co-existence and interaction between different components of the medical system is one of the important themes in medical anthropology. Whereas most anthropological essays focus on the mutual relationship between African and Western medicine (Janzen 1978; Chavunduka and Last 1986) my point of interest is the mingling of indigenous and Christian healing traditions. However, in order to complete the picture of pluralistic medical culture in Lusaka, I felt it necessary to take into consideration also issues of biomedical treatment with an additional study at the Chainama psychiatric hospital in Lusaka. I decided to deal with the biomedical point of view in order to obtain the necessary comparative data for the analysis of the phenomenon of "therapy shopping".

In Lusaka a large variety of available medical systems constitutes the complementary pluralistic medical culture within which patients circulate and experiment in the quest for the best option. As I observed, the patients do not hesitate to undergo different treatments simultaneously and tend to appropriate and creatively combine the elements from different healing systems in their lay medical knowledge.

The patient's pragmatic therapy-seeking behaviour is reflected in the phenomenon of so-called "therapy shopping". The metaphor "shopping" is illuminating for two reasons. Firstly because it connotes the financial transactions standing behind the therapy purchase, and secondly because the system of the distribution of medical health care seems to work on the same principle as the market economy, i.e. supply and demand. Moreover, shopping in some contexts maybe considered to be a leisure activity as well as an economic one.

Schema 2: Medical Pluralism And "Therapy Shopping" in Lusaka

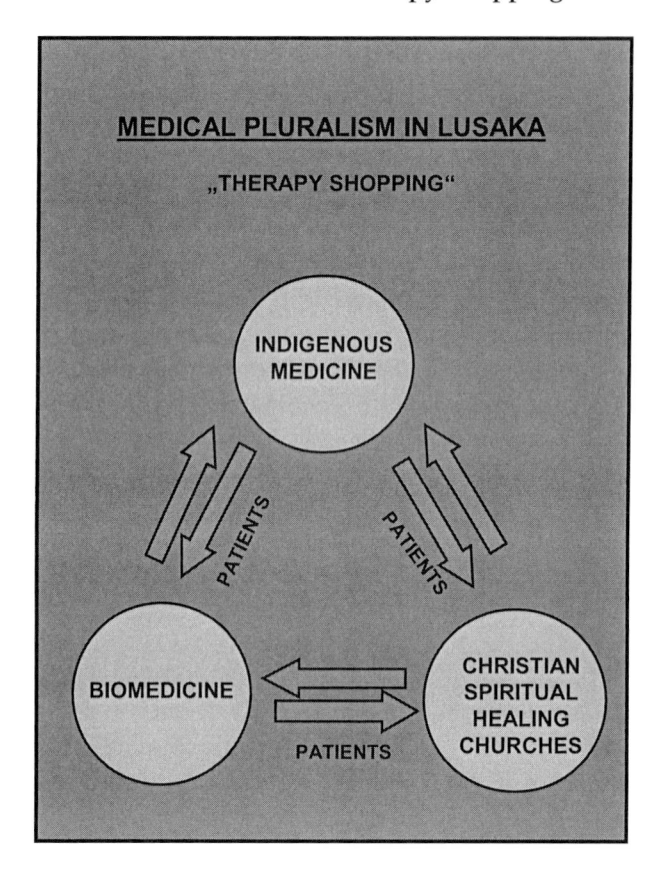

MEDICAL PLURALISM IN LUSAKA

„THERAPY SHOPPING"

- INDIGENOUS MEDICINE
- BIOMEDICINE
- CHRISTIAN SPIRITUAL HEALING CHURCHES

PATIENTS

Patients in a quest for therapy select from a variety of therapeutic offers (see schema above) in the expectation of finding an optimal solution to their problems. However, their demands are not always successfully met, so the shopping becomes more exhausting than exciting. Regardless of the therapeutic facilities in their neighbourhood, patients do not hesitate to move large distances to visit reputable healers or prophets who have been recommended. The patients, in particular those suffering from chronic disease, can be easily trapped in a circle of therapy shopping.

Patient's typical therapy seeking behaviour can be expressed by the chiNyanja term *zunguluka* which means "circulating" or "move around in a space". Patients circulating amongst different medical options tend to make decisions on somebody's recommendation. Neighbours, friends or family members as well as commercial advertisements in the Media[6] play an important role in the patient's decision-making. Another effective way of persuading people is so-called "testimonies" often seen in the Pentecostal churches. These are presented at the beginning of every church service by the patients who were healed miraculously through spiritual healing. The testimonies delivered in front of the other church members are intended to convince them about the reliability of the Holy Spirit's healing power. On the other hand the testimonies serve as social cement reinforcing the social cohesion in the church. Sometimes, a patient receives the recommendations directly from the spiritual world in the form of "a prophetic dream" in which God instructs him where to go to be healed.

It is also commonly shared folk medico-religious beliefs that play an important role in the patient's decision making. Although the traditional and Christian healing is based on similar aetiologies drawing on common cultural resources and shared symbolism, they might interpret it differently. Let me now illustrate typical therapy shopping behaviour with the example of one patient whom I met in the Mutumwa church in January 2009.

Mr. Zulu was a 40 year old man who was married and lived with his older sister, wife and six children in a house in Chipata (the Eastern Province). Mr. Zulu has suffered from an eye disease for more than two years. He has already tried several biomedical facilities as well as traditional healers without any success. As a result, he decided to travel 500 km to Lusaka to visit a specialised health clinic there. Whilst he received treatment he stayed in his brother's house in the Mtendere compound in Lusaka. Although he came to Lusaka primarily to visit a recommended ophthalmologist, he did not hesitate to go across the whole town to consult the healing prophets in the Mutumwa church in Chawama/Kuku compound. He visited the Mutumwa church on his sister's in-law

---

[6] According to Constitution of THAPAZ, the commercial advertisement of therapeutic services is forbidden for traditional healers. However, the most reputable *ng'anga* (usually the heads of these associations) advertise their services on the radio, in television or in the newspapers.

recommendation regardless of his membership to the Reformed church of Zambia. During our interview, he asked me whether I could recommend any competent and reputable traditional healer from Lusaka to him. As emerged from the conversation, Mr. Zulu was convinced that he had been bewitched by an unknown family member because he experienced heat in his body and was bothered by several strange dreams.

In the Mutumwa church, Mr. Zulu underwent the "prophesying", a divination through the Holy Spirit, that disclosed that he was possessed by demons. He was advised by the prophet to undergo several cleansing procedures. The statement from the prophet differed from the diagnosis he was given by a traditional healer whom he had visited before. According to the traditional diagnosis, Mr. Zulu was bewitched, whereas the official documents from the hospital showed that he suffers from ceratitis. To my surprise, Mr. Zulu did not consider these different diagnoses as contradictory but complementary. He was using medicine for his eyes prescribed by a medical doctor, as well as traditional herbs prescribed by *ng'anga* for protection from witches. At the same time he received blessings in the Mutumwa church and prayed several times per day in order to get rid of the demons. Mr. Zulu, after having experienced the variety of different therapeutic treatments preceded by the consultations with his family and friends, finally accepted the witchcraft diagnosis which seemed to be the most appropriate for him.

As this example shows, Mr. Zulu´s "explanatory model" (Kleinman 1980)[7] or in other words the patients way of understanding illness, was conditioned both by the opinion of his family members and his friends as well as by his own experience with different therapies. As Kleinman affirms, "patient and family explanatory models often do not posses single referents but represent a semantic network that loosely link a variety of concepts and experiences" (Kleinman 1980: 106 –107).

As Susan Reynolds Whyte (1989) showed on example of therapy seeking behaviour of the Bunyole from Uganda, people in a quest for optimal therapy try different cures and healing methods, which she calls a

---

[7] "Explanatory models concern aetiologies, time and way of symptoms emergence, pathophysiology, duration of an illness and therapy" (Kleinman 1980: 106).

"therapeutic trial". According to the effectiveness or ineffectiveness of this trial, patients finally construct the diagnosis that they identify with. In this sense, the therapy itself establishes the diagnosis (Whyte 1989). Going back to our example, Mr. Zulu's explanatory model changed according to the situational context. The permanent questioning of the meaning of an illness through experimentation with different therapeutic options helped Mr. Zulu to define his final diagnosis. As he moved from one sector to another he dealt with different beliefs and normative systems. In this respect Kleinman noticed that, "contact with another system of meaning and norms may simply shift between conceptual frameworks and behavioural styles the patient himself possesses or has had experience with and can negotiate with" (Kleinman 1980: 99). The example of Mr. Zulu among others showed that patients do not consider the different illness interpretations as contradictory but complementary.

Medical anthropologists have noticed, that the role of the sick is socially negotiated and changes according to the situation and respective medical context. "In each setting the illness is perceived, labelled and interpreted differently and a special form of care is applied" (Kleinman 1980: 52). To illustrate this argument, I will proceed to show how the interpretations of spirit possessions change according to the different medical settings in which it occurs. The spirit possession represents a common socio-cultural phenomenon associated with spiritual healing in Lusaka. It is a culturally specific behaviour which in different contexts and situations is endowed with different meanings. For instance, the spirit possession of church members accompanied by the trance behaviour (shaking body, falling down on the ground, rolling in all directions, sometimes even screaming) in the Pentecostal or prophet-healing churches is, in the majority of cases, interpreted as a "demon possession". Consequently, a person possessed by the spirit different to the Holy Spirit is recognised as spiritually sick within the church community. Respective therapy therefore consists of "deliverance" or exorcism of this spirits and a series of blessings. However, the same behaviour can be, in a different medical setting such as western medicine, labelled as psychopathological. A patient having similar symptoms as those described above is most of the time considered to be mentally ill or designed as epileptic. In the setting of indigenous medicine, the spirit possession is considered to have a highly positive value since it is associated with the manifestation of an ancestral spirit (*mashabe*) which would like to be recognised and worshipped.

To sum up, the patient's interpretation of his illness changes as it is socially constructed in the process of therapy according to the situation and the medical setting in which it is embedded. As a result, the same symptoms can lead to different interpretations. As will be shown later in the text, the borders between the being sick and being healthy are thin and permeable and shifts according to the social as well as cognitive consensus within the particular context or situation.

Analysis of Therapy Shopping in Lusaka

The following analysis based on data obtained through structured questionnaires focuses on the decision making factors involved in "therapy shopping" in Lusaka. In my analysis I am interested particularly in the patient's motivations and strategies during the health seeking process. I deal with the questions of how the illness is socially constructed, negotiated and maintained in the therapy shopping circle. What are main decision-making factors in the process of therapy shopping and on which social, cultural and economic variables a decision-making mechanism is based?

My research disclosed that the patient's decision to consult prophets or traditional healers does not depend on their age, marital status, ethnic origin or place of residence, but rather on the nature of their illness and recommendation of kin, neighbours or friends. Therapy seeking behaviour also differs according to gender. Generally women are more predisposed to "experiment", to change therapy options than men. Moreover, women proved to have more trust in Christian healing methods within the prophet-healing church than men. This is probably due to the fact that the majority of the respondents from these churches are women, whereas men comprised only 10–15%. The prevalence of women in the churches may be determined by a variety of other factors such as the quest for their children's health care, the sense of communitarians among Zambian women, pastime activity (or women´s socio-economical vulnerability.

On the contrary, the sample of respondents using the traditional healers showed that even if the women in Lusaka tend to visit traditional healers more regularly than men, there is no such noticeable gender discrepancy. Neither geographical distance, nor the ethnic identity of a healer plays a role in the process of the patient's decision making.

The research also focused on the relation between a respondent's educational background, economic status and "therapy shopping" behaviour with regard to the nature of the illness. As follows from the data obtained, biomedical care as the first therapy option was appreciated by 55 % of all the respondents regardless of their education or economic status. However, the economically self-sufficient and educated patients tend to have more trust in biomedical treatment and use it more frequently than the uneducated[8] or unemployed. This finding can be explained by their higher intellectual awareness of the health care system's functioning, the occurrence of health hazards and modes of prevention. To my surprise, the economic factors did not play such an important role in the decision making process in the majority of cases. The costs of treatment by traditional healers sometimes exceeded several fold the expenses for biomedical care. However, people who have trust in traditional medicine are ready to pay any amount in the pursuit of a cure.

As follows from inquiry, the ineffectiveness of biomedical treatment is generally attributed to its incapability to deal with social and spiritual problems. As a belief in spiritually caused illnesses pervades the minds of all Lusaka dwellers, the option of indigenous or Christian therapy logically ensues. The failure of biomedical help – both on the level of diagnosis and therapy – is generally interpreted as proof that invisible forces are involved in their illness. This only deepens their insecurity about the origin of their suffering and pushes them to continue in therapy shopping. Consequently, it opens the space to a wide range of speculation about the origin and the cause of an illness, of which a suspicion of witchcraft prevails. As a Doctor Mukanda, the prominent witch-finder from Lusaka said: *"People go to see ng´anga because they always think that they are bewitched, but it is not like this most of the time. They don't know what might be the cause of their problems"*.

---

[8] By the term „uneducated" I mean a person who did not complete the grade 7 and therefore do not know English, calculating and writing.

On the contrary, the biomedical practitioners do not conceive their failures in terms of the ineffectiveness of their therapy but in terms of a hermeneutic discordance between them and their patients. This discordance issues mostly from the incompatibility of the patient's lay explanatory model and the explanatory model of biomedical practitioners. The patient simply does not understand the medical language employed by doctors. As a result, this crucial cognitive disparity leads patients to label the therapy as ineffective. Biomedical practitioners most often complain that patients do not adhere to their therapy instructions and do not come back for check-ups. In most of the cases, their patients come to consult them when it is "too late", and they do not understand the notion of chronic ailments. One of my informants from the range of biomedical doctors affirmed that: *"patients do not follow the dosage, they believe, as many traditional healers proclaim, that every disease can be healed within seven days, if not, the treatment is ineffective"*.

A short survey among students at the University of Zambia (UNZA) that I carried out in January 2009 showed, that more than 80 % of the total amount of 30 respondents expressed distrust of traditional healing methods and even more than half of them claimed their antipathy to *ng´angas*. The negative image of traditional healing is not only conditioned by a higher level of education, but is gradually enhanced as a consequence of the proliferation of the Pentecostal Churches in Lusaka that enjoy popularity notably amongst the educated middle class. The discourse of Pentecostal churches is primarily aimed at "demonization" of cultural traditions, in particular of traditional medicine.

The Conceptualisation of Health and Illness

In defining what illness is and how it is socially constructed, I draw on the theoretical assumptions of the Anglo-Saxon medical anthropology[9]

---

[9] Medical Anthropology was established in the 1960s in the USA. Norman Scotch defined medical anthropology as an empirical and theoretical research in anthropology and social sciences aimed at cultural representation of health, illness and medical care. He distinguished three subfields –
... footnote continues on next page

(Kleinman 1980; Young 1982; Hahn 1995) and French anthropology of illness (*anthropologie de la maladie*) (Héritier 1979; Augé and Zémpleni 1984). The later was established at the beginning of the 1980's in France by András Zempleni and Marc Augé in their publication *Le sens du mal* (1982). Unlike ethnomedicine that focused on cultural aspects of health and illness at the level of medical praxis, *anthropologie de la maladie* concentrated on the cross cultural and social aspects of health/ illness. French researchers emphasized that an anthropologist should not be interested in illness as an objective category of biomedicine, but as a category that is constructed in the process of social praxis (Augé 1982). Unlike ethnomedicine[10] whose main interest was in the human body and *materia medica* (medicinal herbs), the anthropology of illness and medical anthropology is interested in socio-cultural representations of health and illness embedded in the symbolic system of given society. "Illness is best regarded as a semantic network (a culturally articulated system) that interrelates cognitive categories, social experiences, physiological states and social relationships" (Kleinman 1980: 364). However, the illness pertains to both biological and a social order. An illness is always anchored in the reality of the suffering body, as well as in changeable social relations (Augé, Zempléni 1984).

For the purpose of later analysis of the conceptualisation of illness/health in Lusaka, I draw on the theoretical concepts of Young (1982) based on the distinctions between *disease*, *illness* and *sickness*. From his perspective *disease* represents a nosological entity referring to biomedicine in terms of organic pathologies and abnormalities. On the other hand, *illness* refers to the personal perception of a *disease*. Finally, *sickness*

---

ethnomedicine, epidemiology and public health. Anglo-Saxon medical anthropology was closely related to applied anthropology.

[10] Ethnomedicine was established in the 1960s as a field of study within "ethnoscience" in anthropology. Ethnomedicine focused on the study of medical systems of archaic societies (such as Indian, Chinese or African medicine). The research focused primarily on the collection, classification and typologies of medicinal herbs (ethnobotany) in order to create taxonomies by ethnical affiliation. The theoretical approach of ethnomedicine is based on the premises of culturalism typical for anthropology of the 1960s.

is defined as the state of the *illness* that is socially recognised and makes reference to "the process through which worrisome behavioural and biological signs are given socially significant outcomes" (Young 1982: 270). As a result, *sickness* simply indicates a process of socializing *disease* and *illness* in a given social environment. As we will see later, healers, prophets and medical practitioners skilfully manipulate and shape a patient's health at level of *disease, sickness* and *illness* at the same time

I am especially interested in the process of social construction of patient's *sickness* characterised by the linking the level of symptomatology to aetiology that is in the medical pluralistic culture situationally and contextually conditioned. In different medical systems the same symptoms may lead to different aetiology as we saw in the example of spirit possession in the previous chapter.

As indicated, the concept of *sickness* refers not only to the social construction of an illness but also of the role of the sick. In some cases a patient may feel ill, even though the people in his social environment do not perceive him as ill, or are not disposed to accept his role as sick. As a result, a patient's *illness* and *sickness* must be negotiated. The stronger a social pressure is exerted on patient, the more probable it is that he finally identify with his illness. The task of an anthropologist is thus to analyse respective medical cases carefully by focusing on the motives, strategies and attitudes of all social actors involved in the therapy in order to be able to determine the changing aspects of a patient's *illness* and *sickness*.

As it has been demonstrated by many Africanists (Evans-Pritchard 1937; Turner 1968, 1970; Janzen 1978 etc.), Africans conceive an illness in broader terms as a sort of misfortune including bad luck in business, school or marriage, the loss of property or job, unhappy love, bad harvest or even a natural disaster. The typical feature of African healing traditions is that they are holistic in nature. They draw on the idea that physical, mental, spiritual, social and environmental aspects of health/illness are closely interrelated which represents a point of departure both for diagnosis and the therapeutic process. This approach is contrary to western medicine that is traditionally considered to be secular and based on the Cartesian distinction of body and mind, focused on the treatment of symptoms and syndromes without searching for an original cause of the illness. For many Africans biomedicine is considered to be ineffective as it is not capable of dealing with the social, personal and spiritual context of the illness. As Janzen states, "the dimensions of the illness such as anxiety, social conflict, anger, witchcraft and magic were traditionally seen as outside the western medicine range (...), it leaves the social context of his illness in pathological chaos" (Janzen 1978: 250).

The definition of illness requires necessarily the definition of health, which may be perceived from different points of view. A negative definition of health as "the absence of disease" which has been abandoned gradually in medical discourse is replaced by a more complex definition employed by The World Health Organisation (2006) that specifies health as "a state of complete physical, mental, and social well-being and not merely the absence of disease, or infirmity". With respect to this multidimensional definition, the notion of health in an African context can be defined similarly but supplemented with the spiritual dimension, as the domains of health and religion are closely interconnected.

Dealing with the social aspects of illness and healing in Africa necessitates taking into consideration the anthropological concept of social reproduction[11] as applied for example by Turner, Marwick, Douglas or others. The social dimension of health refers to using and maintaining different networks representing characteristic support groups and redistributive chains in a society. The various solidarity networks whether constituted in the core of family, church community or among healers[12] are involved in the process of healing and play an important role in the negotiation and maintenance of a patient's health. The role of the sick is to a certain extend influenced by the normative order embedded in a given social group. Consequently, each occurrence of sickness defines

---

[11] Social reproduction is a sociological term referring to the processes which sustain or perpetuate characteristics of a given social structure or tradition over a period of time, it is society's ability to regenerate itself (Bourdieu 1977).

[12] *Mashabe* communities in Lusaka consist of spiritual healers (spirit mediums) who gather together on account of the overcoming of common spiritual diseases and initiation into the cultic group according to the respective spirit. In Lusaka we can find the *mashabe* communities of healers possessed by the spirit of a lion, snake, monkey or a hunter.

and mobilizes the awareness of rights and duties within a community (Janzen 1978). The health-seeking process in which the respective social body is involved is linked with cementing certain social relationships while excluding others. This holds especially for witchcraft accusations where a latent social tension or conflict in the background of a patient's illness has to be revealed through divination and remedied in order to find harmony and peace within a community. As will be shown later, the dynamics of the social networks as well as power of their normative order shapes significantly both the identity of a patient and healer.

When speaking about health (*umoyo*), informants in Lusaka connect it to the notion of peace (*mtendere*). Like peace, health is considered not to be a permanent condition, but an ideal order that has to be "fought for". In their eyes an illness is regarded as an "impurity" that makes the body contaminated (*ukukowesha*). Illuminating are other local expressions such as "confusion" (*chisokonezo*), or "disorder" that refers to Douglas's notion of "matter out of place" (Douglas 1970). Consequently, the treatment is conceived as the restoration of purity, peace and order. To express the recovery, my informants use expressions such as *kupeza mtendere mu nyumba* meaning "find peace in the house", or *kupeza mtendere mu mtima* meaning "find peace in the heart".

Linguistic analysis of the chiNyanja term *matenda* reveals that it corresponds on one hand to the biomedical notion *disease* in English on the other.[13] The term denoted an affliction caused by a human, non-human or supernatural agent as shows the local term for witchcraft – *matenda yakubantu* – meaning a "disease coming from people". In order to express *disease* in the sense Young´s definition my informants use also the term *chironda*. Although *chironda* could be translated in English as "sore", it broadly refers to any physical disease connected to the condition of a prolonged suffering body such as AIDS or cancer. To express a condition of illness, the term *kudwala* meaning "to be sick" is widely employed.

---

[13] A disease is a pathological condition of a part, organ, or system of an organism resulting from various causes, such as infection, genetic defect, or environmental stress, and characterized by an identifiable group of signs or symptoms (www. freedictionary.com).

As indicated above, the illness is not seen as merely a disruption of the physical and psychological integrity of an individual but also as an affliction caused by conflicting social and spiritual relationship manifested in the intervention of different invisible powers such as spirits, demons, ghosts and witches that are believed to penetrate the whole of life. In particular, witchcraft is perceived as the main explanatory mechanism for the presence of evil and misfortune in life. Contrary to our fragmented and dualistic conception of illness/disease that does not take into account the social and spiritual contexts and refer only to a dysfunction of the body, illness conceived by Lusaka dwellers corresponds to the findings of Fabrega and Manning (1973) in the example of Mexican medicine formulated as an integrated homeostatic theory of illness. From his point of view, the local theory of disease can be labelled "integrated" "as a number of alternative domains frequently viewed in an analytic sense by others as separate and non-overlapping are treated as conjoined and continuous. Among these domains we may include mind vs. body, social vs. psychological, and genetic vs. environmental" (Fabrega, Manning 1973: 233). The integrated theory of illness is particularly applicable when analysing witchcraft.

Let me give an example of a witchcraft medical case dealing with a local illness designated as *muchezo* that refers to a magical contagion by unintentional contact with a magical object (*chinyanga*) baited by an alleged witch. *Muchezo* is generally expressed by a collocation *kuponda pa wanga* "stepping on medicine" and manifests in the painful swelling of the legs.

Witchcraft case 1: AGNES

Agnes is a 41 year old patient of the traditional healer Kunda Kaleni, she suffers from swollen legs and believes that she has been bewitched. She has been married for 20 years and has five children. She lives in the Chazanga compound in Lusaka in a rented house together with her husband and her children. Agnes has nine siblings, her mother died a few years ago. She also takes care of two orphans (children of her elder sister who died in 2007), her ill elderly father and HIV positive older sister who both live in Lusaka. In 1981 she passed grade eight at Kabanana Primary School in Lusaka. She has good knowledge of English because she used to speak it with her elder brother who works as a teacher of English. Although Agnes has sufficient education, she does not work and depends financially on her husband who is a self-employed electrician.

I met Agnes for the first time in January 2009. Her problem started three months before when she had found a strange magical object[14] in her garden under the tree where she used to sleep. Afterwards she started to have dreams about flying or being chased by a cow. As a result, she stopped sleeping outside. However, every night she heard a strange noise as if *"someone was walking on the roof"* of her house. One day when she went to the hairdresser´s in the compound to have a chat with her friends, on the way back she felt pain in her legs. Agnes narrated: *"My legs were tough I was stuck there and could not move, my legs felt like they boiling. Maybe it was because of my high heels shoes, I thought, but when I came home I could not even move because of the pain"*. As a first option she called a pastor from The Zion Christian Church she knew to come to her house. He prayed and sprinkled Holy water over her body and in the corner of her house to protect it from witchcraft As Agnes did not notice any improvement she decided to ride her bike to the traditional healer Kunda Kaleni who lived nearby. He examined her by means of magical mirrors and told her that she suffered from *muchezo*, illness that came from people. *Muchezo*, as he explained, means that she *"stepped on the charm"* and someone took her footprint to make *nyanga* (magical object) to bewitch her. Furthermore she was told to collect the soil from the place where she found the strange object and mix it with *unga* (maize flour) and the herbs he gave her. Doctor Kaleni prescribed herbal concoction to be taken as a drink once a day and as a bathe three times per day. After having this medication Agnes admitted that she continued to sleep well, however the pain in her legs persisted.

During the second visit of Doctor Kaleni she underwent a special divination that revealed the diagnosis through writing on plain paper. She learnt that her husband had a lover who was trying to steal him from her. Furthermore, the divination revealed that Agnes was arrogant and showed off amongst people. Doctor Kaleni acknowledged that the

---

[14] She describes this objects as a tin in which white powder, herbs and needles were stuffed. All these objects were wrapped in a plastic bag and beads.

lover of Agnes's husband used *kavundula* a charm used to split the couples. As a result she had to undergo special medication together with her husband. Agnes was also told that the *muchezo* with which she was afflicted came from "other people" such as neighbours. Although she insisted that Kaleni tell her who was involved in the witchcraft, he refused as he respected the Witchcraft Act (1995) explicitly forbidding denoting someone as a witch.

Agnes was aware of a possible witchcraft attack from neighbours. She admitted that she was not very popular among people in the compound, especially among women because she was "too sociable" and provokes condemnation by wearing short skirts and trousers.[15] "*People are jealous they say I am too proud. They make a mockery of me by saying hallo, hi in English*", which proved their negative attitude. Contrary, she could not believe in her husband's infidelity and insisted on his faithfulness. Doctor Kaleni made several *ndembo* incisions on her chest and legs and rubbed a special herbal medicine in order to prevent *wanga* (charm) from "*coming up, to reach her heart*", otherwise she could die. After this consultation Agnes claimed to be able to walk a little bit again. However, she acknowledged that bad dreams occurred again when she slept outside under the tree.

Agnes' symptomatic dreams:

(1) *A dream about a lion chasing her*
"I met a tall man under the tree in some village I greeted him zikomo (thank you) when passing around him. When I turned my head I saw a lion just behind me who was chasing me and I ran and ran until I found a big river, something like the Victoria falls, then I flew over that river but then I dropped into the river and it was me now swimming".

(2) *A dream about cadaver*

---

[15] For people living in compounds, it is morally unacceptable that a woman wears a short skirt or trousers as traditional customs say that a woman should wear long *chitenje* (traditional African cloth) and cover her knees.

"Sometimes I dream that there is a person completely rotten with maggots saying to me: "Come, I take you".

(3) *Oppressive dreams*
"Sometimes I can see, and I can feel, that someone who is very fat and heavy is sitting on me so that I cannot breathe properly. I want to open my eyes but I can't then I want to scream "people help me" but again I can't as if there were something pressing down on me. When I wake up finally I find myself very wet and shivering".

(4) *A dream about adultery*
"Sometimes I can have funny dreams about another man making love to me but it is not my husband".

(5) *A dream about fat women*
"I dreamt about a very fat woman. I could see her only from one side from the other side I could not see her. She was fat with a lot of tattoos on her body and big breasts. She was singing but I couldn't exactly hear what she was singing. She was telling me "I told you to give me something you couldn't give me". I was screaming "eee eee" I was so scared the way she was looking at me, she looked like an animal. Her breasts were so big that I couldn't see her face.

As a consequence Agnes decided to visit Doctor Kaleni again. This time, he took action to protect her house by burying a protective medicine under the tree and sprinkling the corners and roof of the house with *mbosha*, protective herbal medicine. A few days after Agnes told me: "*I woke up a little bit late, my children found blood all over around base of the tree. Black blood was following the shade in the same way as I do during the day. I called my neighbour 'come and see!' The blood marks were going up to one house, the second, and the third house and then disappeared*". Doctor Kaleni explained this event with words: "*That tree was the meeting place of witches. I shot them so that medicine came up to their anus and they started bleeding*". Since that time the house has been protected and Agnes claimed to have slept peacefully. Soon after Agnes discovered (by checking his diary and SMS in his mobile) that her husband was really unfaithful with another women from the compound as Doctor Kaleni had indicated during the first divination. She commented: "*He* [her husband] *starts coming back very late. A few days ago he came back home in the morning, so I decided to act and told him everything. He was very upset and beat me so I had to call the police. ...when I talk to him he never listened to me, he sees me only as ugly and does not want to sleep with me. It has to be kavundula"*. After being convinced about *kavundula* witchcraft employed by the love rival, she agreed to undergo another course of medication consisting of a series of cleansing procedures as prescribed by Doctor Kaleni. When I spoke to Agnes for the last time before I left Lusaka, she admitted that she feels much better after the medication. Even I could observe the progress in her physical and mental condition. However, she told me in confidence that she was still afraid that the problems will return.

As we could see in this example, Agnes's illness was interpreted by a traditional healer as multi-causal, i.e. having several causes both in the social and spiritual realm that are both dialectically interconnected. The jealousy of a love rival employing the *kavundula* charm as well as the envy of her neighbours employing the magic called *muchezo* was interpreted as witchcraft. As follows from the schema below, the interpretation of illness is primarily grounded in the disturbed social relationship reflected in the sphere of religiosity (the use of magic, intervention of a witch). The symptomatology is manifested both on the level of psychology, (oppressive dreams, nightmares and paranoia) and on the level of psychosomatology (feeling pain – hotness, nightmares – tiredness). There is also the environmental aspect of an illness which should be taken in account. Agnes got contaminated by the magic through direct bodily contact with a magical object that has had a malign impact on her body causing the painful swelling in her leg. Moreover the magic was made from the soil containing her footprints considered to be an integrated part of her biological body. In conclusion, we can assume that the Lusaka dwellers conceptualise illness as a comprehensive category embracing social, spiritual, environmental, physiological and psychological aspects. These are considered to be all interrelated in an integral whole and play an important role in the process of diagnosis and treatment.

Schema 3: Medical Case 1 – Integrated Theory of Illness

Psychology	Oppressive dreams and nightmares
	Auditory hallucinations
	Frustration (husband's infidelity, unpopularity among people in the community where she lives)
Physiology	Painful swelling of the legs
Psychosomatology	Bodily symptoms described in terms of feeling hotness, tiredness (not sleeping well at night)
Environment	Contagion through the touch of a magical object
	Footprints as an integrative part of the biological body
Society	Envy of the neighbours
	Conflicts with a husband
Cosmology	Intervention of a witch
	Belief in efficacy of contagious magic

Dealing with the local conceptualisations of health/illness, I would like to dwell on an idea concerning the balance of "distribution of health and illness in the world". As I observed, Lusaka dwellers share the opinion that one cannot be healed unless his illness is transferred to someone else. Consequently, an illness is regarded as the manifestation of the omnipresent evil "circulating in the air ready to afflict anyone". The commonly shared idea that one can become afflicted with an illness at the same time when someone else gets rid of it and recovers refers to the logic of the distribution of health and illness which can be compared to the principle of balances or communicating vessels.

As I noticed during several healing sessions, a witch-finder employs contra-magic as a healing strategy in order to send the patient's illness back to a witch. Reversing the charm against a sender is a prerequisite for a patient's successful recovery which means that a patient can be gradually cured at the same time as a witch becomes afflicted. To control the effectiveness of the contra-magic, some witch-finders use a special glass bottle filled with water and small wooden sticks. By checking the surface of the water in the bottle, they can estimate if their procedure was effective or not. If the water surface in the bottle gradually raises it means that the witch is afflicted. When the water suddenly turns to red, it means that the witch was finally killed. As we can see, the process of healing and affliction are implicitly interconnected.

This rule does not proceed only in the case of contra magic but also in other healing practices such as cleansing procedures called *kusamba*. This purgatory ritual consists of "washing out" the illness from the surface of patient's body by means of bathing in a special herbal concoction. After the patient's body has been cleansed, the used concoction, as well as the patient's clothes are buried at the crossroad in the forest so that the first man who passes there becomes afflicted – "take the reins". As Doctor Bongo explained, "*If you throw an illness on place where no people walk then it will not leave you. You know, the cross must be always carried by someone! Sickness is always here* [pointing his finger in the air] *just waiting for another one*".

The logic of illness distribution based on the principle of communicating vessels lies at base of the idea of witchcraft. Someone who has suddenly advanced, gained wealth, power or was promoted at work is most often designated as a witch. People believe that one cannot succeed in any other way than "at the expense" of another. This implies the idea that the good (health, wealth and happiness) is limited in the world. This principle corresponds to the model of limited good developed by Redfield (1952, 1960) and Foster (1965). Foster, who deals with the nature of cognitive orientations of peasant societies and its relation to economic behaviour[16], noticed that "peasants view all the desired things of life, such as wealth, health, status, etc., as existing in a finite quantity and as being in short supply" (Foster 1965: 296). As the good things in life are perceived as limited and it is not possible to expand the quantity. Consequently, people believe that if one profits in life, it must be at the expense of others. This type of reasoning is closely connected to the local conceptualisation of a witch as someone embodying insatiable greed,

---

[16] According to Kearney (1969) the "model of limited good" seems inadequate to explain facts in the peasant economic sphere. However, when it is used in connection with non-economic aspects of life, the reasoning becomes more strained.

acting anti-socially and driven by the desire to harm. In this logic any kind of "surpassing" such as success in work, business, school or even politics is conceptualised locally in terms of individualism and selfishness. The individualism or individual accumulation of funds is seen as a threat to the collectively shared egalitarian norms of reciprocity and therefore implies the notion of witchcraft.

The Conceptualisation of Body

Current anthropological studies treat the body as a physical and symbolical artefact, as a meaningful object. It is supposed that the cultural order takes shape upon the physical body interweaving ecology, cosmology, society and physiology into a coherent whole. As a result, it is difficult if not impossible to abstract the individual body from the environment, social and spiritual realm. These assumptions about body are closely linked to the conceptualisations of person and a self that are culturally biased. The African conception of a person and self differs substantially from our western recognition of the category of individuated person separate from the rest of the society and the universe. In many parts of Africa including Zambia a person is regarded as inextricably linked with other members of society as well as with the invisible word inhabited by different nonhuman beings. Collectivism and shared reciprocity is thus the basis of personal identity and his moral anchorage. Whereas the Western conception of a person assumes that one can be endowed with only one self, Africans believe in the existence of a multiple self as is shown in the examples of witchcraft and spirit possession. The notions of person and self are closely linked to body imagery, i.e. "individual and idiosyncratic representation about the individual body in its relationship to the environment, including internal and external perception, memories, affects, cognitions and actions" (Lock, Sheper-Hughes 1987:16).

At the level of theory I draw on the concept of individual, social and political body elaborated by the famous medical anthropologists Margaret M. Lock and Nancy Sheper-Hughes in their challenging article *The Mindful Body: A Prolegomenon to Future Work in Medical Anthropology* from 1987. The authors define the *individual body* in spirit of Marcel Mauss (1938) as "lived experience of body self as existing apart from other individual bodies" (Lock; Sheper-Hughes 1987: 7). They point out that the conceptualisation of an individual body varies cross-culturally. The classical western dualistic vision of an individual body as separated from and opposed to the mind issuing from the long European history has been contested by socio-centric notions of self-prevalent in many non-western societies including sub-Saharan Africa.

The concept of *social body* inspired by famous symbolical anthropologist Mary Douglas (1966) lies in assumption that the body is conceived as an integrated system, a natural symbol with which we think about nature, society and culture. The individual and social body intermingle and influence each other. In Africa, the bodily disorders are seen as directly caused by social tensions and conflicts for which the cultural idiom of witchcraft is deep rooted. As a result the healing is not directed only at the individual suffering body but also act on the social body, the community.

Finally *politic body* refers to the ways in which the individual and social body is linked to power and social control. The interconnection amongst individual, social and political body is the most visible on examples of witchcraft-eradication movement[17], ethnic violence[18], or political enemy hunts. In this respect Mary Douglas (1966) points out that when a community experiences itself as threatened it will respond by expanding the number of social and political controls regulating "undesired" individuals or groups in the process of constructing both internal and external social boundaries. For the purpose of my later analysis of illness and witchcraft I decided to enrich this tripartite scheme with a construct of *spiritual body* referring to interconnection and anchorage of the individual and social body in the spiritual realm. This category helps to elucidate how the intervention of witches, spirits and other invisible agents are inscribed in the individual and social body and vice versa. Society, its hierarchy, structure, social roles and values are undoubtedly reflected in the religion that in return exerts influence on individuals through the institution of ritual. As we will see later, the spiritual body plays an important role in the process of body imagery, for example

---

[17] See Auslander 1993.
[18] See Taylor 2012.

projection of the internal processes in the individual body (ideas about blood, reproduction, sexuality etc.) on beliefs about witchcraft techniques the magical plane consuming the human blood, the witch's ability to tie the womb etc.), or projection of a social body and its social norms and ethics (communalism, reciprocity, sharing wealth among the family members, respect for elders etc.) into the ideas about witches as anti-social beings, representing the reversal of a given social order.

Another theory I decided to employ for the interpretation of indigenous conceptualisations of body is the *hot and cold theory*[19] based on the assumption that one must maintain the body's internal "temperature", the balance between the opposing powers of hot and cold to insure good health. This implies the avoidance of extreme or prolonged exposure of one quality or another, i.e. an excessive high temperature or low temperature in the body which denotes an illness. Consequently, the therapeutic process endeavours to restore health by re-establishing the "temperature balance" in the body. However, in the local classifications, the hot and cold elements do not only pertain to the actual body temperature, but refer to a symbolic power contained in the diverse substances such as food, herbal medicine and human fluids. As a result, an afflicted person who experience physical changes in his body, in terms of excessive coolness, hotness, dryness or wetness endeavours to restore the proper balance in his body. In this respect, the most common therapeutic technique is the use of the appropriate herbal medicine to withdraw excess heat or cold from the body. The local conceptualisation of health, as a proper balance between hot and cold, wet and dry elements in the body, is in its inner logic similar to the humoral theory of disease developed in the 5 century B.C. by Hippocrates.[20]

---

[19] Many anthropologists dealt with the dialectics of hot and cold in the symbolism of the body: Bouchner 1980; Bourdillon 1972; Comaroff 1985, de Heusch 1987; Devisch 1993; Héritier 1979, Kaspin 1996, Turner 1967 etc.

[20] In the humour theory, health is viewed as a state of balance among four humours: blood, phlegm, black bile and yellow bile. The humoral theory of disease can be found not only in Europe and Africa but also in South America and Asia.

The hot–cold theory applied to the African medical setting discloses that natural processes metaphorically correspond to processes in the body. As Deborah Kaspin showed in her study of the *Chewa cosmology of the body* (1996), human reproduction is symbolically linked to agricultural production. According to Kaspin the local conceptualisation of the body pursues two main principles: Fluidity and temperature that draw on the ecological and biological organisation, and the principle of "body as a map of territory" that draws on cosmological and physiological organisation. In her interpretations, a metaphorical linkage between physiology and ecology is expressed in parallels between the seasonal processes in nature and life processes in the body. This means that coolness which is conventionally linked to water (rain) irrigating dry soil to make it fertile is metaphorically associated with the process of human reproduction. The "cool and wet" sperm of a man is believed to fecundate a woman's womb which is metaphorically regarded as hot and dry soil, waiting to be irrigated.

Local Conceptualisation of Body

The starting point of my analysis of the local conceptualisation of illness in Lusaka is the concern about the individual body as a "man's first and most natural instrument" (Mauss 1938), that we are fully aware until experience of the suffering, being trubled (*kuvutika*). Lusaka dwellers conceptualise the ill body as weak (*foka*)[21] meaning that it is vulnerable, it is not able to resist, and it is easily to be attacked by invisible powers. The health of the "biological" body is especially linked to the proper functioning of three domains considered to be most important: 1. reproduction, 2. digestion/secretion and 3. blood circulation.

Maximal use of the capacity of reproduction, i.e. having as many children as possible in one's life, is considered to be one of the most important tasks of a human, proof of his health, a well-functioning body and an unimpugnable duty towards society. The ability of reproduction does not lie only in the physiologically functional human reproductive

---

[21] In the Christian context a „weak" person is vulnerable, easily attacked by evil spirit as he/she has no faith.

system but it is also a question of being on good terms with one's kin and ancestors who exert a significant influence on this sphere. A vengeful witch from the close family or a wrathful ancestor has allegedly the capacity to "tie the womb" of a woman or "make the man's sexual organ disappeared" in order to obstruct reproduction.

The various disorders of the digestive system figure predominantly in the process of diagnosis and treatment of spiritually caused diseases such as witchcraft, spirit possession or magical contagion. Whereas a healthy individual is seen as having full, fat body with proper digestive functioning, the sick is often linked with an image of thin, shrunk body. The functioning of the digestive tract from "up to down" is metaphorically designed as a "tube" (*chubu*) or a "snake" (*njoka*). The digestive system with its centre in abdomen conceived as a "seat of life" includes other organs such as stomach, intestines, spleen, pancreas, liver and even the whole urinary system. Nausea, indigestion, diarrhoea, vomiting, constipation and other digestive disorders are diagnosed as emanating from disturbed social relations within the close family or neighbourhood and interpreted as a witchcraft attack. Since the digestive system is considered to be the only "open" system in the human body capable to receive the material issues from the outside word (food and liquids), it is regarded as the most vulnerable, particularly to witchcraft attack. The local idea of hated kin embodied in a witch that attacks the reproductive system by feeding his victim in the night with poisoned food or drink, is wide spread throughout the whole of Lusaka. The purgatory ritual prescribed by witch-finders consists of a special medicine eliciting vomiting and diarrhoea.[22] This therapy helps the body get rid of the "impure" substances and thus be healed. As we can see, the digestive system represents a place where the individual, social and spiritual body are the most interconnected.

Human blood as well as sperm which come under the same category is believed to contain a vital force *moyo* ("life" in chiNyanja). "These

---

[22] This procedure is practiced not only by traditional healers but also by prophets from Zion Christian Churches in Lusaka in healing the bewitched patients. The only difference is that prophets use the blessed water instead of herbal medicine.

bodily fluids generate, sustain, and invigorate life, while their diminishment leads to infertility and death" (Kaspin 1996: 569). Consequently the lack of sperm or amenorrhea is often linked to infertility – *chumba* [for woman], *chibola* [for men]. As I found out, the *moyo* changes throughout the course of life. Children and young people are considered the most vital as their blood is *"quick, fresh, powerful and abundant"*. As a person ages, blood becomes slow, weak and dries out which leads to death. The witches are supposed to choose their victims preferably among children and youths as their quick and powerful blood can figuratively kick start the business generating money.

As in many other African societies, healers in Lusaka strictly distinguish between pure and impure blood. The later represents menstrual blood, lochia (blood after childbirth) or spilled blood on the ground in consequence of a murder or slaughter in a fight or hunting. As the holder of impure blood is regarded as highly contaminating and thus dangerous for the rest of society, special attention is paid to his seclusion and ritual cleansing.

As I observed, the Lusaka dwellers understand the healthy/ill body in terms of open/closed flow. It is not only the flow of blood, faeces and bodily fluids that are experienced at the level of an individual body, but in a broader sense also the flow of communication in interpersonal relations embodied at the level of social body. The individual and social body are interfaced in the realm of religiosity, where the projection of social relations as well as the feeling of corporality is experienced. The communication between man and invisible powers intermediated by healers seem to play an important role in the process of medication of both the individual and social body.

Let us first focus on the individual body. The unobstructed and appropriate flows of blood, faeces and different bodily fluids such as urine, lather, saliva, sperm, milk and others are generally seen as essential to maintaining good health. On the contrary, the blockage in the flow (for example amenorrhea, constipation, and hypogalacie), its slowdown (for example hypomenorrhea) or fast flow (for example hypermenorrhea, menorrhagia, diarrhoea, amnesia, hypergalacie etc.) indicates illness and necessitates therapeutic intervention.

As the imagery of body is reflected in the social sphere, well-being is more broadly defined as the fluent unobstructed flow of communication between people that helps to construct the relationship of mutual trust, help and reciprocity. This behaviour is especially expected among close family kin. Stagnation in communication, quarrels or other sorts of tensions issuing from the violation of a binding norm of sociability opens the space for diverse speculation in terms of the involvement of witchcraft, ancestors or divine wrath.

It is not only fluidity that serves as a measure of man's vitality and health, but also the feeling of coolness and hotness and seeking the proper balance between these two elements. People in Lusaka believe that as the body acquires, shares, and loses fluids through its lifetime, it heats and cools and therefore strengthens or weakens its power. According to Deborah Kaspin who made the research in a similar cultural setting among Chewa, cold is linked to low sexual capacity such as of children, postmenopausal women (old men) and barren women, whereas hot refers to sexually active adults. She argues that "at one extreme the corpses are cold when dead, at the other extreme menstruating women are hot as is the food they cook" (Kaspin 1996: 569).

French structural anthropologist Françoise Héritier showed in her study *Symbolique de l'inceste et sa prohibition* (1979) that the symbolic logic of incest among Samos of Burkina Faso is based on binary oppositions whereas two principles are significant: the balance of oppositions and the accumulation of similarities. According to Héritier, "similarities repel and opposites attract, warmness attracts coldness and humidity" (Héritier 1979: 285). She attempts to show that the sexual taboo for men is symbolically constructed through the prohibition of having sexual intercourse with an immature girl, or with a woman in the menopause. In her opinion, Samo people attribute the principle of hotness to a man and his sperm, as the sperm is inherently linked to blood. Consequently, procreation is perceived as the mixing of blood from two kin groups, in the sexual act of the spouses. Whereas menarcheal women are considered to be cold because they lose blood (hotness) every month, a premenstrual, menopausal, and pregnant woman is linked to the principle of hotness because she does not lose her blood and thus accumulates warmth.

According to the "logic of difference and similarity", binary opposites such as hot and cold, optimally lead to an equilibrium, i.e. reproduction among Samo while the similarities lead to disruption, i.e.

sterility (see the figure below). As a result, symbolic of the prohibition on having sexual intercourse with pre-menstrual or menopausal women is constructed around the local conceptualisation of hotness and coldness of the body. Samo men thus can have sexual intercourse and get married only with a menarcheal woman whereas a pre-menstrual girl or a menopausal woman is "taboo" for them.

Man + pre-menstrual girl = warm + warm → dryness → sterility
Man + menopausal woman = warm + warm → dryness → sterility
Man + menarcheal woman = warm + cold → wetness → fertility, reproduction

In Lusaka, the classification of sterility and fertility is made on a similar structural principle, except that the local conceptualisation of the male–female body is reversed. A man is linked to the coldness because of the wetness of his sperm which is metaphorically associated with rainfalls. On the other hand, woman symbolises dryness and warmness as she is linked to the dry hot land. The exceptions are pre-menstrual, menopausal and barren women who are considered to be cold. On the other hand, a woman who is just having menstruation, a woman after giving birth, or one who has just aborted is considered to be excessively warm ("like a fire") because her blood is impure and therefore dangerous for men. The belief that a man who has sexual intercourse with a woman who has just aborted without being ritually cleansed becomes mad is widespread in all Zambia. In the same way, intercourse of an immature girl with a sexually-active adult considered as a transgression or taboo results in severe punishment from ancestors in the form of a "strange" disease known as *mdulo* showing symptoms such as swelling of the legs, malaise, coughing, weakness. This disease that has been ethnographically documented also in neighbouring countries[23] is considered to be magically contagious and may be easily conveyed from transgressor to a third party. Clyde Mitchell mentions this illness (*ndaka*) among Yaka in Central Africa. According to him "Ndaka affects the sexually inactive when they are brought into contact with those who are

---

[23] In Malawi (Marwick 1965, Schoffeleers 1978), Democratic Republic of Congo (Mitchell 1956).

sexually active" (Mitchell 1956a: 137). In general, this disease occurs when a vulnerable person who is considered cool (such as a new-born, pre-menstrual girls, menarcheal women and neophytes) comes in contact with people who are hot because of sexual activity, menstruation or even involvement in witchcraft. As will be shown in the next chapter, in order to avoid mystical contagion it is necessary to adhere to the socially binding norms – taboos.

Another commonly accepted idea concerning sexuality in Zambia is that a woman should not be wet and cold inside her vagina when having sexual intercourse with a man. Her coldness and natural wetness are in the same manner as excessive hotness believed to be dangerous to men, leading to sterility and death. In fact, Lusaka dwellers regard prostitutes (*mahule*) as infertile, because they accumulate too much wetness in the form of sperm due to the fact that they regularly change sexual partners. This excessive wetness inside the vagina and womb causes that the foetus cannot take root there and slips out. In this way promiscuity, as an undesirable and high risk behaviour due to the prevalence of H.I.V/AIDS is symbolically linked to sterility.

As I observed, a common physical problem of women in Lusaka, described in terms of *choka manzi* meaning "the water comes out (from the vagina)", was often diagnosed by traditional healers as well as prophets. A woman with excessive wetness (perhaps because of some gynaecological problem) is regarded, not only as repulsive to a man but infertile at the same time. To prevent a woman from the natural wetness occurring before sexual intercourse, a special herbal medicine called *nyang´anya* is prescribed by healers. "*Nyang´anya makes women dry and warm so that a man can enjoy the sex (…) otherwise women which are wet and thus cold inside are like a cadaver and repeal man*", said Doctor Kasanda. As I noted, the traditional practise of so called "dry sex" is widespread all over Zambia. From the biomedical point of view, this practice is considered to be highly risky because HIV is transmitted more easily in this way. As a result, the health education provided by many NGO's in Lusaka is aimed at fighting against it in order to prevent the spread of AIDS.[24] However,

---

[24] The demystification of the belief that "sex with a virgin can heal AIDS" by a massive health educational campaign (planting billboards in Lusaka city)
… footnote continues on next page

from the local point of view, the abandonment of "dry sex" would go against the local image of a successful procreation.

Another point I would like to highlight here is the local conceptualisation of excessive hotness. As data obtained during my fieldwork showed, excessive hotness in both the female and male body is often linked to magically and spiritually caused illnesses. The wrath and anger of spirits as well as witches is believed to "heat up the body" and thus bring illness. Those bewitched are believed to have spoilt impure blood, which has a dark colour and lumpy consistency, in contrast to healthy blood which should be light and diluted. The cooling effect of water in combination with "cold herbal medicine" involved in diverse purgatory rituals prescribed by *ng'anga* towards mourners, women after giving birth, or those afflicted with spirits, or witchcraft.

The fact, that witchcraft as magical contamination of a body is linked to hotness is apparent from the use of the local expression *kupya* "to be heated" as a synonym of *kulodza* "being bewitched". In particular, hotness in one's legs is attributed to witchcraft through "stepping on *wanga*" (charms) concealed by an alleged witch in a certain place in order to afflict their victim. Moreover, witches themselves are associated with the element of fire. Doctor Mukanda told me that some of the witches use fire medicine (*mankhwala ku mulilo*) in order to afflict their victims from a distance by means of *chilubi* (a voodoo doll representing the victim) burnt to ash. The ash is then mixed with other herbal medicine in order to bewitch or "heat" a victim.

However, the excessive hotness in the body is not associated with witchcraft attacks only, but with spirit possession as well. The local expression *kuvina pa mulilo* meaning "dancing on fire" refers to the *mashabe* spirit possession. I had an opportunity to assist in *ngoma*, the traditional healing ceremony during which the spiritual mediums possessed by the spirits danced on live coal, exposed their bodies to flames, drank the hot blood of a sacrificed goat (*mbuzi*),[25] ate live coal and smoked cigarettes[26]

---

took place five years ago and was one of the most famous and successful fights against the "traditional prejudices" in Lusaka.

[25] The sacrifice of a goat during the *ngoma* initiation ceremony symbolises the death of a sufferer in exchange for the new life and identity – that of a healer.

in order to demonstrate the presence and strength or the spirit entering their body. The attributes of hotness are thus associated with spirits who are considered to be dangerous (afflicting). A medium afflicted with the spirit has to undergo the *ngoma* ritual in order "to calm down" or "cool" the spirit. As I found out, the "coolness" is used as a synonym of calmness and peace and refers to the practice of appeasing the ancestral spirit (*mashabe*) in a spirit medium.

Similarly, the healers from The New Jesus Disciple Church, in order to demonstrate the presence of the Holy Spirit in their bodies, employed the metaphors of hotness in their songs. For instance, the song *napieyne* "I am burning" which was sung several times during the healing session in the church should, according to my informants help to induce the prophet's Holy Spirit possession so indispensable for healing patients.

In order to describe the bodily symptoms, the patients in Lusaka preferably employ a variety of metaphors. These do not reflect only on physical feelings, but also to emotional and social considerations. The pain, as a feeling, is not given independent status it is interlinked to particular emotions, anatomical entities, interpersonal tensions or even

---

[26] A possessed medium usually smokes cigarettes. This ritual behaviour occurs during the *ngoma* healing ceremony as well as during the individual divination séances. It is not clear, what exactly smoking cigarettes symbolises. According to Shoko (2007), dealing with Karanga *shave* spirit possession in Zimbabwe, the spirit mediums smoke cigarettes and drink tea (or beer) to imitate the European way of life. When asked, spiritual healers in Lusaka claimed that *mashabe* ancestral spirits like smoking because they did it when they lived. It seems probable to me that in the past smoking cigarettes prevailed among men as this habit was not as negatively perceived as nowadays when the overwhelming majority of Zambians do not smoke because they consider smoking sinful and unhealthy (Christian propagandas). The ritual smoking of cigarettes may also refer to the symbolic therapeutic value attributed to smoking itself. It is believed that by smoking one can "call and bring" whatever is asked for. Finally, the ritual smoking of cigarettes may in my opinion refer to the symbolism of hotness in the body of possessed mediums and thus represents another "hot element" involved in the ritual settings of *mashabe* healing ceremony.

From Where Does the Bad Wind Blow? 63

situations as a whole. The following interpretation of the most common metaphors employed by the patients in Lusaka leans on "semiological translation" a shift between the semiological system of informants and the semilogical system of a researcher (de Sardan 1995: 89). The semiological translation of symptoms as experienced by a patient enables us to better comprehend the patient's explanatory model, i.e. how the illness is constructed from their point of view.

To illustrate the use of metaphors, let me give an example of the description of backache or headache. Although the patients are acquainted with chiNyanja expressions *msana ku wava* (backache) or *mutu ku wava* (headache), they tend to use the metaphor of heaviness instead. Having a headache, patients complained about "feeling like carrying a heavy load" or, "feeling as if someone was walking on them". This metaphor can be explained by the fact that the chiNyanja term *kulema* means both "heavy" and "tired". Furthermore, a sharp pain in the stomach is often expressed by saying "something is eating my intestines" or "rising up the snake". The experience of dizziness is described in terms of drunkenness whereas bodily weakness is expressed in terms of laziness. Respiratory troubles, experienced by the majority of patients due to the high degree of car pollution in Lusaka, are commonly described by a locution "someone or something is kneeling on my neck" or, "someone or something is sitting on me". The depression troubling many patients in Lusaka, in particular women, is often expressed by collocation "thinking too much", "having restless heart", or "feeling to be in the bottle".

Let me now demonstrate the conceptualisation of bodily symptoms on the narrative of David Chamba,[27] a 26 year old patient of a traditional healer who suffers from epilepsy (a biomedical diagnosis)[28] and believes he is bewitched by his mother (a traditional diagnosis). When I interviewed David, he described his ailments in the following words:

"I feel like dying for some minutes without knowing [the epileptic seizure, he suffers from a blackout which lasts for several minutes], when I

---

[27] The complete medical case of David Chamba is described in chapter 7.
[28] David Chamba was hospitalised in the Chainama psychiatric hospital for the first time in 2007, the provisional diagnosis was seizure disorder.

wake up I feel lazy [body weakness] and powerless. I feel more like drunk [dizziness], not myself (…). Sometimes I become mad just like that. I am possessed by the spirit of lion (a powerful mashabe spirit inherited in the family) which is fighting in me and beating all who touched me [restlessness, aggressive behaviour] (...) I feel like something is moving in my throat like a snake [respiratory problems] (…) Sometimes when I am sleeping and I feel as if someone is kneeling on my neck [respiration problems, fitful sleep], I feel like dead and then I become alive again. It is like I feel lot of air coming into the house without a person coming inside [hallucinations connected to witchcraft]".

Illness Aetiology

The first task of an anthropologist concerned with the study of medical culture is to find out the simplest local taxonomy of causality beliefs (Foster 1976). The causality classification I suggest here is based on my observations and interviews with different traditional healers, prophets and their patients. It corresponds in a certain measure to the central and south Bantu aetiological model proposed by other scholars such as Janzen (1978), Foster (1976) and Oosthuizen (1989). Unlike their classification which is triadic, mine includes a forth causal level, that of mystical contagion. What has to be stressed here is that in African nosology no fixed relationship exists between specific causes and symptoms. Particular aetiologies such as witchcraft can be applied to a wide range of sensations and, conversely, similar sensations may be associated with various aetiologies (Horton 1967:16).

Illness caused by God or nature

This comes under the category of the biomedical notion *disease* to which correspond the chiNyanja term *matenda*. The diseases such as tuberculosis, sexual transmitted diseases, AIDS, malaria, diarrhoea, asthma, cancer, influenza, cholera and hepatitis and other diseases are generally considered to be natural, thus not spiritually caused.

Illness caused by the magical aggression of a man

This aetiology is associated with witchcraft (*mfiti*). The diagnosis of this kind of illness is generally known under term *matenda yakubantu* meaning "diseases caused by people", or under the English term "African disease".

Illness caused by the mystical aggression of a spirit

It is believed that a spirit can afflict one by possessing him (*kukunena*), or "hanging on him" (*chamukwerera*). Spirit possession is common illness aetiology in Lusaka, both in the indigenous and Christian medical setting. One can get possessed and therefore afflicted either by powerful ancestral spirits *mashabe*, by dangerous intrusive ghosts called *chivanda*, or graveyard revenants *chipuku*. Spirit possession can be explained either negatively as a spiritual punishment for improper behaviour, mystical contamination, or witchcraft, or positively as spiritual selection. The medium is believed to be involuntarily chosen by an ancestor who wishes to be recognised and worshipped. Traditional medicine treats the former case by means of exorcism or body cleansing (*kusamba*), whereas the latter is often linked to adorcism in Luc de Heusch's words (1962). It is believed that any possessing spirit whether ancestral, Christian or foreign announce their coming in the form of an illness. The spirits can afflict a medium by an accident, or as a result of inattention. They can be also transmitted, or inherited within the family. Additionally, spirits in particular *chivanda*, might be intentionally manipulated by a witch and transferred to someone by means of charms.

Illness caused by mystical contagion

It is believed that one can be afflicted by direct contact with an impure, spiritually dangerous entity. The notion of contagiousness in the Durkheimian (1965) sense of the term is closely linked to the transition between the domains of the sacred and profane. As it is conceptualised in the study of religion, the transition between these two domains is charged with ambiguity, endowed with both dangerous (afflicting) and potent (healing) powers. A person suddenly possessed by a spirit, bewitched by a charm, or contaminated by an impurity is involuntarily involved with the sacred. As the access to the sacred is regulated by a whole system of ritual prohibitions that are needed to protect themselves from being contaminated by the sacred.

One can become mystically contaminated either by accident and therefore unintentionally, or through one's own unintentional fault, or finally as a consequence of the infringement of taboos. The first type of contagion can be illustrated with the example of the stepping over a harmful concoction that Oosthuizen (1992) classifies as "an environmental hazard". *Kuponda pa wanga* – stepping on a dangerous charm in a form of an invisible medicinal herb (*wanga*) – is the most common sort of magical contagion in Lusaka.

Another example of unintentional mystical contagion is *kusewera ndi wanga* – "playing with magic". One can be stricken unknowingly through the improper manipulation of the protective medicine that had been enchanted before by someone, or if it has not been applied properly. As a result, a protective medicine turns into a dangerous *wanga*. In both of these cases, the charm turns against the user or his relatives and afflicts them. As Doctor Kasanda told me, *"there are people who protect their fields or relatives secretly on their own, it is better if your child is told, your wife is aware, because in the case that you die then your wife is not able to defuse that thing* [charm] *to stop it working (…) or maybe you just shift and somebody who buys that field will die."*

Mystical contagion as a cause of illness, or death can also come through disrespect of certain taboos concerning restrictions on touching impure persons. According to the local conceptualisations, the person is considered to be impure after having sexual intercourse, after having delivered or aborted a child, or while menstruating or mourning. There are also ritual restrictions concerning the manipulation with small children as they are considered to be especially vulnerable and can thus be easily contaminated. For instance, the Lusaka dwellers share the opinion that a child can become ill with respiratory problems if they are touched by someone who just had sexual intercourse, or that a child can be born ill or can even die if the woman who is pregnant is breastfeeding another child at the same time. This is due to the belief that a child who is breastfed sucks the life (energy) out from the one in the womb. The similar folk aetiology can be found in Uganda to explain the *kwashiorkor* an acute form of childhood protein-energy malnutrition in a child recently weaned. It is believed that the unborn child is jealous of its older sibling, whom it tries to poison through the mother's milk, thereby forcing weaning (Burgess and Dean 1962: 25). The mothers must also be cautious about the removal of the umbilical cord because if after being dried, the cord drops from the right side of the child, it is believed it will be impotent in the future. Unless the umbilical cord is buried a child can be bewitched and cannot grow any more. Such a child stays underdeveloped and does not gain height or dies shortly after its birth. It is also believed that a man becomes mad (*ofunta*) if he has sexual intercourse with a woman who miscarried or delivered a dead baby without being ritually cleansed. As will be discussed further in the text, the collecting, storing and use of medicinal herbs (*mankhwala*) is also subjected to diverse ritual restrictions.

It is important to stress that the aetiologies outlined are not exclusive, but rather complementary. The different causal levels often intermingle during the process of diagnosis. For instance, diseases such as cerebral malaria or AIDS commonly considered as natural can be caused even by witchcraft. People in Lusaka believe that a witch can simulate AIDS by applying the *chizimba* (a medicine of animal base) of chameleon so that a victim starts suffering and shrinking until he dies. It is believed that witchcraft is an advanced science and those who master it can easily imitate complicated diseases such as AIDS or malaria to kill their victims. Witchcraft as an illness aetiology can interface both with spirit possession, or mystical contagion. In the former case a witch is believed to send *vivanda* of his dead victims to possess, i.e. bewitch other living people, or to exploit them for work in "invisible plantations".

The aetiological classification suggested above is, to a certain extent, common for both indigenous and Christian therapeutic systems in Lusaka. The only difference is in the terminology. As my research revealed, the Christian healers (prophets) tend to simplify the traditional spiritual world by embracing a number of different spirits under the united category of a "demon" (*demoni*) or a "bad spirit" (*mzimu woyipa*).

Typology of Healing and Afflicting Spirits

With respect to a given aetiology, I attempt to outline a typology of afflicting and healing spirits involved in the process of diagnosis. As indicated before the border between the healing and afflicting aspects of spirit possession is thin and permeable. This assumption raises the question, why is the presence of the incoming spirit in the body always accompanied by suffering? Here, I draw on the widespread cosmological idea that spirits are distinguished by a permanent search for a place, or sanctuary where they could dwell or materialize themselves. As Josef Kandert pointed out, "only one spirit can reside in the material container (...), if a spirit enters a container (body) where another spirit (self, or soul) is already dwelling then it leads to the health troubles of the container" (Kandert 2009:1). As a result, a spirit that chooses its medium cannot manifest itself otherwise than in the form of an illness. The occurrence of an illness is in fact an allegoric form of "collision" between the self and the in-coming spirit.

However, the objectives and reasons for spirit possession can differ. Spirits can be auspicious, coming to possess a chosen medium in order to carry out a "mission", to "do some work" (*ndili nchito*) as my informants say, or to warn of a danger. This is the case with *mashabe* spirits which come under the category of healing spirits. Besides the auspicious spirits, there are also dangerous spirits (*chivanda, chipuku*) that can possess one either by themselves or might be sent by someone in order to cause a misfortune.

Ancestral Spirits

The first significant group consists of ancestral spirits called *mashabe* in chiyNyanja, or *ngulu* in Bemba. These spirits manifest themselves in the form of a wild animal such as a lion (*mkanko*), snake (*njoka*), baboon (*kolwe*), or a hunter (*shabinda*). As I was told, "*mashabe stay within and follow the family tree*", which means that they can be inherited patrilineally or matrilineally. They represent healing spirits that make "one dance" (*kupanga kuvina*) referring to the *ngoma* drumbeating ceremony. Another subgroup of ancestral spirits encompasses spirits of dead persons who are ethnically affiliated to the afflicted person such as chiefs, prominent healers or famous warriors. Although this type of *mashabe* comes under the category of healing spirits, it does not figure in the *ngoma* ceremony.

Due to the fragmentary written documentation, the precise history of belief in *mashabe* spirits in Zambia remains unclear. Some authors such as Ter Haar and Ellis (1988), or Elisabeth Colson (1969) suppose these spirits are of Shona origin[29] and were transmitted to Zambia from the neighbouring Zimbabwe where they are known as *shave* spirits.[30] Others connect the occurrence of spirit possession cult in Zambia with the Ngoni[31] and Nsenga people[32] from the east.

Christian Spirits

The healing spirits of Christian origin are generally called *mizimu*[33] and embodied Biblical personalities such as Saint John, Moses, Gabriel or Ezekiel to mention some which are commonly represented in Lusaka. Unlike *mashabe*, *mizimu* are not involved in traditional but Christian healing ceremonies. These spirits are possessed predominantly by healers of prophet-healing churches such as Mutumwa or Zion The most powerful spirit of this group is *Mzimu Wyera*[34], the Holy Spirit.

---

[29] The Shona (or Mashona) is a large ethnic group of south Bantu living in Zimbabwe and in the north of Mozambique encompassing Karanga, Makorere, Bamanyika, Ndau (Vandau), Rozwi (Amalozwi, Barozwi), zezula (Mazizura). A small group of Shona speaking migrants of the late 1800s also live in Zambia, in the Zambezi valley, in Chieftainess Chiawa's area (Malina a kol. 2009).

[30] See Buchner 1980.

[31] The Ngoni people are an ethnic group living in Malawi, Mozambique, Tanzania and Zambia (Lundazi district) The Ngoni trace their origins to the Zulu people of kwaZulu-Natal in South Africa (Malina a kol. 2009).

[32] The Nsenga is an ethnic group living in Eastern Zambia, Malawi and Mozambique (www. britannica.com).

[33] *Mzimu* (sing.)/ *mizimu* (pl.) is a general term for a spirit (of someone who is dead or who is living). My informants refered *mzimu* to the Biblical spirit whereas *mashabe* to the ancestral spirit.

[34] *Oyera, wyera* means "white", "holy" and "pure" in chiNyanja.

Alien Spirits

The third group is made up of alien spirits coming from outside, from different ethnic groups or countries. These spirits are considered to be numerous, wondering in the air searching for a suitable sanctuary. They can possess anyone regardless of his ethnic or kinship affiliation. As I was told the alien spirits "come through blood", which means that they primarily possess those involved in ritual manipulation with animal blood. These spirits are usually not involved in *ngoma* ceremonies unless they appear in the form of *mashabe*.

In Lusaka, it is possible to encounter the spirit mediums possessed by spirits of eminent personages such as Queen Elizabeth, David Livingstone or Mahátma Ghándí. These types of spirits are considered to be particularly powerful due to their historical significance. This is also the reason of their primacy in witch-finding.

Another prominent spirit, figuring in spiritual healing in Lusaka, is *Kilimanjaro*, the spirit originating from Tanzania. As it is believed this spirit comes from dead hunters or warriors, in particular soldiers who were fighting and died in World War II in Tanzania. Those possessed with this spirit speak Swahili and use an imitation gun as one of the principal ritual paraphernalia.

The spirit called *mansalamba* another popular alien spirit spread in Lusaka represents a female water spirit in the form of a mermaid. According to my informants, the *mansalamba* spirit originates from the Tanzanian coast. It remarkably resembles the spirit *Mami Wata*, a popular mermaid spirit widespread throughout the Western and central Africa and African Diaspora.[35]

Ghosts

The traditional healing system also includes afflicting dangerous spirits, known under the name *vivanda* (pl.) or *chivanda* (sing.). These are ghosts of dead men who died in a misadventure or under unknown circumstances such as in a natural disaster, war, or in a car accident. People,

---

[35] See Drewal 2008.

who were murdered, shot, drowned or struck by lightening, as well as numerous perceived offenders such as thieves, murders, witches or adulterers, are believed to turn into *chivanda* after their death. The ghosts are believed to be wandering around the world and can "hang on to someone" (*chivanda chamukwerera*).

To express the experience of being troubled by this kind of spirit, informants used expressions such as "the spirit is sitting on you", "the spirit is hunting you", or simply "the spirit is using you". One can become possessed by *chivanda* either through witchcraft – a witch afflicts a victim by sending *chivanda* to him, or through a mystical contagion. *Chivanda* can be more properly defined as the wandering spirit of a man who does not yet rest in peace, and who can be ritually manipulated by witches. Although *vivanda* connotes mostly a negative spirit that cannot heal, in some cases it can warn of a danger. As Doctor Kasanda explained, *"vivanda can come to inform you that they did not died a peaceful death, they can even avert you from danger. Other vivanda come only to trouble you or to revenge their death"*. *Chivanda* as a sort of "shadow" (*mthunzi*), or double soul of a dead man, is closely connected to the dead body and therefore to the grave. As a result, graveyards are considered to be highly dangerous places where witches operate in order to get *chivanda* for their charms.

The main difference between *vivanda* and *mizimu* is, according to my informants, that, *"vivanda are connected to the ground, grave and earth, in heaven there are no chivanda, and there are only mizimu"*. According to the local conceptualisation of death, when one dies his personal spirit or soul, also called *mzimu*, leaves his body to go to Heaven to join God. On the other hand the spirit of those who died by mysterious or violent means turn into *chivanda* and stay and wander in the terrestrial world. Unlike *mizimu* which are invisible even to *ng'anga's* eye, *vivanda* can be seen under different forms such as animals, magical objects or human beings. When asked, spiritual healers described *mzimu* in terms of wind or the fresh air (*mhpepo*). *"Mizimu you cannot see them physically, they can just talk, that's why they enter you. When you dream about them you can see them, they appear in the form they were alive, but actually they are shadows"*, explained Doctor Bongo.

Another dangerous afflicting spirit, similar to *chivanda*, is *chipuku*. It is a sort of revenant[36] that appears near the grave and can afflict someone by calling him. *"Once you turn your head and answer, you are dead, chipuku takes you with him"*, elucidated Doctor Kasanda. There are different popular stories about *chipuku* going around in Lusaka. The most famous story is one about a *chipuku* called Rosemary. Rosemary was a beautiful girl who became a prostitute and died in a car accident in the 1970s. After her death, she turned into *chipuku* and started hitchhiking around the Copperbelt province. When people stopped their car to give her a lift, they immediately died in an accident.

---

[36] Schmitt (1994) defines a revenant as a dead person who comes back to the world of the living in various forms.

3. The Figure of a Healer

"Ng´anga is a chief of all witches"
— Doctor Mukanda, Lusaka

Categories of Healers

According to the Constitution of the Traditional Health Practitioners Association of Zambia (THAPAZ), the Zambian traditional medico-religious system recognises five categories of healers – herbalists, diviners, spiritual healers, faith healers and birth attendants. These categories figure in the official documents and constitutions of different associations of traditional healers[1] which have been established by the Zambian government since the 1970s. Every traditional healer who runs his craft has to be registered and obtain a Competence Certificate (or International Certificate for healers from abroad) in one of the healer's associations otherwise his activities are considered illegal.[2] This typology is not clearcut, as actual practices and the specialization of healers often overlap and mingle. The term *ng´anga* means traditional healer (also in many

---

[1] Several governmental institutions involved in organising the activities of traditional healers are located in Lusaka. These are: the Traditional Health Practitioners Association of Zambia (THAPAZ), the Zambian National Council of Ng´angas (ZNCN), the Zambian Herbalist United Organisation (ZHUO) and the Zambian Institute of National Medicine and Research (ZINARE).

[2] Every member shall upon Admission pay a registration fee of 1.000 Zambian Kwacha. To obtain a membership card, the fee of 5.000 Zambian Kwacha is required. Every registered healer has to pay the fee of 3.000 Zambian Kwacha as an annual Renewal contribution. The Competence Certificate costs 10.000 Zambian Kwacha, this shall be renewed every five years according to Clause 6: Admission Fee. THPAZ Constitution (2001).

other Bantu languages), in particular that who is involved in spiritual healing.

Herbalists

Herbalists are healers who use traditional herbal medicine (*mankwala*) to cure "natural diseases". They gain their competence through a process of apprenticeship through patrilineal (from father to son) or matrilineal (from mother to daughter). Emphasis is placed on technical skills and the preservation and transmission of the healing tradition within their generation.[3] Unlike other healers, herbalists are not involved in divination or spiritual healing. They carry out a diagnosis on the basis of observing a patient's symptoms. However, the diagnosis is not the primary aim for a patient. In most cases these specialists are consulted principally for therapeutic purposes. As Nicole Sindzingre (1995) showed with the example of the *Senoufo* of Ivory Coast, diagnosis does not necessarily condition the therapy. The logic of diagnosis and therapy are not always complementary and they do not need to be carried out at the same institutional level. According to Sindzingre, some healers such as diviners are specialised in diagnosing, but they do not heal, whereas others such as herbalists are not involved in diagnosing, but merely in healing. The herbalists in Lusaka treat simple ailments or well-known diseases such as malaria, venereal diseases, bronchitis or influenza. They always rely on the symptoms expressed by patients and do not deal with complicated medical cases. If they receive such a patient, they recommend him to consult a diviner or a spiritual healer, or to try biomedical care. According to the THAPAZ Constitution (2001), the traditional herbalist must be able to recognize at least thirty different medicinal herbs that should be clearly labelled and specify the dosage.

---

[3] Unlike in the past when medical knowledge was passed only orally, nowadays we can see herbalists who keep records about their patients, treatment of diseases as well as about the use of medicinal herbs.

Spiritual Healers

The largest category of traditional health practitioners operating in Lusaka are spiritual healers. They represent spirit mediums possessed either by ancestral (*mashabe*), biblical (*mzimu*) or alien spirits whose power they use for diagnosing and healing patients. There are two main types of spiritual healers, those who get possessed by spirits directly and those who communicate with spirits through night dreaming. Unlike herbalists, they acquire knowledge of healing and medicinal herbs through the instruction of the respective spirit that are believed to "work through" them. Healers can be possessed by several different spirits, whereby not all of them manifest with the same intensity. Every spirit is used for a different therapeutic purposes and their "hierarchy" may change with time. Each spirit has a delineated field of activity – for instance, some are used for healing "women problems", others for detection of witchcraft. Many spiritual healers cannot recognize particular medicinal herbs only if they are possessed and instructed by a spirit. After being dispossessed, they claim they do not remember what the spirit had diagnosed and therefore ask their patients to tell them what the spirit had revealed.

To become a spiritual healer one ordinarily needs to experience a serious chronic illness leading to a prolonged state of suffering and the ensuing recovery accompanied by a mystical spiritual call to become a spiritual healer. This typical "*ng'anga* syndrome" will be more properly analysed in the following chapter. A medium constantly troubled by the spirit is recommended by a healer to meet the claims dictated by the spirit in order to be recovered. In the case of *mashabe* spirits a drumbeating medico-religious ceremony must be organised as a sort of therapy. Unlike the herbalists who choose their occupation voluntarily, traditional spiritual healers claim to carry out their work against their will.

Faith Healers

Faith healers are those involved in Christian spiritual healing. Most of them use Christian prayers, the Bible, Holy water and other Christian paraphernalia to heal their patients. Although some operate independently from their home, the majority of them work as prophets under the patronage of some Pentecostal or prophet-healing churches.

Unlike the spiritual healers, faith healers rarely get spiritually possessed.[4] For diagnosis of the causes of a patient's illness they mostly use the Bible. Divination from the Bible consists of giving the Book to the patient who has to randomly open it. According to the respective chapter, the analysis of a given problem is then carried out. The therapy through faith healing consists of blessings, praying, laying hands on a patient, exorcising demons and fasting in the mountains. The faith healing of a person can be brought about by religious faith in the healing power of the Holy Spirit that is transmitted through prayer sand rituals that, according to adherents, stimulate a divine presence and the power toward healing a disease that often takes the form of a miraculous recovery.

Diviners

Whereas spiritual healers are possessed by spirits, diviners consult the spirits through mechanical devices for diagnostic and therapeutic purposes. As there is no standardised way of divining, a large variety of divinatory techniques can be recognised in Lusaka.[5] The category of diviner mingles closely with the category of spiritual healer and herbalist. A diviner, in the same way as a herbalist, has to undergo the process of apprenticeship provided by an experienced *ng'anga* either from a family member or from an unrelated person. As I observed, the art of divining in Lusaka is solely practised by men and is passed on customarily from grand-father to grand-son or directly from father to son. However, there are also diviners who learnt their craft after paying money to a foreign *ng'anga* usually from Tanzania. It is common for diviners to communicate with the spirits of their dead relatives that materialize themselves in divinatory paraphernalia.

---

[4] The healers (prophets) from the Mutumwa church who are directly possessed by the Holy Spirit represent the exception.
[5] See the chapter 4.

Birth Attendants

Birth attendants represent the last officially recognised category of healers in Zambia. Traditional midwives provide basic and emergency health care services to women and their new-borns during pregnancy, childbirth and the postpartum period. Birth attendants are partly medically trained to attend childbirth at home and to recognize and respond appropriately to medical complications. These specialists are not involved in spiritual healing or divining.

There are another two interstitial categories of healers – Christian prophets and witch-finders – that are not officially recognised and distinctly organised in a separate category. Prophets are commonly included into the category of faith healers, despite the fact that they have much more in common with traditional spiritual healers. The witch-finders on the other hand are officially forbidden and thus profess as diviners.

Witch-finders (mchape)

This profession is not officially recognized by the Constitution of Traditional Health Practitioners Association of Zambia since the Witchcraft Act (1995) forbids witch-finding activities and sets the "penalty for naming, accusing or imputing witchcraft" and the "penalty on the professional witch-doctors and witch-finders". In spite of this prohibition, there are many witch-finders all around the country hiding themselves under the certificate of proficiency as herbalists, diviners or spiritual healers. They practice witch-finding by means of divination and heal both victims and witches by diverse methods such as cleansing the body and space with medical herbs, sucking the magical substances from the patient's blood through a cupping horn, making "tattoos" etc.

Although *mchape* often criticize the Witchcraft Act that in their opinion has led to the proliferation of witchcraft today, they respect it in the way that they do not openly denounce the name of an alleged witch. The majority of them also do not publicly advertise their services and stay hidden in the compounds. Those well-known and with a good reputation often travel all around the country or even abroad to solve individual cases or to assist in the cleansing of villages from witchcraft.

Some witch-finders fall into several categories of healers at the same time, as will be shown in the biography of Doctor Samuel Mukanda who performs as a witch-finder, spiritual healer, faith healer and diviner at the same time.

Prophets

The term prophet, *profeti* or *mneneri* (in chiNyanja), or *kasesema* (in Bemba) are used to indicate a Christian charismatic prophetic healer who was chosen by God and sent to Earth to carry on the healing of Jesus Christ among African people. Prophets consider themselves as real African apostles whose vocation is to heal people from different diseases, poverty and witchcraft through the Holy Spirit (Bible, Mathew 4/ 23–25). They sharply distinguish themselves from traditional healers for ideological reasons following from their religious convictions. Prophets emphasize that the Holy Spirit is an entirely different power which is in a continual struggle with harmful occult forces symbolised in the traditional spirits and witchcraft. „*We use the same kind of herbs and we use tattoos that traditional healers do. But the difference is that they don´t believe in God. What they believe is that themselves they have got a power to heal, but in our case, we believe that a power of God uses us through these herbs so that a man or woman would be healed*".

However, the personal history of African Christian prophets as well as their healing activities has much in common with African traditional healers. Mathew Schoffeleers claims that this fact reflects a widespread "*ng´anga* paradigm" according to which, "the medicine person (*ng´anga*) provides a framework within which [Africans] conceptualize the person of Christ and the role of the Christian minister [prophet]. Christ and the Christian minister in turn provide the framework within which to reconceptualize the *ng´anga*" (Schoffeleers 1994: 85). Actually, in many African societies Jesus Christ is conceived as a true *ng´anga* because of his healing powers, clairvoyance and capacity to intermediate between the supernatural and human world. This dual view of Jesus as a healer and visionary coincides with the role of the traditional healer. Whereas the source of *ng´anga*'s healing power resides primarily in the world of ancestors, a prophet draws on the healing power from Jesus and the Holy Spirit. Although the traditional healer represents a negative point of reference for most of the prophets, their healing methods are strikingly similar. Dillon-Malone (1983) calls the holy men from Mutumwa churches "neo-traditional healers" as they use the same traditional healing practices and are involved in the same explanatory models as *ng'angas*. There are for instance the Christian prophets specialised in witch-finding called *chilansengo*. The only difference between them and traditional *mchape* is that prophets incorporate "traditional" cultural ideas and practices within the "new" biblical religious framework where the Holy Spirit is considered to be the new and only source of healing power.

The Characteristics and Role of Urban Healers

The traditional healers in Lusaka operate either from their homes located in compounds, or from the Lusaka city market known as "Soweto". There is a substantial difference between these two types of *ng'anga* in terms of their quality, credibility, healing competences and the fees they charge for their service.[6] The "home healers" frequently expressed their disappointment with the Soweto healers´ practice. They reproached them for blemishing the reputation of traditional medicine as well as charging an exorbitant price for their services. As Doctor Bongo, director of the THAPAZ, explained, "*Soweto healers are commercial (...) they are spoiling medicine. On the market you can see people aborted, menstruating, people that have just had sex... they go around the shrine, they touch medicine* [exposed medicinal herbs] *and they spoil it. You cannot market medicine like this. It is something sacred you must keep it pure otherwise the medicine like this would kill people*".

His colleague, Doctor Sushita Kalolo adds, "*our friends* [Soweto healers] *want just money. Our friends are hungry they are looking for customers. If you are a good healer people will find you. Our parents never did it like this.*" Both of the healers work at THAPAZ and have a botanical garden where they plant their medicinal herbs (*mankhwala*). However, not many

---

[6] The majority of my informants were healers working from their homes. I had very few dealings with those from Soweto as they were not willing to cooperate with my research unless paid.

healers I met have such good fortune, some of them have to buy *mankhwala* at the Soweto market, or travel to the nearest bush to extract it.

Many traditional healers in Lusaka advertise their service on placards alongside the road, in newspapers, or on the radio and all of them charged money for healing. The table of charges differs from one healer to another. The basic consultation fee ranges from 20 to 30 Zambian Kwacha (5 – 7. 5 US Dollars)[7]. Fees, charged for complicated cases concerning witchcraft, can even range from 1 000 to 2 000 Zambian Kwacha (250 – 500 US Dollars). To my surprise the charges for a traditional healer's services far exceed the charges for services in the medical centres.

Unlike the *ng'angas* the Christian prophets provide their healing service for free. They often criticize their counterparts for the exorbitant sums of money they charge for their healing. As pastor Sikwefu from Mutumwa church clarified: "*Our friends* [traditional healers] *use also wanga* [charms] *and vizimba* [magical objects] *to practice witchcraft. They are allowed to kill a human and they require money for their service. We don't use blood in the way as traditional healers do and we don't get any money from our patients. The Bible advises not to get money from them* [prophets], *our reward will be in heaven, because God is going to check my files, about what I was doing here on Earth, we follow what the Bible says.*"

The urban healers both traditional and Christian are real specialists in problems that urban dwellers experience and encounter. These are mostly financial, such as poverty or unemployment accompanied by alcohol abuse among men, and social, in which the marital, family and love problems prevail. However, healers do not only deal with socioeconomic issues but also with physiological and psychological problems. Among the typical health problems experienced by Lusaka dwellers are infertility, malaria diverse respiratory problems, alimentary and skin problems. Life in town and its predicaments commonly lead to the diverse psychological problems such as depression, frustration or a low-level psychosis.

---

[7] These prices were valid for the years 2008/2009. In 2014 the price doubled, increased to 50 up to 70 kwacha.

The healers represent social and health experts whose eclectic skills are involved in the process of "bricolage".[8] Their ability to appropriate and redeploy the terms, ideas and symbols from Christianity, western medical science, the commodity market and other areas and construct new and for patients "comprehensible" arrangements is a typical feature of the urban healers. The healer compared to a handy man (*bricoleur*) "creates improvised structures by appropriating pre-existing materials which are ready-to-hand" (Lévi-Strauss 1974: 16–33). He or she works with signs, "constructing new arrangements by adopting existing signifies as signifiers and speaking through the medium of things by the choices made from limited possibilities" (ibid: 20–21). The healers are thus creative and experimental figures par excellence. As Comaroff and Comaroff noted, "the ongoing revaluation of signs has always been a palpable feature of African creativity" (Comaroff and Comarroff 1993: 22). The healer's ability to introduce innovations in their "art of healing" conforms, on the one hand to the demand of clients, and on the other hand it represents the way how "everyday experience is recasting prior meanings as it confronts new signifiers themselves variously empowered" (ibid: 22).

Many traditional healers I met appropriated symbols of western medicine such as a white coat, a book of patients or herbal medicine dosages. The ongoing process of medicalization and bureaucratization of traditional healing has been manifested even in the language the healers use when advertising their services. They call themselves "doctors", or "researchers" and their consulting room "surgery" or "clinic". Not only traditional healers, but also prophets from the spirit-healing churches in

---

[8] Claude Lévi-Strauss's (1974) notion "the bricolage" refers to the nature of the reasoning of the archaic societies. Unlike Lévi-Bruhl (1923) who claimed that pre-logic reasoning of a savage man is qualitatively different from and inferior to the logic of a civilised man, Lévi-Strauss attempted to prove that the "primitive logic" of archaic societies is able to generalise, classify and analyse the reality in the same way as the "logic of modern complex societies". The only difference is that the primitive logic is based on the principle of totemic logic that employ the analogies between different levels of ecological, economical, social, and religious conditions (Budil 2003).

Lusaka appropriate some of the medical terms in their vocabulary. For instance, they use the expression "vaccination" when talking about the traditional chirurgical healing method known under the name "tattoos" or *ndembo*,[9] or they used the phrase "to take an X ray" instead of "prophesying through the Holy Spirit".

It is not only creativity and "bricolage" in which healers excel, but also in their pragmatism. Since their authority and legitimacy is threatened by many competitors in the city, it must be constantly reaffirmed and negotiated by introducing innovations. The ability to keep clients and to gain a good reputation depends on the originality of their therapeutic procedures. For example the most common divinatory techniques of mirrors traditionally attributed to witch-finders (as well as to the witches) have been now substituted by methods of automatic writing or spirit possession. Doctor Mukanda expressed his doubts about using the traditional techniques: *"You have to be innovative, because witches are very clever. They use the same mirrors as we witch-finders. If they want they are able to break the mirrors of mchapi* [witch-finders]. *I saw many mchapi coming to the village with their mirrors to cleanse the villagers all failed. Then, I went there and I could stop them* [witches] *because I used the spirit. The witches cannot destroy someone who is dead (...) it is not possible to kill the ghost, it is like to trying to kill the death ...* [laughing]."

In order to draw innovations, healers, in particular witch-finders travel a lot, meet other healers and gain new herbs. By travelling they ensure material and intellectual sources for successful work in the future. The circulation of persons, objects and ideas, typical for the process of globalization, is thus reflected in African contemporary healing. In the act of crossing geographical and ideological borders, the healers themselves participate in the reproduction and construction of the borders themselves. At the same time as they transcend the bounds of locality and tradition and act on the broader social scale through engaging in different institutions such as healers' associations, churches and cults of affliction. "Insofar as healers facilitate or restrict their client's affinities

---

[9] "Tattoos", or *ndembo* is a razor-blade skin incision made around the vulnerable or afflicted area on the body where a medicinal herb is rubbed in order to reach the bloodstream quickly.

with and/or differences to novel therapeutic resources, they articulate their client's affinities with and/or differences from others who use these resources" (West, Luedke 2006: 15).

Biographies of Healers

In order to become a spiritual healer one needs to experience a serious illness leading to a prolonged state of suffering sometimes even to "death" and the ensuing recovery or resurrection crisis accompanied by a mystical spiritual call. This typical *"ng'anga* [healer's] syndrome" is presented in the autobiographies of all the traditional spiritual healers as well as Christian prophets I interviewed. However, the modalities of their vocation and transition vary in each case.

Whereas the crises of possession by *mashabe* ancestral spirits is often accompanied by a set of strange dreams, the spiritual calling that precedes a prophet vocation consists of a sort of visions, (such as seeing dead people, foreseeing danger), prophetic dreams, or an extraordinary mystical experience in which the afflicted encounters personally with spiritual beings.

The occurrence of dreams and visions plays a more important role in the process of diagnosis than physical symptoms themselves. Whereas the symptomatic level is often emphasized by traditional healers, in the case of prophetic possession it is not as clearly recognizable. The symptoms are rather vague, described in terms of mental confusion or madness, weakness or solitude. Unlike those afflicted by *mashabe* spirits have to undergo a sort of initiation, the prophetic vocation also affirmed by a social consensus usually lacks any institutional background.

The process of transition from the role of a patient to the role of a healer is different in the case of prophets and spiritual healers. Contrary to spiritual healers, the prophet's mediumistic qualities are never inherited. As I observed, the shift between the status of prophet and patient is double sided and reversible, and involves on the one side social consensus within the church community and on the other side the individual endeavour from the side of the prophet. Whereas the prophet's vocation is self imposed based on personal charisma and social affirmation, the vocation of traditional healers is conceived as a sacrifice, an involuntary fate. Unlike prophets who claim they were lucky to have been chosen, to be gifted by God to serve people, all of the informants from the field of spiritual healers affirmed an initial resistance and defiance to becoming a healer.

Biographies of Prophetic Healers

To illustrate common patterns of the prophet's vocation and the way how their charismatic identity is constructed the two following extracts of biographic narratives are presented and analysed.

1. Mrs. Mwembe, a prophetic healer from the New Jesus Disciples Church (Lusaka)

> "I started being the prophet here in the church in 1980. What moved me to go to this church was that I experienced, I felt the spirit [mzimu]. I had an uncle who was too clever [meaning a witch] he was practicing witchcraft. When I was sleeping I could see a big tree outside the house where my uncle put different things inside a trunk. There were birds, there were different animals. I could not sleep. The following morning I woke up, I just picked a stick and I went to search that big tree, where I saw the animals in the dream. There was something like a hole and things stuffed in it. I tried to move those things out from the hole, but then those birds came out. After this I became mad. I went to the bush for a week. In the mountains, right there I started to live with angels, who put white clothes on me. I started preaching there. I stayed there for weeks without eating, I was not hungry or thirsty, no, I used to be kept nicely by angels (…) there were no villages, but only mountains and angels. People from my village were searching for me, they visited a certain prophet, they consulted him about me and they were told that I was not dead. 'She is somewhere there, ehee [an interjection used to confirm a statement] let us go and look for her she is in the mountains!' So they went there and they found me there sitting and praying. This is how I started to be a prophet."

2. Mr. Kisimba, the charismatic prophet, a founder of the New Jesus Disciples Church.

"I was born in Toloko village in the Northern Province. To become a prophet I started getting sick, it was 1956 by that time I was 7 years old. My father worked in Tanzania as a driver so I stayed just with my mum. My sickness was that I spent many nights in my bed without having any sleep. So from 1956 until 1960 I was lost in a bush somewhere in the Nyika Plateau [North Malawi] where you can find short people like Bushmen they are called Poka. I went in the bush without knowing what I am doing. I was in the bush for six month, and then a headman of the district made a call out to summon the chief of the district. They grouped themselves and went to the bush to search for me but they could not find me. My father in Tanzania when he heard that I was missing came back home. He decided to go to see a certain person who lived just near Nyika Plateau.

This person was Nyawezi, a prophet and he had a special spirit. He said to my father: 'your son is around, he is not lost' and gave him a direction to Nyika Plateau. 'You cannot find him unless you use my charms and spirit, so I need to go with you', he said. So father accepted and they went in a group. Before they left that place, they kneeled down to pray to ask the power from God. Nyawezi also said: 'If you find your boy then you will have some problems in the village.' When they came to the bush they kneeled down and started praying again. After praying Nyawezi took the charm in a cup, it is called mbojo. Mbojo it is a tree you can find along the river. They put water in a cup and add the mbojo in a water to make a medicine. Nyawezi started to spring mbojo into all direction wherever they were going and singing songs [referring to the Hebrews chap 9/19][10]. From that moment I had no power to move from place where I was, because of their prayers.

---

[10] "For when Moses had spoken every precept to all the people according to the law, he took the blood of calves and of goats, with water, and scarlet wool, and hyssop, and sprinkled both the book, and all the people" (Hebrews 9:19).

They continued sprinkling mbojo on me and they surrounded me. I stopped talking, because I stayed long time without talking in the bush. I communicated just with animals and I was eating wild fruits.

Then I went back to the village. Before entering the village I was thrown down [possessed] by the Spirit peum, peum, peum, peum... After that I received prayers until the Spirit settled down. Afterwards, they started narrating me that I was lost in the bush and what, what ... [he does not remember]. 'The reason you went to the bush was that the Spirit that have been given to you by God is a gift to heal. Through this Spirit you will be guided by God' [he was prophesied]. I agreed and I stayed in that village for two weeks with my dad. Before we reached our home they asked father to go alone. I said to my father: 'I will not use the same way as you are using. I will use my own way to go to the village.' So my father went directly but me, I used a bush pathway to go to the village.

When I reached village I was not able to unite with people because of that spirit. I could foresee and foretell if a person is good or bad. What happened during those days, we used to have a pallas [a sort of duiker]. When you don't have a food in the evening whereas the whole village is cooking food you go and gather before the headman's palace and you eat with others. Before starting eating pallas I was able to see, to tell, this plate contains a poison, so I refused to eat it. People in the village were wandering 'why is he always saying these things?' Then the headman called me and my parents to his palace. I told him that I was able to foresee, to detect if somebody is doing something bad. I could see also charms when somebody wanted to kill somebody. But I was advised to just avoid it, not to tell it off, because I was very young and people would kill me very quickly.

After three years my father went back to Tanzania and I started to have a lot of dreams. I had a dream that my mother was dead, but what's more, I was given a snake. There were many snakes under the tree and I stepped on them. The following day I told to my mother that I had a bad dream about bad snakes. There was also a big tree and I saw a funeral [in the dream] which means that somebody will die in my family.

My mother told me, 'These kinds of dreams are very bad ones.' One month after, she really died. But before she died she told me, 'this is a dream that you had I am going to die.' This is when a problem started.

People from the community realised this boy is able to foresee what will happen so kill him! They wanted to kill me. There were people using charms to protect their cattle from stealing. So what happen, I would go to cowshed and steal this charm. Another day one of the breeders discovered that the charm is not there. They accused me, 'it was Victor Sivamba!' They broad Chikanga [a famous witch-finder] he came to witness that I have mzimu [a spirit] which does not allow killing people. From there, I experienced a terrible headache.

In 1965 I came to Lusaka. I was called by my uncle, young brother of my dad. He said, 'there [in the village] people are going to kill you, better you come here to Lusaka.' When I came to Lusaka, I found two traditional healers there: Kabwaza and Nganyareone was at Kamwala [in Lusaka centre], the second in Matero [a compound in Lusaka to the north-west]. I wanted to find out more about what happened to me. Was I bewitched or what happened? I met the traditional healer and I saw that he had something under his seat [bad charm] like a horn which was stuffed with some chemicals inside. This was a horn from the head of a goat. Then I fell sick, so sick! All this side [pointing at the left part of his body] was swollen. So I decided to go and see Doctor Konoso, a specialist in Matero compound… that was in 1968. He examined me and found out that there was nothing bad with me. Then I received a letter to go the UTG [University Teaching Hospital in Lusaka]. That morning when I should have gone there, my heart told me, you should not go there! In that time we had a meeting, because my dad used to go to the Seventh Day Adventists Church. During that meeting I suddenly fell down and people said: 'This person has chivanda [a ghost, bad spirit].' I continued going to the S. D. A church and they continued telling me, it's chivanda, it's chivanda.

From there, I decided to visit Milingo, do you know him? [Bishop Emmanuel Milingo, a famous spiritual healer.]. I started to go to the Roman Catholic Church and pray and pray. Milingo told me: 'you have some spirit. What you should do is to continue in prayers.' Milingo has got a powerful spirit and from that time I know that I have the powerful spirit too.

From there, I stayed in Matero and I had a swollen stomach. I went to UTG and I was told that I had to undergo an operation. I was vomiting whole night. I was directed by the Spirit to use a razorblade and to do just some cuts [ndembo incision] on the place where I had a problem. So I did these cuts and from that time my problem went away. My family, they were all shocked what happened. But the problem came to my family now.

So from there, I started to heal all members of my family and they started to believe that I am a healer. I started visited prophet Suali from the Mzimu church. He came from Tanzania, he just started to heal. He also had a powerful spirit. I went there often and I was anointed by the spirit. I was drunk with the Holy Spirit! Those people in the church accepted me and they encouraged me to come and congregate with them. It was in 1969. Up to now I have still mzimu [the Spirit] and I believe that I have the spirit from God."

As we can see, the experiences and visions described by prophets refer to the category of "liminal" experience. The "wandering in the mountains" during which one receives the spiritual calling and his identity is radically transformed is included in the majority of the collected biographies. In fact, the symbolic structure of the prophet vocation evokes the "rite of passage" as described by van Gennep (1960) and Turner (1969). Wandering in the mountains far away from civilisation or *societas* represents a typical "liminal" experience that corresponds to the phase of seclusion. Receiving a spiritual call and an encounter with a spiritual power during the seclusion then symbolizes the passage from the profane to the sacred.

The examples of the biographical narratives show that the common theme of "wandering in the mountains" is accompanied by starvation, a feeling of being lost, communicating with angels or spirits, praying and not talking. In the mountains, the sort of spiritual *communitas* is experienced as the following statements illustrate: *"I stayed there with angels for* weeks without eating but I was not hungry or thirsty, no! I used to be kept nicely by angels"*, or *"I communicated just with animals and I was eating wild fruits"*. During this stay a strong tie between a man and God is created. This tie is confirmed symbolically by receiving white clothes which represents the purity of *mzimu* (prophetess Mwembe) or by the sprinkling *mbojo* (prophet Kisimba). As I was told, *mbojo* represents the sacrificial blood of calves and goats as referring to the Bible: "This is a testament which God hath enjoined unto you" (Hebrews 9: 19–20).

Coming back from "wild nature" to a native village represents the transition from nature to culture in Lévi-Straussess's sense of binary opposites. The transition may be accompanied by conflict, as we saw with the example of prophet Kisimba: *"When I reached the village I was not able to unite with people because of that spirit"*. The acquisition of the new role of prophet necessitates the need to be socially recognised and affirmed by significant others. As personal biographies of prophets disclosed this social recognition is always accompanied by conflict. People in the prophet's vicinity either do not believe in his extraordinary qualities, or interpret them negatively. This follows from the narrative of Mr. Kisimba who claimed he was accused of witchcraft by the people from his village and labelled as "demon possessed" by the prophets of the Seventh Day Adventists Church.

The liminal experiences at the base of a personal metamorphosis may also be embodied in the experience of biological "death" and the ensuing resurrection as the following narrative of another prophet (from the same church) Mr. Shaka shows: *"In 1972 I was taken to the hospital in Chilaompwe after being sick for a long time. I was certified dead and they put me in the mortuary. I was in the mortuary, it was on eleven March. I died at 23 p.m. the previous night and I was revived at 5 a.m. the next morning. When I woke up I found out that I was in the mortuary. It was the time when my friends came to check my body to prove that I was dead so that they could arrange a coffin for me. When I woke up, I was taken by my fellow policemen to the hospital. On the way there was a place, where a certain man was dealing with spirits (mzimu). That person told them, that I was not dead. He said, 'It was just a spirit that had taken him. He is a prophet.' Since that time I have started to go to the Mutumwa church. I have started to experience the Holy Spirit in my body. That is how the Spirit called me."*

Biographies of Traditional Healers

The following examples of biographic narratives of traditional spiritual healers help us to analyse "ancestral calling" leading to their healing career that varies substantially from that of Christian prophets.

1. Samuel Mukanda, a prominent witch-finder from Lusaka

Samuel was born 35 years ago in Choma, a village half way between Lusaka and Livingstone. His father was one of the most famous healers and witch-finders in Zambia at that time. He died under mysterious circumstances, when his son was five years old. Samuel interprets the family tragedy with these words:

> "My father was fighting with an organised group of witches that were stronger than him. One day he became a seriously ill and he told us: 'I am bewitched and I will die today. Cleanse yourselves but do not mourn. In two days my murders will follow me'. After these words, he really passed away. We obeyed his wish and we all underwent the kusamba [ritual cleansing]. We did not mourn because our tears could disturb the spirit of our father who was still fighting with the witches at that time in order to revenge his death. That day when we buried our father, people in his surroundings started to die. He succeeded in destroying those witches who killed him, but his life was lost forever."

After the death of his father, Samuel stayed with his mother and his other seven siblings. As the local custom required, his mother after the death of her husband sold the house and moved with the children to another village close to Kabwe (in the north of Lusaka). As her family lived there, it was not difficult to buy a house and start a new life. Samuel started attended primary school and found new friends. When he was ten years old he suddenly became ill. He repeatedly suffered from severe headaches, dizziness and concentration problems. Every night he had terrible nightmares in which he was chased by a lion and other wild animals or pressed to dance in graveyards. His mother anxious for his health recollected that her husband had suffered the same symptoms after his father's death when he became possessed by his spirit. With the suspicion that her son was also afflicted with the "unnatural disease" she took him to the local Mutumwa congregation. This church had a well-known reputation for dealing with witchcraft and spirit possessions. The Mutumwa prophets discovered the cause of Samuel's disease with the help of the Holy Spirit. Samuel remembers:

> "They told my mother that I had been possessed by the spirit of a lion that I inherited from my father. This spirit is very strong and does not leave you without being heard of. My father used this spirit for healing and witch-finding. I soon realised that it is my fate that I have to continue the family vocation. At the very beginning I defied it. I refused to listen to the spirit. I did not want to become a healer! No! My dream was to finish the school and be a carpenter. Soon after I understood that I cannot defy the wish of my ancestors, that they are stronger than me."

Samuel's health condition deteriorated from day to day, his headaches grew to migraines, to dizziness and sharp pains in the heart. The spirit of lion that was visiting him in his dreams gave him a clear ultimatum – either you respect my wish and you will become a healer or you die. The spirit also ordered Samuel to marry only one wife and forbade him to consume alcohol. Other instructions concerned the sexual purity to which he must adhere to when manipulating herbal medicine. Further the spirit indicated that he should respect the black colour that symbolises the spirit of the lion and the red colour that connotes power and the fight against witchcraft. If Samuel did not respect these rules, the spirit could cause the illness again and make it even more severe than before. In the Mutumwa church, that Samuel continued to attend, the spirit of the lion manifested several times by possessing his body on the occasion of drumbeating and singing Christian songs. Although the prophets usually in this type of case carry out exorcism, this time they decided to appease the spirit.

> "They realised that the spirit was too strong, that to expel him from my body would cause my death. They recommended that I undergo the drumbeating ceremony. We agreed. During this occasion, the spirit revealed to me all the mystery about healing, which herbs I should use for which diseases, where to go to search for them in the bush."

Although Samuel became a traditional healer, he continued to visit the Mutumwa church together with his mother who by a coincidence was promoted from an ordinary member of the congregation to a prophetic healer. It is difficult to estimate how these two events were interconnected, however several months after his mother had become a healer Samuel started to have another health problem, this time of the psychic order. He was distracted; his mood fluctuated, one time laughing one time crying, the people around him thought that he had gone mad. Samuel recollects:

> "Mutumwa prophets prophesised me that I am possessed by another spirit, mizimu [spirits of biblical origin] – that of Moses and Samuel. They both troubled me day and night (...) we have work for you they were saying Here you are the Holy Bible, respect it as Gospel. It helps you to catch the thieves and witches and heal the innocents."

At the request of his mother, Samuel obeyed the calling of the biblical spirit and started to use them along with the spirit of his father.

Today Samuel is a well-known witch-finder who has a wide clientele. During the divination séances he consults the "old man" as he calls the spirit of his dead father. Before divination starts, Mukanda puts forward a white plate where a patient has to hand in some money (*ndalama*) and maize flour (*unga*) as an offering to the spirit.[11] Then he places the plate under his bed and covers himself with a white blanket. By smoking cigarettes and speaking Tonga got possessed by his father. With a deep and slow voice he reveals a patient's problem. He carries out this kind of divination in spirit possession solely in the evening from 6 p.m. to 6 a.m. To detect witches and their magical objects he relies on the Christian spirits of Moses and Samuel. Possessed by these *mizimu*, he uses the Bible to detect witches by opening it and reading some chapters as well as to catch dangerous witchcraft objects by snapping the Bible. This technique Mukanda uses uniquely during the day from 6 a.m. to 6 p.m.

---

[11] This procedure is common for all spiritual healers I met in Lusaka.

2. Sushita Kalolo, a spiritual healer from Lusaka

This seventy year old charismatic *ng'anga* with a gleam in his eyes whom I met for the first time in the Association of Traditional Healers in Zambia (THAPAZ) soon after my arrival in Lusaka introduced himself in an unforgettable manner: "*Good morning Madame, I am Sushita Kalolo, Mulenga, Chilenshie, Emanuel, Kasanda, Konyumbashalumba, Sakukuwa, Sakukuwa Kuvaloshi, Panfilda, Nomela Nine, Kafua Ubila, Nine Kanindi, Mupika Potalala...*" and he continued by naming other spirits that possessed him during his life in order to help him to heal people.

Sushita Kalolo lives with his wife in a small house in Mtendere compound where he receives his patients and plants herbal medicine in the garden. He works in town as a general secretary at THAPAZ. Apart from this job, he is *ng'anga* specialised in the treatment of venereal diseases. He recollects the time when he experienced the crises of possession for the first time:

> "I was sixteen; it was in 1954, I was very sick. The bad wind fanned me, I felt it all around me and it made me talk. I was like drunk. My head was heavy and I felt dizzy. My father took me to Sakukuwa Kasanda, who had a well-known reputation as the best witch-finder in Zambia at that time. Sakukuwa told me that I was possessed by a chief Kasempa from the North-Western province and that I will be possessed by many other spirits during my life including his own spirit when he dies. He was right. After Kasempa, the spirit of Gabriel, Michel and Ghandi came, some fade away, some stay with me up to now. Divination of Sakukuwa predestined the whole of my life. He also told me that I will live in Mtendere compound in Lusaka because Mtendere means peace and I have a pure white heart. For the same reason I have to dress in the colour white. He foretold that I will work for some time as a clerk at the court and that I will become a healer when I am 36 years old. This happened when Sakukuwa died exactly as he said. His spirit possessed me and asked me to become a healer. Thanks to him I know which herbs to use for which disease and how to treat patients. This sage man also foretold me that this country would gain its independence in 1964. He told me that I will live until I am 121 years old if I do not use public transport. His spirit ordered me to walk otherwise I will die in an accident.

Sakukuwa's son Kasanda (senior) was my good friend. We knew each other very well, as we were neighbours for some years. He was a well-known witch-finder in Lusaka. I was even his patient when people in the compound tried to bewitch me. That time he told me: 'You have our spirit you don't need to be worried'. Kasanda gave me the calabash for destroying witches from a distance, but I don't use it often, only in extreme cases. When he suddenly died due to witchcraft his spirit also possessed me and asked me to revenge his death. But the spirit of Sakukuwa refused it by saying that I have a white heart that never kills. And so, the death of Kasanda was revenged by his son who in turns became a witch-finder, one of the best in Lusaka today."

As follows from the narratives, the crises of spirit possession comes suddenly and unexpectedly as a result of accumulated anxiety issuing from certain events such as the death of an intimate family member or a friend, or the inability to conceive a child.[12] The crises is always accompanied by a set of symptomatic dreams such as flying, swimming under water, being chased or bitten by certain animals such as a lion. These dreams play a much more important role in the process of diagnosis than the psychophysical symptoms themselves. A common set of these symptoms referring to *mashabe* possession consists of a persistent headache, tachyarrhythmia, dizziness, seizures, loss of appetite, insomnia and weight fluctuation to name some of the most common. In the case of women, problems linked to the reproductive system occur.

An afflicted person receives various "spiritual demands" in his dreams. These demands have in fact in the form of "instruction" referring to the specific forms of a patient's behaviour that must be respected if one wants to recover from his illness. If they are ignored or resisted, the patient's health would get worse or could even lead to his death. The instruction may vary according to respective spirits, most often they consist of ritual prohibitions concerning sexuality, marriage, consumption of certain food[13] and liquids.[14] The spirits also instruct a medium

---

[12] According to biographic interviews with Doctor Aron, Irene and Sato.
[13] Such as babel fish (*mirmba*), pork and goat meat (*nyama ya mbuzi*), or some vegetable leaves (*delele, nakatapa*).

which colour of clothes he should put on and which paraphernalia he should use. Sometimes *mashabe* can even indicate where one should live or work as we saw in the example of Sushita Kalolo.

The spirits of male and female ancestors choose the spiritual medium regardless of their sex. However there is a rule, that the ancestral spirits are inherited either matrilineally or patrilineally (the case of Mukanda), or as an alien spirit comes out of the family circle (the case of Sushita Kalolo). Whereas recovery from an afflictions caused by family *mashabe* spirit necessitates the participation in *ngoma* therapy, the afflictions caused by alien spirits manage to be healed without.

The Relationship between Healers and Patients

The social relations of the patient, as well as the relationship between a patient and the healer play an essential role during the whole process of healing. The social body comprised of a patient's kinsmen as well as the close non-kin intimates represent a patient's solidarity network on the one hand, and an active agent of therapy on the other. As aforesaid the illness conceived by Lusaka dwellers always has social implications. As Victor Turner observed among Ndembu, sickness of a patient will not get better until all tensions and aggressions in the group's interrelations have been brought to light and exposed to ritual treatment. (…). "The doctor's task is to tap the various streams of affect associated with these conflicts and with the social and interpersonal disputes in which they are manifested and to channel them in a socially positive direction" (Turner 1970: 392).

The role of *ng'anga* as a mediator of social conflicts is incontestable in this respect. In the course of divination, a healer focuses primarily on the reconstruction of a patient's problem by analysing his family background and his social relations within the neighbourhood (both on a synchronic and diachronic level). The objective is to reveal the causes of social tension in the patient's vicinity, in other words, to assigns the social and psycho-physiologic symptoms to the respective aetiology,

---

[14] Such as alcohol (beer).

remedy the distorted relationship and redress its balance by employing the respective therapy.

Therapy management itself is never a matter of individual choice. Rather it is a process of negotiation between a healer, a patient and his significant others (kinsmen, friends or neighbours). The significant others and their model of authority that form a "lay therapy managing group" (Janzen 1978) constitute an indispensable critical decision making body determining the therapy choice. In most of the cases the patient's relatives also help with the payment of the treatment and travel. The mediatory role of the patient's therapy managing group is also dependent on their available social and economic capital. Disposable financial resources, a good knowledge of English, useful social contacts, access to health care facilities, available transport options and many other factors influence the whole process of decision making and therapy negotiation.

It needs to be stressed that the situation in urban settings is rather different from that of rural areas. In towns, the intervention of a kinsman is limited because of their job obligations, dispersed residences and transport requirements. The patient's therapy management group in town is not so large and efficacious as in a village because relatives live either out of the city and do not have an intimate relationship, or are simply absent due to the high HIV/AIDS mortality in town. In town, the cohesive force of family seems to be replaced or functions parallel to alternative solidarity networks comprised of friends, neighbours, or religious associates. The mechanism of negotiation and decision making involving the patient's relatives is however incontestable in the cases of children's affliction. In most of the other cases, a patient is accompanied either by one or two relatives (husband/wife, or parents) or comes alone. Although the active participation of a patient's relatives during the medical consultations is rather rare, they exercise a latent but significant influence on the patient's decisions about therapy options. This means that they help to evaluate treatment that they have undergone in the past and search for an optimal solution for the future.

It is not only the opinion of relatives that shapes the patient's view about his illness and modes of therapy, but in a broader sense, it is the whole society. In everyday life health problems are discussed at different public places such as bus stops, waiting rooms, churches, markets, or on public transport. Patients share their medical experiences with other members of the community and acquire new practical knowledge from the Media, work, or school they attend. The public opinion thus considerably forms and reshapes their explanatory model of illness. The way how patients supported by their significant Others and acquainted with local medical discourse conceptualise the illness and evaluate the therapy determines, not only on the further process of therapy seeking itself, but also changes the course of actual treatment. This usually goes independently of the symptomatic progress of the illness.

The limitation or absence of a kinship solidarity network in the urban setting is also reflected in the recent discussion about the process of individualization and the general crises of communal solidarity in Africa.[15] Refusing to provide the necessary help to close relatives is generally regarded as anti-social behaviour and leads to witchcraft accusations amongst family members. However, as I observed the moral obligation of communitarian reciprocity in a situation of someone's need is for the most part respected in Lusaka. As the majority of Lusaka dwellers are Christians, the idea of "aiding your fellowman" is highly valued. The predicament of everyday life in the compounds calls for generally accepted solutions such as gathering money for someone's funeral (*ndalama ya maliro*)[16], or in-church collections designated to pay for the medical care charges of someone who is ill.

The relationship between patient and healer both traditional and Christian is always unequal. It is a relationship between those "who know", who have access to medical knowledge and those "who don't" which gives rise to and reinforces the social distinction between them. Moreover the spiritual authority of the healers assured by symbols of healing (for example exposed paraphernalia, or the Bible) evoking the power of the involved spirits is considered uncontested. As patients have implicit trust in the authority of the spirits the healer "works

---

[15] See Marie 1997.

[16] Young mourners walk around the compound and collect money; they are furnished with a home-made document where a photograph of the deceased, a date and a cause of his death is indicated. Each donor has to write down his name and the amount of money he contributed to the burial.

through" or "works with" they are reconciled with the final diagnosis they receive. They hold the locution "spirit never lies". According to the research carried out among patients of both traditional and Christian healers, 100% respondents affirmed their agreement on the given diagnosis.

As I have already pointed out, the patient's identification with a particular diagnosis as preconditions of successful therapy does not depend only on the social consensus but is also conditioned by cognitive consensus, i.e. agreements on ideas and symbols. In other words, the patient and a healer have to "understand each other" – to share a common symbolic universe. Cosmology, in the context of healing, thus provides idioms for the explanation, prediction, and control of the disrupted experience (Horton 1967). As we will see in the following chapter, it is in particular during the course of divination when a healer "by a subtle symbolic manipulation with particular metaphors of multiple resonance," (Comaroff 1980: 646) imposes meaning upon disorganized patient's experience.

4. Indigenous Spiritual Healing

> "When ng'anga dies it is like
> when a computer burns down"
> —Doctor Bongo, Lusaka

Each category of *ng'angas* is distinguished by their specialization in the healing of certain kinds of diseases. As their practices are not standardised, healers employ different methods of divining and healing. In this chapter, I attempt to outline some of the common ways of diagnosis and therapy involved in traditional spiritual healing in Lusaka. Special attention is paid to the interpretation of the process of divination.

By the term "spiritual healing" I mean the complex of diagnostic, therapeutic and prophylactic practices carried out by spiritual healers, diviners, witch-finders and prophetic healers associated with so called spiritual diseases, i.e. those caused by spirit possession, witchcraft and mystical contagion. The definition of spiritual healing proceeds the term healing by which I do not only mean the final redress of sickness, but the whole process of restoration of the healthy state of the sick. This also includes the mitigation of suffering and harmonisation of the relationship between a patient's individual and social body. The patients themselves are not seen as mere passive recipients of therapy, but as active agents participating in the whole process of healing. As it has been shown in the preceding chapter, there are also other agents such as kin, friends or even non-personal forces that play an important healing role and should not be thus overlooked. Spiritual healing is conceived as a comprehensive, dynamic process that is socially constructed and situationally conditioned.

Before we proceed to particular healing methods, I would like to stress that diagnoses and therapy are never separate processes. The divination, i.e. spirit revelation's of causes of illness that draws on the psycho-social analysis of a patient's social profile and interpretation of his dreams leads to an identification of the agent causing the affliction and recommendation of an appropriate therapy and modes of prophylaxis.

All these practices are usually carried out simultaneously and intermingle during the consultation.

Divination (Illness Diagnosis)

The process of diagnosis consists of the recognition of symptoms as well as the identification of the cause of the illness. In other words, a healer puts stress on the symptomatological as well as the aetiological level. To diagnose the cause of a patient's affliction *ng´angas* use t diverse divinatory practices based on the use of the spiritual power of ancestral or biblical spirits. There are two types of divination that can be recognised in Lusaka: divination through spirit possession, and divination through the manipulation of divining tools. Whereas the former method is typical for spiritual healers, the latter is employed by diviners.

Spiritual healers who reveal the diagnosis through spirit possession do not rely on the patient's description of the problem. It is believed the spirit as an omniscient entity will reveal the diagnosis itself through the healer without asking the patient any questions. In contrast, diviners – not directly possessed by the spirit – communicate with it through diverse divining tools. The essential part of this type of divination is the examination of a patient's history, his family and social background and the interpretation of his dreams. In both cases, the setting in which the divination séance takes place plays an important role. To persuade a patient about the veracity of a diagnosis, a healer has to establish an intimate atmosphere open to discussion.

In Lusaka, the divination through mirrors, or "screening", is the most common technique. It is based on the use of a special divining tool – a "mirror" made of shards of mirrors fixed on a turtle shell or on a wooden spoon, to which red and white beans are added.[1] This divinatory technique is based on the principle of screening i.e. seeing things and events in a reflective material medium such as crystal, glass, mirrors or

---

[1] The divinatory technique of mirrors has also been documented among the Chokwe. The southern ethnic groups use a cord of multicolour beads instead of mirrors. The technique of twirling a cord of beads is provided even in Lusaka.

water. Before starting a séance a diviner first has to "wake up" his mirror by cleaning it with white clay (*mpemba*) and by drawing a cross on its surface. A diviner never uses just one mirror, but two or three of them. Each of the mirrors has a different shape and size. The ritual manipulation with several mirrors enables a diviner to "piece together" a complete picture. In the course of a divination a healer checks all the mirrors at the same time. Whereas the smaller one is held in their hand, bigger ones are placed in front of them.

By shaking rattles (*chibalala*) three times, a diviner calls his spirit. Subsequently the mediatory relationship between patient, healer and spirit has to be established. Some healers ask the patient to press the finger of his right hand against the small pad or a "box" located on the mirror in order to establish the contact with the ancestral spirit too. Others for the same purpose make patients hold a special stick covered with multi-coloured beads. There are also diviners who use a special hallucinogenic medicine called *mwavi* to get in contact with their ancestral spirit. They also give this medicine to their patients so that their "eyes can be opened" and see the future and past on the "screen".[2]

For this purpose, some diviners in Lusaka are equipped with a special consultation room where a white cloth is attached to the wall. The bench placed in front of the screen evokes the idea that a patient is in a cinema. This metaphor is even used by informants. The divination consists of watching the screen where the story – most often connected to witchcraft – is revealed. As a result, the patient can encounter an alleged enemy or a witch face to face.

In order to illustrate the process of divination I will use an example of one of my key informants, a reputed witch-finder Doctor Kasanda. This forty years old *ng'anga* uses three mirrors that he inherited from his grand-father Sakukuwa, one of the most well-known witch-finders in Zambia who died when Kasanda was a small boy. He uses his father's spirit for divination and healing. When entering his small dark consultation room one sees him sitting behind the table where different

---

[2] Some healers claimed that divination might fail if a patient bursts out crying during the consultation. As Doctor Kunda told me, "*tears chase the pictures.*"

paraphernalia[3] including magical mirrors are exposed in front of a patient. This setting plays an important role as a "hallo effect" in the first phase of divination. This consists of establishing a suitable mediatory relationship between patient and diviner in order to build up their confidence. The exposed paraphernalia represent evocative memorials of the diviner's personal history, wisdom and knowledge accumulated both in the history of the family and in the course of his life. They confirm his spiritual authority and power in the eyes of his patients.

Doctor Kasanda uses two old mirrors with bigger shards decorated with blue beads and one small, newer mirror decorated with red beads. As he explained, he uses all three mirrors to compare the pictures he obtains during divination in order to prove the veracity of the revelation. To identify an agent responsible for a patient's illness, Kasanda has recourse to a bigger mirror. The more complicated the case the more mirrors will need to be consulted.

At the beginning of the consultation a patient is asked not to interrupt the process of divination by questioning or by statements about his state of health, but only to agree or disagree with what was said by a diviner. Consecutively the situation changes and a sort of dialogue is established between the diviner and the patient who is now asked to specify his problem depicted before. By following the patient's answers, a diviner alternately looks into mirrors where the reflections of colours and shapes can be seen.[4] As I was told, every mirror is spatially divided into several fields by the shards whereas each of it corresponds to the field in the patient's life.

What however plays a crucial role in the process of interpreting signs emerging in the mirrors is a diviner's knowledge of colour

---

[3] Kasanda's paraphernalia consists of divinatory mirrors, kauri shells, bead necklaces, a tiger head, small calabashes, sea shells, a walking stick and a wooden bird.

[4] The signs differ according to individual diviners. Some claim to see only colours and shapes while others talk about *"pictures move like in the cinema"*. In the latter case the identification of an agent (usually a witch) is more explicit. A diviner as well as a patient can even see the face of an alleged witch or speak with him/her face to face.

symbolism. In accordance with Turner's findings about Ndembu's interpretation of colours, a spectrum of three main colours is especially significant. Red is the colour of power, strong emotions, danger, blood and conflict in the family caused by witchcraft, while white refers to peace and harmony. White is generally considered to be the colour of the purity of *mizimu*. That is why the white clay (*mpemba*) is used for cleaning divinatory mirrors and calling the spirit. Turner assumes that whiteness more than any other colour, "represents the divinity as an essence and source (...) and has a quality of trustworthiness, veracity and purity" (Turner 1967: 76). On the contrary, black is embedded with negative qualities such as disease, death and impurity.

As I observed during the divination séances, Doctor Kasanda starts with outlining the patient's general problem by checking only one mirror. Afterwards he proceeds to cross-check two mirrors by means of which he contextualises the patient's problem, both at the synchronic and diachronic level. He sets the problem in a time and respective social setting. The whole divination process is a sort of latent dialogue between a patient and a diviner which develops and proceeds towards a deeper understanding. By probing the alternatives, the diviner attains a higher level of understanding of a patient's problem. At a certain point, the level of analysis proceeds toward synthesis. As Devisch (1979) and Werbner (1989) showed, "a divination is not only analytical, but has also a moment of revelation through verbal and non-verbal communication through paradox, incongruity and evocative synthesis of quite disparate meanings" (Werbner 1989: 25).

According to my observations, a diviner not only attends to the patient's answers and follows his behaviour attentively, but also exerts a considerable influence on his view. This finding corresponds to Werbner arguments that "the course of interpretation is highly methodical, authoritative, yet selective and situational" (Ibid: 58). Moreover, patients perceive the whole divination as a highly sacred event and they have unquestionable trust in the authority of the spirit which governs the whole séance. The power and authority bestowed on a diviner is derived from his ability to communicate with an ancestral spirit as well as from his life history.

If we have a closer look at the whole process, we will see that even if the main aim of divination – common for a diviner and a patient – is to find out the final cause of a patient's illness and to establish a respective therapy, their expectations and strategies differ. A patient's main interest is to discover the *efficient cause*, i.e. to know "who or what caused the illness" (Sindzingre, Zémpléni 1981), while the identification of an *instrumental cause*[5] i.e. "how it happened" plays a secondary role. In contrast, the *ng´anga* believes that the explanation of the *instrumental cause* plays a crucial role in the process of diagnosis.

Their detailed knowledge of diverse magical techniques used by a witch – common for both witches and witch-finders – are exhibited in the course of divination. It seems that, a witch-finder basically draws on concrete information obtained from a patient concerning his health, problems in the family and dreams during the divination. At the same time he draws on his work experience, takes advantage of his general knowledge of the urban social environment and "common pool" of recurring patient's problems. Apart from this knowledge, he also uses material symbols –paraphernalia as well as verbal symbols to reconstruct the particular patient's case. In order to create the "symbolic bridge" (Kleinman 1980) between him and his patient, a diviner relies on a shared symbolic repertoire. As Comaroff (1980) showed in the example of Tshidi of South Africa, "the divinatory session itself is a subtle process of symbolic manipulation in which the healer extends particular metaphors of multiple resonance and the clients respond in the light of their own perceptions of the matter at hand (…) the symbolic clusters generated by the procedure are rich and multiple, and they permit interpretive flexibility" (Comaroff 1980: 646).

A patient, who is generally not well acquainted to with witchcraft, is gradually drawn into the "construction of his story" by means of impressive and nightmarish witchcraft symbolism figuring in the detailed *ng´anga's* description of the *instrumental causes*. We need also to take into consideration that the patients before visiting a healer find themselves in a burdensome situation. They have opaque feelings about their actual situation and see the unhappy events in their life as discontinuous, which leaves them in a state of anxiety and constant uncertainty.

---

[5] "Instrumental cause" refers to the technique used by an afflicting agent (Sindzingre, Zempléni 1981).

As it has already been shown in example of Agnes (witchcraft case 1) the main task of a diviner is to arrange and interconnect to the patient's separate experiences such as nightmares, psychological stress, social problems, physiological complications into a "comprehensible whole", to construct the illness as an integrated whole. By identifying with "his story" constructed during the diagnosis, the patient finally comes to understand the motives and causes of his illness and see his problem in a different light. This brings him relief from the previous anxiety. Comaroff (1980) took the same view in the case of Tshidi: "The act of divination among the Tshidi may be the recognized manner of imposing meaning upon seriously disorganized experience, divination is the most elaborate and conspicuous forum for the creative management of meaning in everyday experience" (ibid: 646).

In view of a patient's willingness to accept several different diagnoses considered as complementary I came to the conclusion that for a patient it does not matter which story a diviner constructs. What is important for him is that the "story" provides him a comprehensible explanation of his illness. The patient's identification or non-identification with a respective diagnosis depends primarily on the efficiency of the therapy itself. If we take into account the patient's trust in the diviner's spiritually inspired healing qualities, we can suggest that the whole of the divination process is about imposing the story created by a diviner on a patient and his persuasion about its veracity. From this follows that the more a patient identifies with his story, the more there is a chance of effective treatment. The efficacy of healing is from the most part based on the "placebo effect" as we will further see with examples of therapeutic practices such as the "cupping horn" or the "cleansing house ritual".

Divination through Spirit Possession

The method of diagnosis used by spiritual healers seems to be more standardised than those of diviners. Spiritual healers diagnose and heal certain types of afflictions by being possessed by one or more spirits with whom they communicate in the trance, or through dreaming. Usually they use paraphernalia such as a white plate in which a patient puts money, maize flour, beads and cigarettes as an offering to the ancestral spirit. Unlike traditional spiritual healers who use a fly whisk with a handle decorated by multi-coloured beads for calling their ancestral spirits, the prophets possessed by *mizimu* (Christian spirits) call them by prayers. The choice of paraphernalia depends on the type of spirit involved. If *mzimu* spirits are involved then a healer uses the Bible and Christian prayers, if *mashabe* spirits then traditional songs, a fly whisk or rattles are employed.

During the spirit-inspired divination a patient may not ask any questions, or otherwise interrupt the séance. It is believed that spirit reveals the diagnosis through the healer-medium directly. The veracity of the message is never challenged as the authority of the spirit is considered supreme. A patient, after being instructed by a healer, is supposed to just agree or disagree with what has been said by the spirit. As follows from my observation, the spiritual healer does not remember the course of divination due to a momentary memory loss.

Unlike the divination through mirrors, it is difficult to offer a plausible interpretation of divination through spirit possession as it is impossible to objectively identify how a spiritual healer establishes the diagnosis of his patient. There is no praxis of patient's questioning as in the case of diviners, the diagnosis is believed to be revealed directly by the spirit. In fact, the spiritual healer as well as a patient depends on the supreme authority and inerrancy of the spirit who governs the whole divination séance.

Divination through "Writing"

The recent divinatory method of "spirit revealing writing" provided by many diviners and witch-finders in Lusaka consists of asking a patient to bring a blank piece of paper and roll it up. A diviner puts the roll under his right arm and with the help of rattles or a fly whisk starts calling his spirits. In a few minutes, he takes the roll out of his arm, unrolls it and reads the "message written by the spirit" to the patient. As I observed the handwriting in red colour connoting the power, was not identical with the handwriting style of the diviner. However, the way of writing corresponded to the diviner's diction.[6] Doctor Lukesha who used the method of writing in combination with "scanning" in order to identify witches asked his patient to put a roll of plain paper under their pillow and sleep on it. The next day when the patient came for a review and brought the paper the healer interpreted the diagnosis written or "revealed by the spirit" on the paper.

The method of writing seems to be quite a recent and innovative divinatory technique. I have not come across any mention of it in earlier studies of local healing systems (Turner 1968, 1970; Frankenberg 1969; Jules-Rosette 1981), my informants also considered this method to be new. I suppose that it may have emerged as a result of cultural syncretism under the influence of the expansion of both education and Christianity. As Zambians consider themselves to be a "Christian nation", they very much appreciate the significance of the Holy Scripture. This might be the reason why "the spirit-revealing writing" as a divinatory technique has occurred and became so popular in recent years when the Pentecostal movement appealing to the authority of Bible experience the boom. West and Luedke (2006) in their analysis of the transformation of indigenous knowledge in Mozambique briefly mentioned this method and interpreted it as the consequence of the progressive bureaucratization of traditional medicine forcing the healers to be literate. In this respect writing as one form of western knowledge is a symbol of power for many Africans. This might be another reason why *ng'angas* tend to include it in their therapeutic itinerary.

Bones Setting

The bones setting is another common method of divination provided in Lusaka that probably came from the southern regions inhabited by Zulu (South Africa) and Shona (Zimbabwe) where it is well known under the

---

[6] During my fieldwork I personally underwent this type of divination. The diagnosis was written in the local language and as the diviner lacked the sufficient knowledge about my family and social background the whole diagnosis was rather vague.

name *pengula*. It is a sort of geomancy[7] which necessitates twenty to thirty different chicken bones. A diviner rubs them against each other and afterwards casts them in front of him. The resulting pattern made of bone assemblages is therefore analysed and interpreted by a diviner.

Interpretations of Dreams

The importance of dreams and visions for the African medical culture has been neglected for many years in African religious studies. Although there were a few scattered references about the role of dreams in traditional African religions (Evans-Pritchard 1937; Nadel 1954; Mbiti 1976), more systematic studies of dreaming later developed within the studies of Independent African churches (Fisher 1978; Fernandez 1982; Kiernan 1985). Recently, the dreams connected healer's "spiritual calling" are viewed in connection with their identity construction, or achieving religious status (Jedrej and Show 1992).

The Zambians consider dreams to be not only parallel to the "real world" but as an intermediary between the visible – terrestrial, and invisible – spiritual world. It is believed that via dreams people can communicate with superhuman realities which influence their everyday life here on Earth. A "dream telling" represents on the one hand, a way how to understand the unpredictable consequences of encounters with these superhuman realities (such as illness, death or bad luck), and on the other hand, it refers to the identity of a patient. The later was shown by Reynolds (1992) with the example of the Zezuru for whom a dream telling represents the way of socialization, individualization, i.e. the constitution of self. The author focuses particularly on the dreams traditionally associated with the ancestral calling on which the identity of healers is based. As many of them tend to resist this calling their identity is gradually negotiated. On the contrary, Kiernan believes that the dream-telling is principally a social act as "a dream told to others leads to an analysis

---

[7] Geomancy is a method of divination that interprets markings on the ground or the patterns formed by tossed handfuls of soil, rocks, or sand. (www.wikipedia.org).

of dreams as social assets which can be manipulated to their advantage or disadvantage" (Kiernan 1985: 304).

As indicated above, dreams-interpreting as a part of a superior knowledge of *ng'angas* represents both an important strategy of establishing and maintaining their authority and a way of exerting an influence on its patients. A patient's dream telling during the witch-finding divination séances serves as a clue for a diviner's construction of his story. A witch-finder, in order to identify a witch, interprets the symbols appearing in a patient's dreams by linking them with appropriate witchcraft techniques unknown to a patient. The dreams (*maloto*) in fact represent an important source of information about a patient's spiritual state of mind as well as about his social, spiritual and psycho-physical well-being. What needs to be stressed is that for healers both traditional and Christian dreams convey more valuable messages about the patient's health state than mere symptoms. They pay special attention to them as their interpretation helps them to assign a particular affliction and its symptoms to an appropriate aetiology.

With accordance to data obtained during my fieldwork, I have come to the two key conclusions: Firstly that the occurrence of symptomatic dreams, their content as well as their repetitiveness are pivotal indicators pervading every type of diagnosis and secondly that the occurrence of symptomatic dreams shifts every illness interpretation to an aetiological level of spirit possession or witchcraft, even if its symptoms are ordinarily attributed to the category of "natural disease".

When collecting dreams of patients I noted, that there is a whole cluster of culturally shared dream symbols—some reveal the wish of an ancestral spirit to be worshiped and call a patient for guidance and divine inspiration, others presage a good or bad future or just warn us of danger.

An analysis of dreams first necessitates their classification. John Mbiti (1976) proposed the multidimensional classification of African traditional dreams into five categories such as threats, warning, requests, directives and revelations. Humphrey J. Fisher (1978) comes with a two-dimensional classification of dreams according to their significance and meaning. Whereas some of the dreams are meaningless and ambivalent, others have a spiritual significance and a clear meaning. This assumption concurred with the opinion of my informants who basically distinguished two types of dreams: The first are the dreams produced in the early stage of sleep the informants call "dreaming time" which content is closely linked to experiences from everyday life and thus reflects the state of one's mind. These dreams have no special importance and are not involved in the diagnostic process. On the contrary, the real dreams (*maloto*) which occur in the "fast asleep" (*mutulo*) that my informants depict as a time when "*a body is without possession of its senses and you have no power to wake up*".[8] *Maloto* are considered to be signs coming from the invisible world that play an important role in the divination process. It is believed that in the "fast asleep" the "shadow" (double spirit of a man) leaves his body and travels to the parallel worlds where one can experience numerous dangers and adventures.

I distinguish three pivotal categories of "symptomatic dreams" that figures the most often in narratives of patients. The first type that concerns encountering dead people is usually associated with either warnings of danger, or the wish of a dead relative to elucidate strange circumstances of his death, or his wish to be revenged. Secondly, there are dreams referring to the encounter of *mashabe* ancestral spirits which is commonly interpreted as an "ancestral calling". As is shown in the schema below the ancestor appears in a dream in the form of a particular animal (such as snake, monkey, or lion) or refers to a specific activity that represents him.

The third cluster of dreams is connected to witchcraft. The "shadow" of a man is considered to be especially vulnerable when it leaves the body in a dream. It is believed that it can be easily attacked, captured and exploited by a witch. The shadow can be "tied" by means of taking the victims' footprint or by use of various witchcraft techniques as is illustrated in the schema on the next page.

---

[8] This phase of sleeping is designated as non-R.E.M in biomedicine. However, in the non R.E.M phases dreams usually do not occur.

Schema 4: Dreams Associated with *Mashabe* Spirits

Content of a dream	Significance
Digging in the bush	Collection of medicinal herbs, healer's career
Stepping on leaves, grass and dry sticks on the ground in the bush	Calling of an ancestor in the form of a hunter
Flying	Ancestor's calling in general
Swimming under the water	Calling of ancestors in the form of a snake, or *mansalamba* (water spirit in the form of a mermaid)
Being chased by a lion or dog	Calling of an ancestor in the form of a lion
Stealing the crop	Calling of an ancestor in the form of a monkey

Schema 5: Dreams Associated with Witchcraft

Dream	Affliction *Header continues on next page*
Feeling of being oppressed, chased or beaten with a stick.	Patients complain of the fear of being pursued (paranoia), having persistent headaches, and elevated heartbeat. These dreams are accompanied by visual hallucination – seeing small hairy beings (*tuyobera*)
Being exploited, "used" for manual work on a farm, mill house or plantations.	Patients complain of being tired, overlaboured, and weak and having backache.
Having sexual intercourse or being raped by a monster (*ilomba*)	Patients complain of having backache (in the case of single women) or having reproductive problems (in the case of married women).
Being fed with poisoned food or human meat	Respiratory problems or diarrhoea. It is believed that the poison contained in the food or drink goes inside the chest and causes a heavy cough, or even tuberculosis, or goes inside the stomach and causes a form of diarrhoea that resists any medicine. After being fed in the dreams the patient claims to *"vomit things that were given to them during the night such as human meat, the hair of dead people, lizards, nails etc."*
Being operated on or being "tattooed" by a witch.	Patients complain of a migrating pain through the entire body. They believe that diverse magical objects, which were inserted in their body during the night witches attack, are circulating in their blood. The treatment of this affliction called *chiposo* consists of the removal of the parasite objects by a witch-finder by means of *mulumiko* – a cupping horn.
Being killed by kalilole, "a magical gun"	Patients complain of chest pains, a strong cough and headache. It is believed that those who were shot by *kalilole* start bleeding from the nose, eyes, ears and mouth and they die quickly.
Being bitten by snake Communicating with dead people Seeing a tall person and a coffin Being burnt or seeing fire	Various

Witchcraft technique	Explanation
A witch uses its witch familiar or ghosts of dead victims	This dream seems to be connected to fears surrounding the acquisition of wealth.
A witch drains blood from the victim, sending a troubling ghost to the victim to exploit him as a labour force	This dream seems to be connected to fears surrounding the acquisition of wealth.
A witch uses his familiar *ilomba*.	This dream seems to be connected to fears surrounding sterility, miscarriage and HIV/AIDS
A witch incorporates magical objects into stomack of a victim by feeding him at night	This dream seems to be connected to fears surrounding witchcraft attacks in general
A witch makes tattoos on the body of the victims and rubs it with the enchanted medicine.	This dream seems to be connected to fears surrounding witchcraft attacks in general
A witch shoots its victim three times in dreams	This dream seems to be connected to fears surrounding witchcraft attacks and sudden death.
A witch sends the snake to afflict its victims A witch sends the *chivanda* or *chipuku* to trouble its victims A witch sends the fire to heat its victims	This dreams are generally linked to witchcraft

Healing (Therapy and Prophylaxis)

Traditional healing is based on the use of medicine that contains herbal, animal and mineral sources. This medicine can be "manufactured, sold or advertised for the use in the diagnosis, treatment, mitigation or prevention of any disease, disorder, abnormal physical states or symptoms whether in man or animals" (Constitution of THAPAZ 2001: 23). *Mankhwala*, a herbal based medicine, is made of dried and pulverised bark and the roots of different trees (*mutengo*). It can be provided as a commercial good by different *ng'anga* either at a market, or in their consultation rooms. Whereas some roots are extracted locally by traditional healers themselves, other are imported from abroad (the Democratic Republic of Congo or Tanzania).

The collecting, storing and use of *mankhwala* is subjected to multiple ritual restrictions. Herbal medicine is believed to be "pure" in essence and sacred because it comes from God.[9] In order to preserve its symbolic purity, the providers as well as users have to respect a special ritual code of behaviour when manipulating it. *Mankhwala,* if not treated according to the traditional norms can become contaminated and impure. Such a medicine is either ineffective or highly dangerous and can easily turn into a dangerous *wanga*. As a result, every *ng'anga* instructs his patients to follow and respect the rules given by the spirits in order to assure effective treatment.

Although the taboos differ for healers and patients, there are some, which are common for both. For instance, the ritual prohibition of touching *mankhwala* by impure individuals such as menstruating women, women who aborted without being cleansed, or someone who has just had sexual intercourse.

For *ng'anga* the rules are generally more complex than for patients. For instance, it is believed that a healer cannot touch the medicine and treat patients after having had a quarrel with his spouse without having "restored peace at home". As I was told, healers cannot touch medicine

---

[9] As herbal medicine is considered to be a "gift from God" (*mpaso ya mulungu*), Mutumwa churches provide it to their patients during the healing services.

and treat their patient without being cleansed after someone from their family has passed away. Restrictions also apply to collections of *mankhwala*. A healer when collecting the "powerful medicine" such as *mutototo* (a stimulating aphrodisiac for men) cannot touch it with his right hand otherwise he/she becomes impotent. Spiritual healers and diviners, conform not only to the commonly shared ritual restrictions mentioned above, but have also to respect the special instructions revealed by their ancestral spirits. Every *ng'anga* has own repertoire of *mankhwala*. He usually mixes from three to five different medicinal herbs to obtain the remedy whose name and composition is a highly guarded secret. As a result, most healers are reluctant to provide detailed information about the herbs they use. They often point out that access to the secret knowledge of herbs requires one to become a healer. To combine *mankhwala* from different *ng'anga* is considered to be highly dangerous, not only due to the risk of an overdose, but mainly for spiritual reasons. It is generally believed that, the medicine from different healers comes from different spiritual sources, which may easily lead to their "collision", and have a negative effect on the patient's health. Moreover, the unprompted and uncontrolled combination of herbs may, according to my informants, cause the *mankwhala* to turn into a dangerous *wanga*.

In Lusaka, herbal medicine is commonly used for the treatment of genitor–urinary diseases, diarrhoea, respiratory and reproductive problems, and problems of locomotion. There is also a whole range of medicine used for treating social afflictions – for example medicine for good luck, job promotion, getting back a runaway husband or stolen money, or medicine to ensure the successful resolution of a court case. Especially *muito* (love potion)[10] and various aphrodisiacal stimulants such as *mutototo*[11], or *nyang'anya*[12] are a particularly much-sought-after good among Lusaka dwellers and can be purchased at almost "every corner".

---

[10] *Muito*, love potion, is a common charm medicine available everywhere in Lusaka. It consists of the combination of four medicinal herbs. It is believed that as a patient smokes it, the smoke attracts the lover.

[11] *Mutototo*, an aphrodisiac for men, also known under the name "gun powder", exists in many variations according to their respective sexual problem. *Mutototo* is generally effective eight hours after ingestion in the form of a tea.

Apart from herbal medicine, *ng'angas* also use so called *chizimba*, a medicine containing animal (or human parts) such as the fat of a lion, animal fur, and the heart of a sheep, hair of a white man, the meat or shell from snails, snake skin, turtle shells or spider webs. They use *chizimba* mainly to ensure a patient's job promotion, being successful in court cases, or to neutralize witchcraft. *Chizimba* is also employed by witches as a necessary part of some of their magical objects – *chinyanga*.[13] The *chizimba* made by witches comes under the general category of *wanga* (dangerous charms) whereas the *chizimba* made by a healer is conceived as a powerful but "pure" medicine designated for the neutralization and protection (*kutchinjirizo*) from witchcraft.

The use of *chizimba* by both healers and witches is based on the principle of *homeopathic* and *contagious magic* (Frazer 1922).[14] In Lusaka, the

---

[12] *Nyang'anya* is an aphrodisiac for women used for the traditional practice of "dry sex". By drinking *nynag'anya* in the form of a tea, a vagina becomes dry and warm which is considered to be a desirable state for having sexual intercourse.

[13] *Chinyanga* – a witchcraft object – is made of frog or snake skin stuffed with black powder which is made of rotten cow bones, and human blood or meat. The bones from a chicken and the talons of eagles are added to make *chizimba* more effective and powerful. To neutralize the most powerful witchcraft *chizimba* made of human blood, witch-finders use a lion's fat.

[14] Frazer defined the *homeopathic* and *contagious magic* in his book *Golden Bough* (1922): "If we analyse the principles of thought on which magic is based, they will probably be found to resolve themselves into two: first, that like produces like, or that an effect resembles its cause; and, second, that things which have once been in contact with each other continue to act on each other at a distance after the physical contact has been severed. The former principle may be called the *Law of Similarity*, the latter the *Law of Contact* or Contagion. From the first of these principles, namely the Law of Similarity, the magician infers that he can produce any effect he desires merely by imitating it: from the second he infers that whatever he does to a material object will affect equally the person with whom the object was once in contact, whether it formed part of his body or not. Charms based on the Law of Similarity may be called *Homoeopathic or Imitative Magic*. Charms based on

... footnote continues on next page

use of traditional medicine is for the most part based on the principle of homeopathic magic. For example, the intended effect of *chizimba* containing the fat of a lion or the hair of a white man (*tsitsi ya muzungu*) is to assure job promotion or the success in business of a patient. According to the "law of similarity", it is believed that a *chizimba* made of the fat of a lion symbolizes power and boldness, and *chizimba* made of the hair of a white man endowed with economic capital, will produce the success in business. Similarly, *chikoka*, a special type of medicine for attracting the attention of people, love or business, is made from a bird nest, spider's web, or anthill mud. According to the "law of similarity" "*it sticks and pulls the things together*". As Doctor Kasanda said, "*chikoka is the medicine which makes that people love you and listen to you*".

Contagious magic employed both by witches and witch-finders is mostly linked to witchcraft. For instance, there is a particular offensive magic used among women called *mukunko* that produces an illness of prolonged period which is made of *chizimba* containing pad contaminated with menstrual blood of a victim. According to the "law of contact", the *chizimba* contaminates the victim with whom the pad was once in contact. As Lock and Sheper-Hughes 1987 showed, in many non-European societies there is a strong concern with matters of vigilance over social and bodily boundaries, i.e. what enter the body (food, drink), what leave the body (disposal of one's secretion, hair cuttings and nail parings). Concern with penetration and violation of body exits, entrances and boundaries are then extended to material symbols of body such as home, doors and gates.

---

the Law of Contact or Contagion may be called *Contagious Magic* (Frazer 1922: 386).

Schema 6: Illustration of the Use of *Chizimba*

Animal ingredients used for the fabrication of *chizimba*	Name of the charm	Characteristics of the charm *Header continues on next page*
Bird nest; Anthill mud; Spider net	*Chikoka*	Good luck
Shell and meat of snail	*Mukunko*	Witchcraft
Skin of an armadillo (*nsoni*)	—	Good luck
Fish scale	*Kavundula*	Witchcraft
Faeces	*Kavundula*	Witchcraft
Fat of lion	—	Good luck
Chameleon	—	Witchcraft
Electric fish[15]	—	Witchcraft
Hair of a white man (*Tsisi ya mutungu*)	*Muito* (love potion) *Tuyobera*	Good luck Witchcraft
Oil and blood from *sandawana* (bush rat)[16]	*Kamboma* (money power oil)	Witchcraft
Human blood	—	Witchcraft
Human bones	—	Witchcraft
Skin of snake (cobra)	—	Witchcraft
Turtle shell	—	Witchcraft Healing
Shell from ant eater (*nkaka*)	—	Good luck
Porcupine spine	—	Healing
Chimba - pelt from leopard	—	Healing

---

[15] An electric fish is a fish that can generate electric fields. It is said to be electro-genic as well as electro-receptive. Electric fish species can be found both in the sea and in freshwater rivers of South America and Africa. (www.wikipedia.org).

[16] *Sandawana* is a sort of wild rat living in the bush. It has red hairs and leaves bloodstains in its trail. As I was told by doctor Lukwesa, *sandawana* it is almost impossible to catch and kill. For this reason the leaves where bloodstains remain are used to make *chizimba*.

Curative or destructive effect
to pull something together, to attract people, love and increase business
to have prolonged menstrual periods, to afflict the reproductive system
to have good luck in work, love, and business
to split a couple, to make love rival smells like a fish
to split a couple, to make a love rival smell like faeces
to give somebody power, to make him terrifying, to win court cases, to get a job, to become a leader in a group
to make somebody shrink and die (simulating AIDS)
to paralyse somebody in order to escape
to get married to a white person; to become rich and powerful at the expense of family members
to become rich at the expense of family members
to make a victim powerless, to increase one's business; to increase the harvest; to get the fuel for magical plane transporting witches
to make magic planes for night transport; to make magic guns to kill a victim
to become powerful
to transport *chizimba* from a distance to cure haemorrhoids
good luck in life
to stop natural bleeding from the nose
to cure skin problems

Purgatory procedures

Traditional therapy consists of a series of purifications of the body and place by means of *mankhwala* – medicinal herbs. The purgatory procedures have both therapeutic and prophylactic function and consist of drinking herbal decoctions, eating dry pulverized herbs in porridge, fumigation, bathing and rubbing *mankhwala* on the body or in skin-incisions.

The most common purgatory practice in Lusaka is *kusamba* – cleansing the body by bathing in *mankhwala* concoctions. *Kusamba* is prescribed in order to "wash out", to rid the body of the symbolic impurity, illness by means of bathing in a special herbal concoction. This method already described in chapter 2 is employed both by traditional healers and faith healers. The later uses holy water in combination with an exorcism instead of herbal bath. *Kusamba* is most commonly employed if a patient is possessed by a *chivanda* or by other malevolent spirits. According to the local traditions, mourners have to undergo *kusamba* in order to get rid of the impurity of death and therefore anticipate the potential affliction by the spirit of a dead person. The cleansing procedure as a part of the funeral rites is aimed at the separation of the dead and surviving family members. It is believed that, the mourner who underwent cleansing is protected and thus cannot be "pulled into the world of the dead". The risk of the contamination is generally high in the following cases: 1) when a family member died a sudden mysterious death; 2) one was *ng'anga* or a witch; and 3) there was an intensive emotional tie between the dead person and the mourner during their life. This is the case when one of the spouses dies. In Zambia, there is a tradition of cleansing widows. A woman whose husband died has to be cleansed by means of sexual intercourse with a brother-in-law. Only the woman who has been cleansed in this way can have other sexual partners in the future and be fertile. If a woman is not cleansed after the death of her husband, potential lovers might be afflicted by *chivanda* (ghost) of the dead husband and the woman can become infertile. Due to the high rate of AIDS in Lusaka, this traditional cultural practice was modified. Nowadays, widows do not have sex with their brothers-in-law any more, instead of it, the symbolical cleansing by anointing their sperm on the widow's forehead is performed. Not only mourners, but also women after giving birth and those who aborted, are preventively cleansed by bathing in a special herbal concoction in order to get rid impurities.

Kusamba as a therapeutic and prophylactic practice is prescribed when witchcraft is involved.[17] The bathing of body before going to sleep, or before undergoing a house-cleansing ritual (*kuchotsa ziwanda*) is generally prescribed as a form of protection against another witchcraft attack. An afflicted person, his relatives and a house have to be cleansed several times to get rid of "the bad wind" (*mpepo oipa*) and to be protected from an ensuing attack. *Ng'angas* in Lusaka do not provide pure prophylaxis against witchcraft to their patients neither provide preventive protection of the body by wearing amulets present.

The magical protection of a field (*kutchinjiriza munda*), spouses from extramarital sex (*lukanko*) or babies by their mothers (*chibere*) is regarded as highly dangerous as the boundary between protective and offensive magic is thin and permeable.[18] The majority of my informants believe that one cannot be protected from a witchcraft attack until it happens. When asked why people do not protect themselves against witchcraft before it takes effect, one of my informants promptly answered: *"It is like going to see a doctor with a broken leg one day before you broke it. How can I know that I will need his help tomorrow when my leg is alright today?"* This citation recalls us to the local conceptualisation of illness as an omnipresent but unpredictable entity as mentioned in the previous chapter. No wander then, that the notion of preventive medical examination as recommended by a physician is completely foreign to the majority of Lusaka dwellers.

Traditional Surgery Methods

Ndembo or "tattoos" are a widespread therapeutic method used by healers in Lusaka. *Ndembo* is a razor-blade skin incision made around the vulnerable or afflicted area on the body where a *mankhwala* in the form

---

[17] *Kusamba* is not recommended in all of the witchcraft cases, but only in the cases when particular magical techniques such as sending a "bad smell" or *chivanda* to a victim were employed by a witch.

[18] See chapter 7.

of dry or fresh pulverised leaves, bark or roots, is rubbed in order to reach the bloodstream quickly.[19] A patient who underwent this sort of chirurgical intervention can be recognised by symmetrical skin scarification.

Mulumiko or the cupping horn used by witch-finders in Lusaka, is a kind of surgical method based on sucking out the parasitic objects (*viposo/chiposo*) such as teeth, claws, bones, stones, or even small animals circulating in the blood of the patients by means of a horn which is leeched onto the affected area where *ndembo* has been done before. A healer puts the horn into his mouth and sucks it for as long as the blood clot rises into the horn. Afterwards, he blows out the contents and starts searching the objects. Nowadays the horn is very often replaced by a cut tennis ball or special polyvinyl sucker because of the danger of HIV transmission. The circulating objects (*viposo*) are believed to be inserted in the human body by witches during their malefic night operations, either through *ndembo* or through "night feeding" victims in dreams. The patients afflicted by this disease usually complain about a sharp moving pain though the whole body. Before the cupping horn is used, a healer has to gather the alleged invisible objects at one place in the body with the help of a special medicine injected into the patient's body through *ndembo*. This medicine also causes the objects, which were until then invisible, to become all at once visible when sucked out by the healer. Janzen (1978) noticed that *bang'anga* from Congo had gradually abandoned the use of this method as "it had become increasingly difficult to convince patients of its validity" (Janzen 1978:198). On contrary, I found out that almost all of the healers in Lusaka use a modified cupping horn for healing the afflictions caused by witchcraft. While some *ng'anga* prefer using a special medicine to kill the parasitic objects in the body rather than sucking them out, others combine both methods. The purification of the blood by getting rid of parasitic objects is employed also by vomiting various objects such as human hair, human fingers, bones, razor blades and frog induced by the ingestion of a medicinal herb called *mugezo*.[20] The blood

---

[19] As a consequence of the health education about AIDS, the healers in Lusaka gradually use sterile razor-blades for the chirurgical interventions.

[20] *Mugezo* (etym. something to vomit).

may be cleansed also by means of sneezing induced by sniffing medicinal herbs generally called *sanga luenge*.[21]

In the frame of cleansing rituals *ng´angas* in Lusaka also provide the purification and protection of a place regularly visited by witches Such a place depicted by the local collocation *mpepo oipa* (bad wind) can be a house, field, barn or outside areas under a tree where, as people believe, witches congregate. In most of the cases, the protection of a house is secured by the method of fumigating. The *mankhwala* such as *lubani* (yellow stone), *jikalangue* (plant with horns) or *mbosha* (fresh herbal leaves) is burnt over live coals and the smoke is driven into the house. In addition, various measures have to be taken to trap the witch inside the house. For this purpose the witch-finders place "magical traps" made of razor blades covered by *mankhwala* placed in the four corners of the house. I was said that, a witch who is trapped starts bleeding so that he can be easily identified according to the bloody stains leading to the house where he lives. Magical traps can be also made of cords stretched in the house so that a witch can be trapped like an animal. In order to protect the house regularly visited by witches, *ng´anga* sprinkles a protective herbal concoction on the walls. This produces an effect that, "*a witch who wants to enter the protected house cannot see the house but just water, a big river. To enter that river a witch has to be very clever to be able to transform himself into a water animal like a rat and pick that person from the house and start witching him*", said one of my informants.

The ritual of "house cleansing" (*kuchotsa ziwanda*) magical objects (*chinyanga*) laid by a witch is provided by witch-finders in Lusaka. This ritual consists of the detection[22], neutralization[23] and destruction[24] of

---

[21] *Sanga luenge* (etym. medicine to sneeze).

[22] To detect or localize a magical object, witch-finders use different divinatory techniques such as spirit possession or communication with ancestral spirits through magical mirrors.

[23] The neutralisation of a magical object means that a witch-finder releases and materialises the harmful power embedded in the object. As a result the object becomes visible.

chinyanga in a patient's house.[25] Unlike in rural areas where the "house cleansing" still pervades, in Lusaka it has begun to wane.[26] Doctor Mukanda, a prominent witch-finder told me, "*Here in Lusaka there is a lot of witchcraft because ng'angas don't check up and cleanse houses any more. They are scared, but in the villages they do. You know it is a very dangerous job, if you don't have the right medicine you can even die. Witches they don't want to be caught by us* [witch-finders] *they are more like thieves who don't want to be caught by policemen. They* [witches] *would rather kill us than be caught.*"

In February 2009 I had the opportunity to assist in a "house cleansing ritual" carried out by Doctor Mukanda in the house of Anna, one of his patients living in the *Ngombe* compound in Lusaka. Anna consulted Doctor Mukanda for the first time in January 2009 complaining about her problem of purulent herpes which had gotten worse. She underwent the divination and was told that she, as well as her ten year old granddaughter Catherine, had been bewitched. She was recommended to undergo the ritual in order get rid of the objects of witchcraft.

The ritual started in the evening around 5 p.m. when all family members gathered at home. Mukanda had prepared a special herbal concoction[27] in a basin in order to bathe and therefore protect all attendants in the house. All of us, one after another passed through two

---

[24] In most of the cases, witch-finders in Lusaka destroy *chinyanga* at a distance. This consists either of turning the *wanga* (charm) against the witch, or destroying *chinyanga* symbolically by a fire made from matches thrown into a special calabash while using a magic formula.

[25] In order to carry out the cleansing house ritual special permission from local police must be obtained. This directive was enacted as a consequence of the destructive and violent course of the witch finding raids into neighbouring houses.

[26] Only one from ten witch-finders claimed to provide the „cleansing house ritual". However, the Christian healers from the Evangelical Mutumwa church claimed to „search houses" (cleanse houses) in order to detect and destroy magical objects.

[27] The concoction was prepared from a pulverised black herbal medicine, red bark and cold water.

cleansing points where our feet, hands, forehead and nape were washed and smeared with grease mixed with red *mankhwala*. Afterwards Doctor Mukanda ordered us to draw the curtains he dusted *mbosha* leaves on live coals in his portable cooker and started fumigating rooms in each of the four corners starting with a bedroom. Then he changed clothes[28], unpacked his equipment he had brought in a suitcase and switched on the tape recorder with his favourite *kalindula* music.[29] The "sniffing around the house" – searching for magical objects – could start.

While praying and listening to *kalindula* music from the tape recorder near to his ear, Doctor Mukanda suddenly got possessed by the Biblical spirit of Moses who he uses for the detection of witches and objects. He describes his feelings as follows: "*It is like a magnet, when I am possessed by Moses I am pushed everywhere and I have to find it* [the magical object]". In his right hand he was holding the open Bible in order to catch the magical object in it. At the same time he was sprinkling *mankhwala* around from the basin with the help of a fly whisk.[30] When sniffing and rummaging around, he made strange sounds such as belching, hiccupping and wild animal noises to demonstrate the presence of the spirit inside his body. The whole performance culminated when Mukanda finally found an *ilomba*, a witch familiar in a form of a magical snake under the carpet. With the help of other men standing in a circle around him, Mukanda started fighting the *ilomba* tooth and nail by gripping it in his hands and teeth in turns. The "mystery combat" with the monster was completed by throwing the *ilomba* into the basin with the *mankhwala*.

---

[28] There was no symbolical meaning why he changed his clothes. He simply changed into working clothes not to be dirty on the way home.

[29] *Kalindula* is a popular musical style in southern-central Africa characterised by an up-tempo rhythm in addition to the *kalindula* bass guitar, one or more hand-crafted guitars called "banjos" and traditional drums. This style originated in the late 20th century in urban areas and is popular particularly in the Zambian southern province where *Chikuni Radio* station broadcasts it. (www.wikipedia.org).

[30] The same fly whisk he uses for calling the spirit of his dead father who helps him with witch finding.

Immediately after Mukanda fell down on the floor possessed by the spirit, others picked him up and brought him into the living room. Doctor Mukanda calmed down lying on the clay floor, head covered by the Bible, and the tape recorder near to his ear when suddenly he got possessed again with another spirit. He stood up, started talking in chiChewa language greeting everyone in the room and explaining what "should be done now" (*tsopani*).[31] As requested, the assistant brought the basin with *mankhwala* where the huge magical snake had been thrown as well as plastic bags and razor blades. As he explained to all attendants, the *ilomba* was thrown into the basin where it suddenly shrank into a small magical object *chinyanga*. When Mukanda drew out the materialised witchcraft substance from the basin and exposed it to all the attendees in the room, all were astonished and became much exited. He captured and neutralised the invisible dangerous power of *ilomba* by channelling it into the visible magical object. Equipped with plastic bags on his hand he started to carefully dissect the *chinyanga* with a razor blade. Dead silence ensued. All attendees curiously observed the scene as he unwrapped the magical object and found human meat (*nyama ya muntu*), three needles, some *mankhwala* and a small horn (*nsengo*) inside. Mukanda started explaining: "*This is the human meat that belongs to Anna. The ilomba was eating the meat from her belly every day that´s why she was suffering with chironda* [meaning disease]. *She felt a sharp pain because of these needles that were pricking her, look at them* (…)". After inspecting the object again a heated discussion about "who is the witch" and "why he did it" opened up among all of the family members. The suspicion was cast on Catherine´s father and his family as the relationship with them was tense and conflicting. While people were discussing the whole situation, Mukanda´s cousin took the dissected *chinyanga* outside the house where he burnt it and buried the ash far in the garden.

---

[31] *Tsopani* means „now" in chiChewa language (spoken in Malawi). During the speech Mukanda repeated this word every three seconds to emphasize the importance of the present time.

Ngoma Medico-Religious Ceremony

A medico-religious institution called *ngoma* (a drum) or *mashabe* ceremony is a typical therapeutic praxis carried out by spiritual healers in Lusaka. There are three main types of the *ngoma* that can be recognised in Lusaka.

The most common type is a ceremony organised for an afflicted patient. It is not only a healing ritual but also a therapeutic initiation of a patient into the role of a healer.

Ngoma organised for an afflicted healer represents a second type of therapeutic ritual that serves to redress the balance between the *mashabe* ancestral spirit used by a healer for healing and his own *mzimu* (spirit, soul). The ancestral spirit becomes usually disturbed by the infringement of binding "spiritual rules" for example when the healer commits adultery, or treats his patients during the impure period (after having sex, during menstruation etc.). In these cases, the spirit afflicts the healer with an illness as a form of punishment. It is precisely the same type of illness that occurred at the beginning of his healing career.

Thirdly, there is *ngoma* organised for a healer who passed away. This second phase of the funeral rite should assure that the *mashabe* spirit that had been working through the healer during his life is appeased and transferred to another living healer, usually in the matrilinea. The objective of this ceremony is to prevent other healer's and mourning relatives becoming afflicted by this spirit.

Due to the limited space of this thesis, only the first type of ritual will be treated both at the individual level as a rite of passage (an initiation of a patient into the community of healers) and at the social level as a process of the patient's social integration into a group of spiritual healers. As *ngoma* is intrinsically linked to the phenomenon of spirit possession it will be looked at in detail in the chapter 6.

5. Christian Spiritual Healing

"Jesus was a true ng'anga and we are his disciples"
— Pastor Sikwefu, Lusaka

In this chapter I explore the phenomenon of spiritual healing within the prophet-healing churches. As there are plenty of different churches of this type located in Lusaka I decided to investigate the one particular church of the Mutumwa type called the New Jesus Disciples Church situated in the Chawama/Kuku compound. After outlining the brief history of the African independent churches in Zambia, my attention focuses particularly on description and interpretation of common modes of diagnosis and treatment and the importance of the social body (church congregation) in the therapy process. I aim to show how the illness is socially constructed by prophets themselves within the church community. Furthermore, I will be interested in differences and similarities of Christian and traditional spiritual healing that although it draws on the same ontological reality, common medical cultural ideas and practices its interpretation substantially differs.

Since the 1970s and in particular in the 1990s under the influence of President Chiluba's declaration of Zambia as a Christian nation, Christianity in Zambia has been significantly marked by the proliferation of so-called African Independent Churches (AICs). These became part of the strengthening charismatic movement, particularly within Protestantism. Charismatic can be defined as "one who attests to an experience of spiritual renewal through the power of the Holy Spirit" (Burgess 2006: 89), and is endowed by a spiritual gift – charisma, such as speaking in tongues, healing, prophesying and exorcising. Leaders and founders of these churches as well as Christian healers called prophet represents the prominent figures endowed with the charisma.

The AICs since their beginnings have strived to make the Christian message, of which they were merely passive recipients during the colonial era, relevant to the African worldview and culture. Their religious activities have been primarily oriented at earthly life – at people's existential concerns – in order to obtain concrete benefits. In the same way as people in the past used to worship their divinities and ancestors and address them with demands for the abundance of children, harvest, success in hunting, trading and good health, they started now to turn their prayers to Jesus and the Christian Saints.

However, Africans have never thrown away their original beliefs but creatively incorporated them into the new biblical framework. As a result, religious syncretism has become the most prominent feature in all AICs. The AICs share but simplify the miscellaneous indigenous spiritual world by embracing a number of different spirits under the united category of demon which is put in contrast to the Holy Spirit considered to be the only source of truth and healing.

The power of the Holy Spirit is evoked and strengthens by means of prayers, spiritual blessings, lying on of hands on the patients, demon exorcism or speaking in tongues. The belief that the Holy Spirit is allowed to possess one, thereby removing the presence of undesirable spirits in him, stands in the core of Christian spiritual healing. It is believed, that only a body rid of bad spirits can receive the Holy Spirit, and thus be healed. For this reason spirit possession in the form of a trance is provoked both on the side of patients and prophets during the healing sessions in these churches. One of the greatest attractions of the AICs is that they agree on existence of witchcraft and evil spirits and offer protection from it.

The syncretic nature of the AICs manifests itself noticeably in the arrangement of liturgy. The leaders promote African music and dance to ensure the authenticity of religious experience for all church attendees. As a result, the choirs singing religious hymns accompanied by traditional dance performances play an indispensable role in every church service. One can be easily impressed by the spontaneous ambiance during the services that differs so much from those calm, well-ordered, reserved known from Europe.

As aforesaid, African Independent Churches represent an extremely important socio-structural component of Zambian Christianity today, especially in urban centres where they occur in large numbers. As the majority of Zambians are strong believers, belonging to a church community is a fundamental part of their social and political life. Churches located in every Lusaka compound represent not only the place where people regularly meet and glorify God but especially a space where strong feelings of *being* (locality and identity) *belonging* (kin, reciprocity, the others) and *believing* (morality, agency) are constructed.[1]

Zambia has a particular make-up that gives the church a special importance from the socio-political point of view. "The manufacturing sector is controlled by expatriates most of whom are South Africans while the trading sector is dominated by Asians. In this sense the only sector opened to Zambians is politics, the civil service and the church" (Gifford 1998: 220–221). As many Zambians living in the compounds lack the sufficient education and their social and economic capital is rather limited, the majority of them are also excluded from participating in politics or civil service. In this situation religion, in particular African Independent Churches remains the only "socio-political field" where ordinary Zambians can gain social prestige and authority.

The History of African Independent Churches in Zambia

According to van Binsbergen (1981) the religious scene in Zambia just before independence was characterised by the growth of prophet-healing churches such as Mutumwa, Watch Tower, different cults of affliction, the witchcraft eradication movements such as the Mchape[2], or Bwanali-Mpulumutsi movement[3]. All these movements were politically

---

[1] See Chabal 2009.
[2] See chapter 7.
[3] The Bwanali-Mpulumutsi witchcraft eradication movement appeared in 1947 in Nyasaland (now Malawi). It inherited many common religious elements from the Mchape movement that had preceded it. The traditional witch-finding practices were accompanied by the reading of the Bible. The adherents of this movement also put "a greater stress on the heaven-sent nature of the witch-finder's tasks, referred to moral precepts, many of which assert simply that witchcraft is "not cricket" (…). Its emphasis on divine inspiration, the sharing of sins by confession, and back-to-God moral rearmament classes it with a religious revival rather than with the patent medicine trade" (Marwick 1950a: 112).

and socially oriented, some of them even engaged in political actions against the colonial authorities.

The general boom of AICs in Zambia, as elsewhere in Africa, came after independence, in particular in the 1960s and the 1970s. It was principally the Pentecostal movement inspired by external models coming from Nigeria and the United States. The Pentecostal doctrine became "a vehicle for the expression of indigenous spirituality, as shown by its strong emphasis on healing, wealth and power" (Ojo 1988). According to Austin M. Cheyeka (2008) the "first wave of Pentecostalism" (from 1960 to 1970) was related to the arrival of the Scripture Union to the Copperbelt province and to the visit of Billy Graham, the famous American evangelist in Lusaka who has conducted many evangelical crusades since 1948 all around the world.

The "second wave" (from 1970 to 1980) is generally considered to be the decade of Christian growth in Zambia[4] represented by "Pentecostal explosion" (Gifford 1998), i.e. the formation of many prominent Pentecostal fellowships, such as the Bread of Life Church International (1975) the World of Life church (1980), the Pentecostal Assembly of God (1971) and others. In the same period the charismatic movement, which had been gradually strengthening, began to face opposition from the main established churches and its influence began to infiltrate into the Roman Catholic Church. This was particularly under the leadership of Lusaka's Archbishop Emmanuel Milingo who gained an excellent reputation as a Christian spiritual healer throughout the whole of Zambia. In the 1970s and later in the 1980s, it was also prophet-healing churches that had proliferated in Zambia. The most prominent churches of this type that occurred in Lusaka were the Mutumwa[5], Zion[6], Apostolic and Spiritual churches[7].

---

[4] By 1980, Christianity constituted 72% of the total population whereas the average in the other states of Sub-Saharan Africa was 53% (Cheyeka 2008).

[5] According to the Registrar of Societies in Lusaka, there are five different denominations of the mutumwa-type church in Lusaka (with their respective number of branches registered in Lusaka). These are: the Evangelical Mutumwa Spiritual church of Zambia (five branches), the Apostolic Mutumwa Spirit church (seven branches), the Mutumwa Holy Spirit church (one

... footnote continues on next page

The "third wave" of development of AICs in Zambia (1990s up to now) was in token of the new boom of Pentecostal oriented churches labelled in recent literature as neo-Pentecostalism (Anderson 1993), neo-Charismatic (Burgess 2006) or Born-Again Churches (van Dijk 1995). The outstanding feature of these churches is that they have no connection to the classical Pentecostal churches and mingle closely together with the charismatic streams of Christianity. Whereas the Pentecostals of the "first wave" were predominantly marginalized in the new, urban and industrial social order, neo-Pentecostals, in contrast, are represented by people fully westernised, urban and well educated of a middle socioeconomic status. Although the literature concerning Zambia in this period mentions only the neo-Pentecostal movement, from the data I recorded in the Registrar of Societies it follows that also a great number of the prophet-healing churches have been newly registered since 1990. This was influenced by two main factors. The first one was political – the proliferation of these churches broke out in the 1990s as a result of the declaration of Zambia as a Christian nation by the president Frederic Chiluba. The second factor was bureaucratic —with the end of the Chiluba governance and the inauguration of Levy Mwanawasa (2002–2008), the politics of restriction and of the uncontrolled mushrooming of Pentecostal

---

branch), the New Jesus Disciple church (one branch) and the Spiritual church (three branches).

6   From my research in the Registrar of Societies in Lusaka it followed that there are seven different denominations of the Zion-type church in Lusaka (with their respective year of registration and number of branches registered in Lusaka). These are: the Zion Spirit Church (registered in 1977, 12 branches); the Zion Christian Prophecy Church (registered in 1997, 3 branches); the Zion Prophecy Church of God (registered in 1974, eight branches); the Zion Christian Church (registered in 1983, three branches); the Zion Holy Spirit Church (registered in 1995, two branches); the New Anointing Zion Church (registered in 2007, one branch); and the Zion International Church (registered in 2007, one branch).

7   For example: the Mzimu church, Spiritual church of Zambia, Paradise church and others.

churches by increasing the fees of registration was implemented.[8] The regulations in turn enabled the bloom of prophet-healing churches in this later period.

Prophet-Healing Churches

The first and the most outstanding feature of these churches is religious syncretism, the process when the local traditional customs and beliefs in dangerous ghosts (*vibanda*), ancestral spirits (*mashabe*) or witches (*mfiti*) are placed within the biblical religious framework where the Holy Spirit (*Mzimu Woyera*) is considered to be the only source of healing power. Daneel (1987) when dealing with the religious syncretism of AICs in Zimbabwe among Shona uses the term "Christian indigenization". According to him, "the AICs provide us with many examples of an innovative approach whereby traditional cultural and religious ceremonies have been adapted and transformed to have Christian meanings" (Daneel 1974: 309–347). Anderson (1990) links the religious syncretism of AIC's to the notion of contextualisation that he defines as "an adaptation that, while displaying parallels with traditional religion, essentially implies a continuing confrontation with and creative transformation of traditional religion and values" (Anderson 1990: 56). Unlike the Pentecostal churches that draw predominantly on Christian healing, the prophet-healing churches adopt some of the elements of traditional healing such as using herbal medicine, traditional surgery methods (such as *ndembo*), cleansing bodies (*kusamba*) and public spaces and healing through spirit possession.

For an outsider, the greatest distinguishing feature of these churches is the use of uniforms for its members – white for Mutumwa and Spiritual churches, green and khaki for Zionists. The prophet-healing churches are situated in almost every poverty-stricken compound and their congregations count from 30 to 100 members, of which the majority are women. Their leaders and members are usually not educated, for this reason the sermons are carried out in local languages, mainly in chiNyanja and Bemba. They form small congregations, in comparison

---

[8] From 250 000 to 2 million Zambian Kwacha.

with the huge spectacular Pentecostal churches and therefore their social impact is not so wide.

As the name itself lucidly shows, the prophet-healing churches focus on divine "prophesying" of patient's problems through the power of the Holy Spirit. The Christian healers in these churches called "prophets" (*profeti*) are believed to be given the gift of prophecy and healing by Jesus Christ. Apart from prayers, blessing and driving out bad spirits, some prophets, in particular from the Zion churches, use various symbolic objects for healing such as holy water, anointing oil, ropes, sticks, clothes, herbs, ash and so on. The Bible the instrument of their liturgy is also used as a ritual object in much the same way as the holy water. For instance healing in the *Mutumwa* churches consists of laying the Bible on the head or body of a patient while praying. On the other side, the Zion churches use the Bible as a divinatory tool for prophesying the patient's future. The patient is asked to open it randomly in front of the prophet who then offers the explanation of the patient's problem according to the respective chapter.

Pentecostal and Neo-Pentecostal Churches

There is a whole range of different Pentecostal churches in Lusaka that vary in their size and number of adherences from small ones based in the leader's house to rapidly growing, vast church organizations counting thousands of members, and having splendid churches based near the shopping malls. In contrast to the prophet-healing churches, the founders of neo-Pentecostal churches are young charismatic men, well educated and materially secured who embody modernity itself. In order to promote their churches, they use mass the Media (in particular TV broadcasting their church services live), door-to-door evangelism, or organise mass open-air evangelizing crusades.

The neo-Pentecostal churches that have emerged in large numbers in urban centres, appeal primarily to the young generation of educated and wealthy Zambians who support them financially. The economic pursuit of these churches by means of clientelistic networks is grounded in the religious doctrine known as the "Gospel of prosperity".[9] The neo-Pentecostal strategy consisting of "helping the poor and ill in the name of Jesus" is particularly effective in towns, where poverty flourishes.

The unprecedented proliferation of the neo-Pentecostal churches and their growing popularity in the last two decades should be viewed from the perspective of the long-term socio-economical crisis in the country. Bad governance, corruption and mismanagement of the resources exacerbated the situation in Zambia. "In this context of daily survival many people began to construct their lives around the discourse of miracle, healing and prosperity" (Cheyeka 2007: 152). During the sermon, the preachers incessantly stress the importance of fighting against poverty, unemployment, the AIDS pandemic, the high divorce rate, the problem of alcoholism embodied in the notion of witchcraft. The proliferation of Born Again Christians is not only a response to the multi-crisis (socio-economic, politic and health crisis) but is also linked with the advent of market economy, development of entrepreneurship, and growing number of the middle class in Zambia.

An idea of conversion as a way to being spiritually reborn and thus healed represents a pillar of the religious doctrine of contemporary neo-Pentecostal churches. "The promise of a reward in the afterlife" is conditioned by the necessity of abandoning and condemning one's past life and cultural traditions. The leaders of the churches attempt to persuade the believers to create a distance from their "sinful life" before the conversion, whether it was linked to worshiping ancestral spirits, abusing alcohol, or living in polygamy. For neo-Pentecostals, the adherence to the traditional beliefs generally represents backwardness that leads to poverty and impedes progress towards modernity and prosperity (Meyer 1993). As a result, the prominent preachers of neo-Pentecostal churches strongly promote internationalism and universalism. The challenge of "breaking with the past" necessitates among others the total rejection of indigenous medicine and avoiding practices of *ng'angas* pejoratively

---

[9] The "prosperity gospel" is based on the belief that if people believe in Jesus Christ, he shall bless them with riches as a reward in the afterlife. For this reason the adherence are asked to give financial gifts to the church with the promise that this good deed will be repaided in the afterlife.

called witch-doctors. As one of the Pentecostal priests explained, "*witch-doctors put witchcraft and demons* [afflict] *on their own patients and then they heal them in order to gain money. They are all help-mates of Satan*".

The neo-Pentecostals emphasise the importance of "charismatic gifts" such as *glosolalia*, enduring faith, persistent prayers and the observance of strict religious ethics.[10] There are significant similarities in the spiritual healing of both Pentecostals and prophetic healers such as for example the accentuation of persistent collective and individual prayers, laying hands on the patient's head, the use of holy water and exorcising the evil spirits (demons) and fighting witchcraft. In contrast to the prophet-healing churches, leaders of neo-Pentecostal churches do not practice prophesying and reject the use of traditional herbal medicine within the church.

Spiritual Healing in the Mutumwa Church
(The Case Study of the New Jesus Disciples Church)

The Mutumwa is a cluster of the most known prophet-healing churches in Zambia. Its distinguishing feature is that it combines traditional healing practices with the Christian liturgy. The Mutumwa churches have no homogenous organisation and therefore liturgies vary as they have spread to different parts of Zambia after independence. Hence it seems appropriate to think of Mutumwa churches as a movement "not only because a variety of distinct medico-religious bodies acknowledge the title Mutumwa and a similar inspirational source, but also because their impact has crossed ethnic barriers" (Dillon-Malone 1983a: 205).

The Mutumwa movement has its origin in the Isoka district of north-eastern Zambia in 1920. The founder of the first church, which was called Mzimu church[11] at that time, was Aram Rabson Chinyamu Sikaonga, a traditional diviner and herbalist (*nchimi*) of the Tumbuka

---

[10] Apart from the strict observance of Ten Commandments, it is strictly forbidden for church members to drink an alcohol, take drugs, smoke cigarettes and changing of sexual partners.

[11] I draw on the personal diary of Bishop Victor Sivamba, the founder of the New Jesus Disciple Church.

origin. Both expressions *nchimi* and *mutumwa*[12] indicate a prophetic healer who was chosen by God and sent to Earth to carry on the healing ministry of Jesus Christ among African people. After the proclamation of Witchcraft Act in 1911 and the ensuing prohibition of the use of a poison ordeal as a method of detecting witches, the Mutumwa-nchimi movement became a part of the famous Mchape witch-finding crusade, which was active at the beginning of the 1930s in Northern Rhodesia as well as in neighbouring countries. The charismatic leader and internationally reputable witch-finder named Chikanga from the Rumpi District (by Lake Nyasa in Malawi) had a particularly strong impact on the formation of the Mutumwa church (Redmayne 1970). In 1956 he experienced a typical prophetic syndrome involving a serious illness leading to an experience of "death" and ensuing resurrection crisis accompanied by a mystical spiritual call to become a witch-finder with a special mission to cleanse Africa of all forms of witchcraft (Dillon-Malone 1983a). His fame spread quickly all over Nyasaland and the neighbouring regions including Northern Rhodesia. Sikaonga, a founder of Mutumwa church, knew Chikanga well and spent some time with him learning his healing art. Similarly the founding members of the New Jesus Disciples Church in Lusaka, where I carried out my research, understand Chikanga's healing ministry as a point of reference by claiming that they were healed by him, or just met him.

From the 1930s, the Mutumwa-nchimi movement gradually spread out of the Isoka district to the Copperbelt province and to the Lusaka district where due to large labour migrations and urban development it took its roots easily. While Dillon-Malone claims that the Mutumwa was not formally recognized as an established institution until independence in 1964, the diary of Bishop Kisimba (a founder of the New Jesus Disciples Church in Lusaka), asserted that Rabson Sikaonga had already formally registered the church under the name of Nchimi church of Zambia

---

[12] *Mutumwa* means "sent by God", *nchimi* means a Christian healer (witch-finder).

in 1953. After his death in 1972[13] the Mutumwa churches extended their influence westwards and southwards among Nyanja, Bemba and Tonga. As formally registered they have around sixty different branches in the Copperbelt Province and around more than twenty in the Eastern, Northern and Central Provinces.[14]

A history of the New Jesus Disciples Church (see the diagram below) is genealogically attributed to the Copperbelt branch of the Mutumwa Nchimi Church of Herbalists,[15] which was established in 1977 having the headquarters in Ndola. In January 2004, the church was renamed and officially registered as the New Jesus Disciples church of Zambia. This church with its headquarters in Mbala numbered fifteen congregations in 2009.[16] In my research I focused on one of them the *Kuku* congregation – which is situated in the Chawama compound in Lusaka.

---

[13] After Sikaonga's death, three groups of successors of the *nchimi-mutumwa* tradition appeared under the leadership of Moses Simwinga, Kenan Sichinga and Alifeo Siwakwi according to the diary of bishop Sivimba.
[14] Registrar of Societies in Lusaka, 2009.
[15] It changed its name to the Batumizi Church of Herbalists in 1982.
[16] Congregations: Chongwe (1), Lusaka (1), Ndola (2), Kitwe (1), Mbala (10).

Schema 7: History of the New Jesus Disciples Church

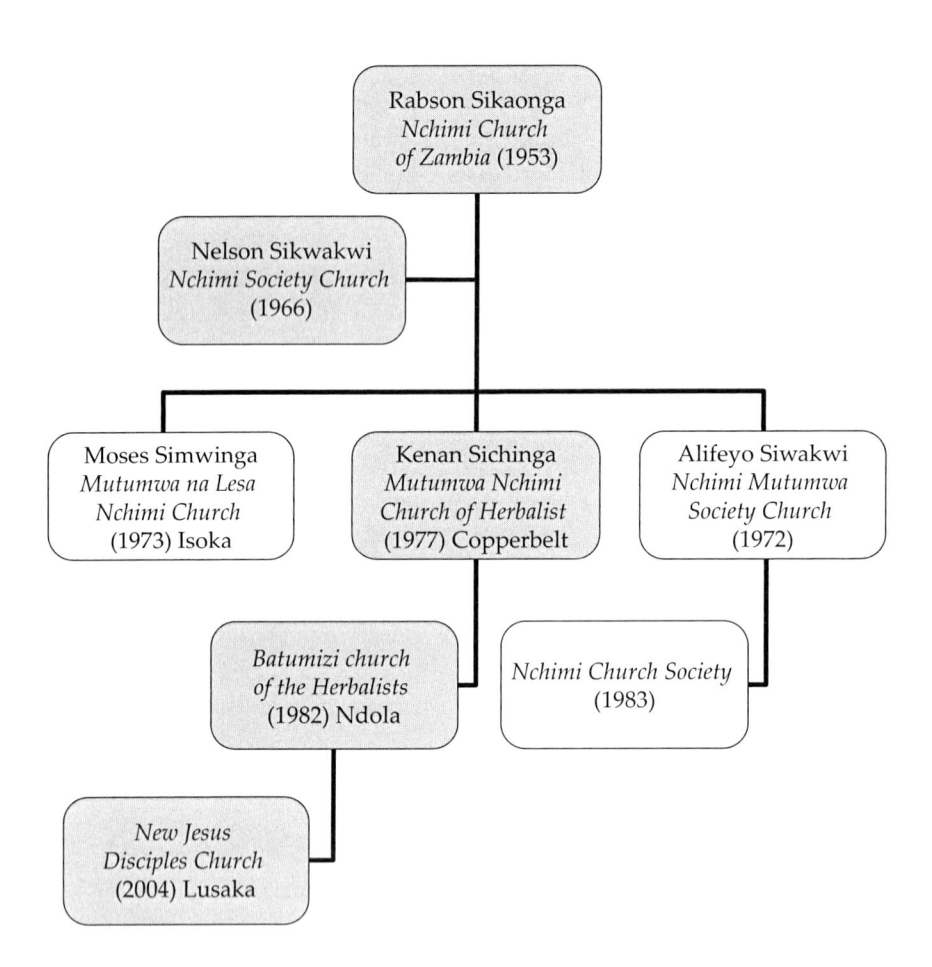

- Rabson Sikaonga — *Nchimi Church of Zambia* (1953)
  - Nelson Sikwakwi — *Nchimi Society Church* (1966)
  - Moses Simwinga — *Mutumwa na Lesa Nchimi Church* (1973) Isoka
  - Kenan Sichinga — *Mutumwa Nchimi Church of Herbalist* (1977) Copperbelt
    - *Batumizi church of the Herbalists* (1982) Ndola
      - *New Jesus Disciples Church* (2004) Lusaka
    - *Nchimi Church Society* (1983)
  - Alifeyo Siwakwi — *Nchimi Mutumwa Society Church* (1972)

The Kuku congregation comprises of about 90 members[17] who regularly visit church services, some of them have undergone baptism[18] and become full-value members. These can be distinguished from others by wearing white church uniforms or white headscarves (*chitambala*) in the case of women. All members have got clearly defined roles and status in the church hierarchy according to the Church constitution[19] such as a bishop, reverend, principal, elder, deacon, secretary and a treasurer. Unlike these roles that can be achieved by appointment, the roles of prophets, collectors and distributors of herbs and choir singers are conceptualised as a special "gift from God" (*mphaso yakwa Mulungu*). In particular prophets holding the most important function in the church had experienced a sort of affliction in the past and have been cured through the power of the Holy Spirit within a Mutumwa or other spirit-type church. This experience serves, as many anthropologists have shown (Sundkler 1961; Daneel 2001; Kirsch 2002), as a pattern of both recruitment of new members and the way to become a prophet. Status of the prophet based on charismatic authority is rather unstable, and open to social negotiation.

Church membership is most often assured by means of baptism. The congregation is mostly composed of individuals who after being converted regularly attend the church. During my research I did not notice any kind of pressure on being converted from the part of Mutumwa members. This strategy is more often employed by Pentecostal churches.

Apart from the members there are numerous shifting groups of patients coming from different Lusaka compounds.[20] However, the majority of members and church attendees dwell close to the Chawama

---

[17] A number of members registered in the church having a special blue card issued increased significantly during my research. The initial number of 30 members multiplied twice during 2008–2009. At the end of the research in March 2009 the total number of the members was 90.

[18] Baptism is done by being dipped three times in a river after attending weekly lessons of catechism for four months.

[19] The Registrar of Societies, 2004.

[20] Some patients however came from distant places such as Kabwe, Kitwe or Livingstone.

compound where the church is based.[21] The church provides diagnosis and treatment for different kinds of afflictions related to the traditional aetiology. Prophets resort to the Christian healing practices by prayers, singing hymns, blessings, laying on of hands, using the Bible, exorcising evil spirits, at the same time they adopt the traditional healing methods such as *kusamba* (cleansing), cleansing houses from witchcraft magical objects (*kuchotsa ziwanda*) and the use of traditional medicinal herbs (*mankhwala*) applied orally, by bathing or through *ndembo*, traditional incisions. Prophets also provide psychosocial counselling in the cases of emotional and domestic problems and analysing the patient's dreams. Unlike their attitude towards western medicine which is quite tolerant, they radically reject traditional medicine. During the church services, patients were systematically discouraged from approaching *ng'angas*.

The weekly main service which takes place every Sunday in the cardboard church in the Chawama compound may take approximately four hours or longer depending on the number of patients. The main service consists of two parts which correspond to a sermon-prayer service and healing service. Although these parts are temporally and spatially distinct, they form the whole, as two parts of the same coin.

For the purpose of later analysis, the description of the sermon-prayer and healing service in the church will be set into a framework analogous to the basic structure of liturgy. The first part sets the course of liturgy in the spacio-temporal context with regard to the particular activities of different social actors. Attention will also be paid to the embodied experience of the ritual that activates our senses by *smelling*, *touching, seeing* actions, gestures, symbols, decorations and *hearing* readings, prayers, music, and other sounds.

Sermon-Prayer Service

Entering the church, everyone takes off their shoes and takes up their assigned position according to sex and position in church hierarchy. The first part begins with an opening prayer in the form of a hymn sung by

---

[21] 80 % of the total respondents come from the Chawama, Kuku, John Lenge or the Mississi compound.

the main priest in Mambwe language. This hymn referring to Jesus' healing ministry on Earth is sung in the special soprano tune that imitates angel's voices and implies an esoteric content to the song referring to the Book of revelation.[22]

After the opening hymn, a prayer to Jehovah in Tumbuca language ensues. All attendees kneel down facing east and bow their head in a silent prayer led by a main priest. During the prayers some of the prophets visibly demonstrate the presence of the Holy Spirit's power entering into them by making strange sounds – *kumbiola* – similar to a loud hiccup. Then the singing of diverse religious hymns alternates with another prayer, sometimes both are carried out simultaneously.

The first part of the service consists in the Bible reading and preaching that concerns moral themes based on the Ten Commandments, themes of healing and casting out demons. As I noticed the priests as well as the prophets have adopted the populist Pentecostal discourse concerning the rejection of traditions, in particular indigenous medicine and *ng'angas'* healing practices pejoratively labelled as witchcraft. What is however interesting is that the anti-traditionalist discourse moulded by church dignitaries implies the rejection of modernity as well. During the sermons, the preachers discourage the church members not only from attending healers, traditional ceremonies but also from attaching to money, consumer goods, attending discotheque or clubs as modern forms of entertainment, or wearing modern cloths (trousers for women).

After the Bible readings and preaching so called "comments" ensue. These focus on elucidation of what had been said during the preaching by illustrating the words of God using examples from everyday life. The comments are usually accompanied by vigorous theatrical performances during which attendees react with enthusiasm. Communication between

---

[22] „And I heard the sound from heaven like the roar of rushing waters and like a loud peal of thunder. The sound I heard was like that of harpists playing their harps. And they sang a new song before the throne and before the four living creatures and the elders. No one could learn the song except the 144.000 who had been redeemed from the Earth" (The Bible, Chap. 14/ 2 – 10).

prophets and attendees during the comments is assured by the singing of hymns which intersect the whole action.

In case that "dear visitors" are announced to visit the Sunday service, the liturgy continues with the ritual of "welcoming guests". The visitors, the most often prophets from other spirit churches or reputable patients coming from far away, are asked to stand in front of the congregation whereby the main priest introduces them. They are called upon to greet all the attendees, introduce themselves more in details, and say the reason for their visit. After the collective prayer to Jehovah is carried out, the attendees start to sing songs and greet the visitors one by one by shaking their hands and embracing them.

I witnessed several times that the friendly and enthusiastic atmosphere escalated into spontaneous dancing and singing that became highly spiritualised. As the interaction between local prophets and "prophet – visitors" increasingly intensified, the later fell into trance manifesting the presence of the Holy Spirit in their body. This trance was often accompanied by a search for magical objects inside and outside the church, or by spontaneous prophesying which made the spiritual atmosphere in the church even more ecstatic. As I observed, the trance behaviour in the church often launched a chain reaction among attendees. In a few seconds several people got possessed during this occurrence – both patients and local prophets. For an external observer, it was difficult to recognise at first sight who from the participants is possessed by the Holy Spirit and who by demons. When the prophet's trance ended and chanting finally came to an end, the leader of the church raised his voice to announce that: "*There was a witch in the church at night and that everybody has to pray strongly to protect the church*". The "circle of praying" conducted by the main church leader ensued in order to neutralise the power of witchcraft in the church and to "cleanse" the *chilansengo*, a prophet specialised in witch-finding. Once I witnessed a visitor, a prophetess from the neighbouring Paradise Spirit Church, falling into a trance, during the "welcoming guest ritual", in such a violent way that she injured herself while running away from the church and searching for a magical object in the field. Being possessed by the Holy Spirit, she was pushed to dig wildly with her nose in the soil while imitating the animal sniffing a capture. The *chilansengo* was then brought back to the church and laid down on the ground, her body was temporarily paralysed, and her face was covered with blood and mud. Other prophets made a circle around her in order to deliver prayers and a blessing.

The whole atmosphere in the church calmed down and the liturgy continued with the collection of tithes and a thanksgiving prayer. When announcements concerning next week's program were delivered all the attendees gradually left the church while singing songs. The church representatives and guests who left the church first ranged themselves in a line outside the church, whereas other attendees when walking singing in a queue shook one by one the hands of those standing in a line. Afterwards they joined the same line, and waited to be greeted as well.

My interpretation of the ritual of welcoming guests and its epiphenomena stem from the image of the visitor as being a highly ambivalent figure, stranger, and outsider penetrating the holy space of the church. On the one hand, the church members received the visitors as "friends" loaded them with love and hospitality, on the other hand the visitors represented sort of "enemy" embodied in danger of potential contamination of the church with witchcraft (new coming patients) or the manifestation of spiritual superiority by means of detecting witchcraft (new coming prophets). In both cases the presence of outsiders stimulated spiritual atmosphere in which the spirit possession occurred. The objective of this culturally biased behaviour was, in my opinion, to clearly demarcate the social, spiritual and even spatial boarders within the church. In other words, the aim was to maintain the boarders between "we" and "them", good and evil, inside and outside, security and danger. By defending these borders that have been blurred by the presence of visitors, the local prophets supported by the social body of church members aimed to affirm their charismatic authority within the church and at the same time to maintain the security of the inner circle of church members.

Healing Service

After a short break while an assistant writes down names and some other details of those patients who came in a register book, the second part of the main service – the healing session ensues.[23] The healing service starts with a thanksgiving prayer to Jehovah. The spatial distribution of the participants and their sitting order is reversed. The pastor who has faced the East during the sermon service is now facing the West, and attendants are facing the East in order to receive the power of Jesus.[24] After the names of patients have been called out, a special hymn called *napieyne* ("I am burning") is sung in order to "heat the body", i.e. prepare it for spirit possession. Some prophets visibly demonstrate the presence of the Holy Spirit's power entering into them by making strange sounds (*kumbiola*) or making gestures like struggling over a divine stick. It is believed that the Holy Spirit works through the body and mind of prophets and comes into communication with the spirit (*mzimu*) of the patient so that the prophet can have a direct vision of his social and psychological background. Moreover prophets claim to be able to physically experience the patient's body pains.

The healing service is mainly aimed at the illness diagnosis through the Holy Spirit called "prophesying" or "searching" (*kusecha*). Nine to twelve sick, three by three, sit in front of the prophets in a line with their legs outstretched. Patients are asked to respond to the prophets in the terms of "yes" or "no" only if questioned. The prophesying is carried out simultaneously by two or three prophets while the other attendees are singing hymns.[25] The singing women make a ring – "wall of a sound" – around the healers and patients to encapsulate the healing action in a private domain and stimulate the sacred atmosphere surrounding the whole prophesying. The clients undergoing the holy divination are

---

[23] Spiritual healing is not provided only during the Sunday main service but even during the rest of the week. Some healing sessions take place privately in the main pastor's house. Prophets claim to be on duty all the time, ready to help every man regardless of his creed, race or economic situation.

[24] I observed the spatial shifts in the first phase of my fieldwork (from January to February 2008), but not in the second phase (from October to November 2008). The members simply gave up this custom without any reason.

[25] Whereas the hymns during the preaching service are sung discontinuously and are miscellaneous, the singing during the healing service is incessant and the repertoire consists of two or three songs sung over and over again.

usually accompanied by one or more relatives. These sit nearby in order to hear clearly the prophet's words. The average time of an individual prophesying is 15–20 minutes. The prophet manages to prophesy two or three patients during the healing service. It can also happen that he/she switches the patient in the middle of diagnosing them if asked by another prophet to help them with their case.

The chanting of hymns plays a crucial role in the congregation meetings. Their main function during the church service is to stimulate a sacred atmosphere and set the stage for the culminating point of the whole ritual embodied in the experience of "collective effervescence" (Durkheim 1965). The strong emotional experience leading to an altered state of consciousness experienced during the sacred rite helps to overcome the division among individuals and therefore reinforces social cohesion in the community. Those who experience the possession by the Holy Spirit feel a loss of their individuality and unite with God. All participants of healing service who experience both mentally and physically the ritual absorb the sacred power and energy that helps them to overcome the difficulties encountered during the course of everyday life.

Singing Hymns

The omnipresent singing in the church has not only an emotionally stimulating function, but it also serves as a mode of communication between community members, patients, prophets and preachers. The interactional dimension of the Mutumwa Christian hymns is manifested both in their call-and-response form and periodical interruptions when sequences of singing alternate with sequences of prayers and preaching. Hymns serve as markers of the whole ritual structure and facilitate the management of individual transitions (Jules-Rosette 1975). The sequences and cadence of singing not only mark the structure of a meeting, but also serve to introduce speakers when they preach, the arrival and entry of a new person or new topic on the scene. As the hymnody is mostly limited to the church leaders and some church members attending the church choir the orchestration of the whole church service is in their hands. I noticed that men (preachers and prophets) mostly use the hymns as way to acclimate their lively speech, in the same way as saying "hallelujah" or "amen". Women, on the other hand, sing hymns either in the choir as a part of a church program, or individually after receiving the signal from the men. Only wives of preachers or prominent prophetesses could take the liberty to interrupt the preaching with the spontaneous singing of songs, which referred directly to the theme of a preached message. I cannot therefore agree with Kiernan (1990) who claims that women interrupt men's preaching in order to latently criticize their dull speech or to "uplift and enliven the proceedings by compensating for the failure of the speaker to re-awaken flagging enthusiasm"(Kiernan 199: 200).

Jules-Rosette (1975), Kiernan (1990), and Kirsch (2002) who studied the hymnody in the prophet-healing churches assume that by means of singing of songs the attendees may express their affirmation or displeasure with the course or content of a preaching. Kiernan in this respect marked that, "the hymn has the diversionary or correctional purpose of changing the course of the sermon or speech; a kind of warning shot across the bows to leave off the present topic either because it is offensive, distasteful, tiresome or otherwise undesirable and to adopt a fresh one" (Kiernan 1990: 200). According to my observations, the singing of hymns is primarily aimed at reinforcing the spoken word and activating the collective enthusiasm during the sermon and healing service. Hymns refer to the themes of preaching such as the healing ministry of Christ, and the work of the Holy Spirit, or they aim at evoking the moral themes concerning virtuous Christian living.

Healing Devices

Some prophets in the church use a special carved wooden stick called *nkoli*, or *pidgika* for the purpose of diagnosis and treatment. *Pidgika* means "the light of Jesus" and refers to the Biblical Moses who used a similar stick to divide the water in the Jordan River in order to allow the Jewish people to escape and punish the Egyptian pursuers (the Bible, Exodus, Chap. 4). *Pidgika* can be thus viewed as a sacred object serving as a material support of the divine, as a place where the Spirit can be materialised before it possesses someone's body. The prophetess Mrs. Kazembe concurs: *"We believe that the Holy Spirit can go and use this stick as a path, as a way to enter somebody"*. By touching a patient with the *pidgika*, prophets are able to feel the physical pain in their own body. Another prophet Mr. Tembo describes his experience in words: *"When the Holy Spirit enters my body I feel different, I experience a force, all my body is perplexed ...when I see a sick person I can diagnose him directly, if he is complaining of pain in the lungs or back I first feel the pain in my lungs or back. Then I ask a person if it is true and he answers yes (...) I can see also visions of the patient's past and present moving like pictures on a TV. I can be shown by the Spirit something that happened a long time ago and I will tell him"*.

The prophets use the *pidgika* only if they obtain such instruction from the Holy Spirit in their dreams. It is believed that the Spirit also reveals which tree (*mutengo*) the stick must be made from and to which purposes it can be used. Two female prophets from the Mutumwa church told me that they use the *pidgika* for all range of practices such as extracting the medicinal roots in the bush or for healing patients by pressing the *pidgika* against their body. Additionally, the divine stick serves as a tool for detection of witchcraft objects: *"Pidgika is like a magnet it pulls me to the place where the chizimba* (magical object) *is hidden"*, confirmed one of the prophets. The divine stick itself is employed as a protective medicine against witchcraft and evil spirits. A prophet grates a part of the *pidgika* with a knife, mixes the wood flour with medicinal herbs and applies it in a form of "tattoos". It is strictly forbidden for prophetess to touch the *pidgika* during their menstruation, after the death of a family member, or after quarrelling with their husbands or other family members. Its fabrication is a task for the reverend of the church. When a prophet dies his stick remains to be given to somebody else in the church according to the spirit's instruction.

Prophesying (Illness Diagnosis)

"Prophesying", "searching" or *"kusecha"* is a divination through the Holy Spirit. This method of illness diagnosis represents a mixture of traditional spirit possession divination and Christian divine prophesy or vision. It is based on the prophet's ability to reveal the information about a patient's illness history and his social background both from a diachronic and synchronic point of view. A sick is instructed to answer in terms of "yes" or "no" to the prophet's questions. As a result, the whole process of prophesying therefore represents a sort of prophet's narrative monolog.

A prophet firstly establishes the contact between him, the Holy Spirit and the patient by touching him with *pidgika*. Furthermore he starts giving a description of a client's residential place and of his kinship relations both from the mother's and father's side. As I observed the healer generating questions is directed by the patient's previous answers. In order to identify conflicts, tensions and fights "in the patient's heart", a prophet investigates carefully his personal and family history. Sometimes the presence of witches in the family or neighbourhood, or avenging spirits (*chivanda*) is mentioned. The patient's personal biography, as revealed at the beginning of the séance, represents an important clue in the further illness investigation. The symptoms of psycho-physiological ailments are mostly expressed in the form of metaphors. These symptoms are then related to more complex descriptions of an affliction whose causes lies either in the sphere of social relationships or in the spiritual realm. The emphasis is also laid on the psychological temper of the patient and his dreams.

It is important to stress that all these interpretative levels recapitulated in the final diagnosis closely interface. The findings from the Christian prophesying séances fully corresponds to the aforesaid "integrated theory of disease" (Fabrega and Manning 1973) that interlink the different (physiological, psychical, social, religious and environmental) aspects of the illness in the whole and treat them as conjoined. The following outline represents ten overlapping spheres of a patient's problems frequently mentioned during the "prophesying" séance in the Mutumwa church.

1. Household problems

Tensions rising from household cohabitation, quarrels about money shortage and infidelity of men leading todomestic violence and witchcraft accusation.

2. Marriage problems:

The infidelity of men sexual problems of the couple, "run-away husbands", illegitimate children, disputes over dowry and money.

3. Women's problems:

Menorrhoea, gynaecological problems, infertility, difficult pregnancy, miscarriages, and the death of children.

4. Men's problems:

Impotency, sexually transmitted diseases, problems of sexuality ("low performance in bed"), promiscuity and mood swings, alcohol abuse, problems at work and unemployment, problems of paying *lobola*.

5. Love problems:

Difficulties in finding a partner, in getting married, "runaway boyfriend/girlfriend", "love sickness", rivalry in love and jealousy.

6. Problems with neighbours and workmates:

Envy and jealousy leading to witchcraft accusations; thievery and disputes over property.

7. Problems with children:

Common children's diseases, diseases related to witchcraft, looking after orphans.

8. Psychological problems:

Fear, anxiety, nightmares, insomnia, hallucinations, lack of appetite, depression ("thinking too much").

9. Economic problems:

Unemployment, destitution, difficulties in providing food for the children, to pay the rent, the costs of a funeral, to complete education or to pay for health care.

10. Physical bodily problems:

Chest pains, backache, stomach ache, headache, pain in legs, weakness, tiredness, vaginal discharge, nausea, diarrhoea, eye problems.

During the session, the prophet links the problems with relevant cultural aetiologies in order to provide an appropriate diagnosis. Whereas witchcraft is mentioned on average in two from ten cases, negative spirit possession is involved more often, in four of ten cases. As I observed, patients seem to have implicit trust in the authority of the Holy Spirit that "works through" the prophets which leads them to accept the final diagnosis they receive. According to the inquiry carried out among patients, 100% of respondents affirmed the correctness of the diagnosis.

The lack of knowledge of a patient's social background is compensated by the prophet's familiarity with the terrain. Like many *ng'angas* prophets are also very perceptive and susceptible to miscellaneous impulses emanating from their clients. In this respect, Dillon-Malone affirms that "the *nchimi* diagnosticians are keen observers of the manner on which patients react in word or in bodily gestures to their statements and they follow up on those areas which elicit a more manifest emotional response" (Dillon-Malone 1988: 1161). The prophets excel not only at their observational skills, but at the articulation of the problems. All prophets I met shared some of the common personality characteristics. They were all strong personalities endowed with charisma, the gift of empathy and their volubility. Their communicativeness, curiousness and ability to articulate were striking at first sight. I also noted that church members who accomplished aforesaid characteristics, were constantly encouraged by prophets to "work on them" to actually become one of them.

Healing (Therapy and Prophylaxis)

There are several medico-religious practices carried out in the church in order to heal or protect the coming patients from various spiritual ailments. The repertoire of the therapeutic practices predicates the syncretic character of Christian spiritual healing. The majority of these procedures (No. 5 – 9) are employed also by traditional healers. There is no doubt that prophets of the Mutumwa church are inspired by the world of indigenous medicine as they come from the same cultural background. Therapeutic practices consist of:

1. Exorcism, driving out bad spirits (*ntchito yochotsa mizimu yoyipa*)
2. Individual and collective praying (*pemphero*)
3. Healing through contact with the Bible and parts of a patient's body
4. Spiritual blessings (*dalitso kwa Mulungu*)
5. Psycho-social counselling
6. Spiritual cleansing of the body (*kusamba*)
7. Using the medicinal herbs (*mankhwala*)
8. Application of "tattoos" (*ndembo*)
9. Spiritual cleansing of the area contaminated by witchcraft (*mpepo oipa*)

Exorcism as a spiritual healing method generally refers to the expulsion of an evil spirit(s) – demon(s) out of the person possessed or tormented by them (Burgess 2006: 189). This method is a necessary part of the Mutumwa healing. The therapeutic practice of exorcism is based on the expulsion of bad spirits "from the heart" (body) of a patient by the laying on of hands on his head and praying, which is characteristic in its repetitive and zealous form, of a sort of incantation. In a few cases an open Bible is laid on the head of an afflicted person or is applied on other parts of his body. By shouting in the ear of a possessed-person and hitting him with the *pidgika*, the patient becomes fully possessed by the demons that lurk in his body. The "bad spirits" manifest in the body of an afflicted person in the form of ecstatic trance. Such a person starts trembling, falls down and screams. The prophet holds him on the floor and casts out the demon by praying loudly and shouting *"choka"* (go out) into the patient's ear. When the trance fades away, the person is asked to stand up and the healer together with the other church members prays for him. Later on the healer prescribes a variety of herbal medicine for both the body's protection and treatment of physical ailments.

Individual and collective prayers serve as a support to spiritual healing carried out by prophets in the church. It is believed that by praying the power of the Holy Spirit is activated and manifested in the bodies of holy men, the prayers have a purgatory function and prevents moral pollution. Finally by praying the person reinforces his body and mind. As one of the prophetess elucidated to me, *"the person who has no faith and does not pray regularly is very weak. Evil spirits will find him and enter his body"*, whereas an individual whose prayers are freely carried out as necessary several times per day are protected from such evil spirits. Collective prayers are strictly organised within the liturgy order during the church service. The latter are considered to be more powerful and effective in the process of healing.

The religious doctrine of the Mutumwa church is based on the appreciation of the Bible (*Buku laMulungu*) as the supreme authority. The Bible is used as a ritual object in much the same way as the holy water. Spiritual healing is impossible without laying the Bible on the head or body of a patient while praying. On the other side, the Bible is never used as a divinatory tool as it is common amongst faith healers in particular in the Zion church.

The spiritual blessings are carried out by the main priest with his hands over the head of the believers that is covered with white cloth at the signal of purity and divine protection. The blessings serves on the one hand as God's protection against the influence of bad spirits, witches and bad accidents in life, on the other hand it helps to bestow the wish on someone who will thus experience the favour of God. Liturgical blessings are performed not only over people but also over ritual objects (such as medicinal herbs, the *pidgika*, and Holy water).

The psychosocial counselling as a part of the whole process of healing is carried out by prophets in cases of emotional and domestic problems. Whereas prophesising is publicly displayed, counselling is performed privately in the strictest confidence between prophet and patient. Whilst the client feels able to discuss freely his feelings and worries, the prophets tries to clarify more clearly the problem that he has encountered, to help him to resolve it and discover the coping mechanisms. The objective of psychosocial counselling in the church is to help the patient better understand the cause of his illness, release his tension as well as give him consolation.

To cleanse the body of an afflicted person, a special sort of herbal medicine to drink and to bathe in is prescribed by the Mutumwa prophets. This procedure draws on the traditional cleansing employed by *ng'anga*s. The afflicted body gets rid of bad spirits that "hang on it", they are "washed off". This takes place outside the church, usually in the nearest "bush". The washing off of moral pollution caused by infringing traditional taboos, or church rules takes the form of heart-searching prayers, or the confession of sins in front of God and other church members. In the case of some members moral backsliding, a cleansing ritual in the same form as a baptism is done, with a difference that the "sinner" is dipped in the river just once instead of two times.

Another important part of the therapy process is the distribution and application of herbal medicine to the patients. Doses, species of herbs as well as the place of its occurrence in the bush are revealed to the prophet by the Holy Spirit in dreams or directly "seen" in the moment of prophesying. Herbal medicine in the form of root, leaf or bark is distributed for free by one of the prophets either at the end of the service in front of the church or another day in the early morning. Applications of the medicine through "tattoos" and other traditional chirurgical procedures are carried out in the pastor's house after the main service. Herbs are collected approximately once a month, whilst prophets claim to travel long distances to extract and collect them.

Ndembo, the method of razor-blade skin incision in which the herbal medicine is rubbed in is commonly used by traditional healers. The Mutumwa prophets have recourse to this method in exceptional cases when the other methods of healing fail.

As it follows from the history of the *mutumwa* movement, prophets in particular *chilansengo*[26] have always been dealing with witchcraft. The patient who is suspected of being a witch is asked to bring *chizimba* or other dangerous charms that he has in his possession to the church, where they are neutralized and burnt. In some cases the ritual of "cleansing the house" (*kuchotsa ziwanda*), has to be carried out by the Mutumwa prophets. This happens solely on the patient's request and requires police permission. The operation consists of the localization of the magical object in or outside the house by "snooping around" while being

---

[26] *Chilansengo* (etym.poison collector) is a term employed for a witch-finder possessed by the Holy Spirit.

possessed by the Holy Spirit and its detection and destruction in a fire. As the invisible magical objects are most often hidden under ground, *chilansengo* has to dig it with the help of his *pidgika* in order to localise, neutralise and destroy it. The course of the operation is similar to that one carried out by traditional witch-finders (*mchape*). The main difference lies in the spiritual source involved – whereas the *chilansengo* is possessed by the Holy Spirit, the *mchape* draws his power from ancestral or possibly biblical spirits. Traditional witch-finder works individually contrary to the *chilansengo* whose activity is indispensably linked to the complex ritual carried out by the whole church community. Loud singing of the choir and prayers carried out by the main priest plays an important role, as it stimulates the necessary spiritual ambience appropriate for spirit possession and for witch-finding activities. At the same time it helps to neutralise a place encumbered with negative energy (*mpepo oipa*). For the same purpose the *chilansengo* uses medicinal herbs called *mbosha*. In contrast to traditional witch-finders who use the herbal concoctions for deactivation and visualization of magical objects, the Mutumwa witch-findersjust touch it with the *pidgika*.

6. Spirit Possession

> *"When I go to the river, I want to call my spirit chimukele, it is going to rain, the cloud is ready, he wants to drink water, he wants it now. Bring him nkholombe (kalabash)."*
> — Excerpt from songs during ngoma healing ceremony in Lusaka

Anthropological Studies on Spirit Possession

The phenomenon of spirit possession has been of enduring interest to many anthropologists[1] who study religion in Africa. Various theories have been developed in order to explain this specific culturally biased behaviour by contextualizing it socially, culturally and politically. Many scholars have accentuated the importance and the ambiguities of gender and power involved in spirit possession. In this respect the most famous is the Lewis's comparative study *Ecstatic Religion. A Study of Shamanism and Spirit Possession* (1971) that treats spirit possession as a primary social phenomenon having its gender and political implications. Lewis builds his theory on the critique of Luc de Heusch's conception of adorcism and exorcism as two distinct aspects of spirit possession. Whereas the former is defined as the adoptive process of domestication and integration of a spirit in the body of a patient who thus becomes a medium for the spirit, the later consists in casting out the spirit as a part of the therapy. Lewis argues that both adorcism and exorcism are compatible and intermingled processes that are treated at the same level of a medical case. He argues that the uncontrolled spirit possession is always manifested in the form of an illness. To get rid of it means to cast out the spirit from the body of afflicted. If the method of exorcism shows to be

---

[1] Beattie and Middletown 1969; Behrend and Luig 2000; Boddy 1989; Comaroff 1985; Hammond-Tooke 1974; Lambeck 1993; Lewis 1971; Luc de Heusch 1962; Moore 1999; Stoller 1995; Oosthuizen 1992 and others.

insufficient, the therapy shifts into another level which is adorcism or "controlled" possession. The endeavour of healer is to meet the needs of the spirit, calm it down in the body of the patient and integrate him into a cult. A major current within the substantial literature on spirit possession studied in Muslim Africa (Lewis 1971; Boddy 1989; Lambeck 1993) focuses on women's marginality and transient ritualised performances as a source of power, as an expression of overcoming their subordination. In this spirit Lewis's conception of central and a peripheral cult of possession was elaborated. From the funcionalist point of view he interprets these cults of possession as an instrument of oppressed, frustrated and marginalised social groups which have in a strongly structured society only a limited possibility to express their wishes, needs, to draw attention and respect of others as well as achieve the appropriate social status. These peripheral or "deprivation" cults organised around mainly women-healers represent a sort of emancipation over men's dominance and the fight against social inequalities. According to Lewis, the phenomenon of spirit possession has apart from its social and political function also a psychological function as it serves as a catharsis of women's frustration.

Although Lewis was criticized for neglecting the symbolical meanings of possession, and the ambivalence of power relations and of cultural change, some of his assumptions still remain valid today. This is true in the case of the argument that spirit possession appears predominantly in the stratified society structured around the dominant culture which is represented by a given social group endowed with power and authority (for example men in Muslim society). This dominant group tends to suppress freedom and the rights of minor social groups as Janice Boddy (1989) has shown in the example of oppression of women possessed by Zar spirits in Muslim northern Sudan, or Paul Stoller's (1995) on example of the cultural resistance of Songhay people organised in the cult of Hauka against the oppression of French colonial regime in Niger. Unlike Boddy who analyses the Zar possession cults from the point of view of the inner social dynamic, the construction on personhood and maintaining the identity of women, Stoller interprets the Hauka spirit possession cult in the wider historical context of colonialism with a special emphasis on the power relationship and modes of resistance.

Mashabe Possession

Unlike the diviners and witch-finders who are predominately young men, the majority of Lusaka's spiritual healers involved in *mashabe* possession are married women. Whereas Lewis (1971) or Hammond-Tooke (1974) tends to explain the prevalence of the phenomenon of spirit possession among women in terms of the deprivation theory, Oosthuizen (1991a) assumes that this phenomenon which proliferates in particular in the urban setting is linked to the problem of women's adaptation. Studying women in the South African towns, who emigrated from their native villages and faced the difficulties of adaptation to urban living conditions he concludes that "with a rapid social change experienced in a fast-developing urbanised area, traditionally-orientated people experience great difficulties in adapting and fall back on old securities to guard them against what for them are the activities of evil forces in the new situation" (Oosthuizen 1991a: 194). This assumption however does not fit the setting of Lusaka, as the majority of women living in the compounds have immigrated many years ago, were born there, or used to live in a different town before.

Their psycho-physiological problems described in terms of depression and anxiety cannot thus result from the difficulties of adaptation at living in a town as Oosthuizen supposed. Rather, the prevalence of spirit possession among women is linked to their existential insecurity issuing from their economic and marital distress resulting from their dependence on their husbands. Their internal anxiety thus turns into a bodily experience of external danger coming from *mashabe* spirits. As my research disclosed, spirit possessions in present day Lusaka are primarily linked to reproductive problems, i.e. "women's diseases". As it is believed the ancestral spirits can similarly as a witch affect a woman's reproductive system by entering her body and binding her womb. There are *mashabe* communities in Lusaka that gather patients entirely with reproductive problems. From this it would be assumed that through spirit possession women help to overcome their most profound insecurity that might be felt– being infertile. Moreover, the infertile woman is socially stigmatised and devalued by her husband and his family, who is not reluctant to abandon her without any remorse or mercy. The entry to the community of *mashabe* healers can be interpreted as a way that Lusaka women can find psychological consolation, achieve social status in society and thus ameliorate their economic situation.

However, healing through spirit possession has not been not always the domain of women as assumed my informant Doctor Aron: "*A time ago men were also involved in mashabe healing but what turned the balance [gender distribution] was that a lot of men started resisting the commands of spirits when they got possessed and refused to dance* [to participate in the *ngoma* ceremony]". This change in gender composition of spiritual healers in Lusaka is clear even from the patient's letters addressed to a famous Christian healer Emmanuel Milingo,[2] between the years 1979 and 1980. More than half of the letters (of a total sample of 250) were written by men who explicitly state that they believe themselves to be possessed by spirits (Ter Haar, Ellis 1988).

What was the reason for this shift in gender distribution? Doctor Chembe, one of the spiritual healers from Lusaka, attributes this change that occurred within the last thirty years, to the problem of cultural reproduction. In her opinion, "*daughters are closer to their mothers than sons to their fathers and thereby it becomes easier to convince ladies to join the mashabe practices than men. Girls are not forgetting their cultural practices they are closer to the tradition*". Other informants acknowledged that it is not only a problem of gender distribution but of a general decline of *mashabe* spirit communities as modern life in towns and the proliferation

---

[2] Archbishop Milingo became the symbol of the charismatic movement within the Roman Catholic Church in Zambia. Milingo was convinced that God had given him the gift of healing people through the power of the Holy Spirit. In the 1970s he held public healing séances during which he exorcised evil spirits (*mashabe*), healed the sick by touch and gave them blessings. His controversial healing ministry, which did not conform to the Roman Catholic doctrine, became a thorn in the Vatican's side. Consequently in 1982 he was summoned to the Vatican, and in 1983 he was asked to step down from his position of Archbishop of Lusaka which he had held since 1969 (Ter Haar, Ellis 1988). After the ban imposed on Milingo's healing ministry, people continued to write to him letters as they believed that he was capable of healing the sick by correspondence in the same way as by the laying on of hands (Ter Haar, Ellis 1988).

of Christianity affected many people who therefore abandoned their belief in the healing power of *mashabe* spirits. "*People choose rather to worship Jesus then ancestral spirits. Nowadays, people even accept death due to their deep sickness caused by mashabe spirits than undergo the traditional ceremony. Such believers they are.*"

As the written sources mentioning *mashabe* spirit possession in Zambia are very scarce[3], it is difficult for me to provide a comparison of this phenomenon in time. One of the most reliable source of information about the *mashabe* groups in Lusaka in the 1980s are the previously mentioned patient's letters written to archbishop Milingo, who gained an excellent reputation as a Christian spiritual healer throughout the whole of Zambia, especially in Lusaka where he was operating. Ter Haar and Ellis's (1988) analysis of the letter, seems to provide valuable comparative data about different types of afflictions that the urban dwellers encountered in the 1980s. As follows from the letters, possession by the ancestral spirit was manifested by different afflictions among which the typical urban problems of that time such as unemployment, anxiety, depression and the difficulty of getting married prevailed. According to Ter Haar and Ellis these kinds of afflictions resulted from the increasing poverty which struck the urban population in the 1980s due to the huge economic recession in Zambia.

The depression, anxiety and frustration mentioned in the letters, interpreted by Milingo as *mashabe* spirit possession, corresponded with what James Ferguson (1999a) calls the feelings of abjection or disconnection that Zambian urban dwellers, predominantly men labourers experienced due to the disenchantment of the myth of modernity at that time. Spirit possession thus could represent adversely what Stoller (1995) showed in the example of the Hauka, a sort of postcolonial cultural resistance against the loss of economic certainty and Zambia's connection to the world economic market guaranteed by the English during the colonial era. The results of the economic crisis were especially felt by men, single urban labourers who stayed abandoned in town without work and without their families. These "losers" usually took refuge in the *mashabe* communities in Lusaka during the 1980s and 1990s. With the

---

[3] See Colson 1969; Bőchner 1980; Ter Haar, Ellis 1988; Luig 2000.

proliferation of Christianity in particular the neo-pentecostal movement of the 1990s that came with its rhetorical attack against local traditions including the belief in *mashabe*, many Lusaka men appraised a new opportunity for attaining leadership or status as dignitaries in these new establishing churches. They abandoned the *mashabe* cult communities and occupied a new position as Christian healers or prophets.

The Crises of Possession

According to the statements of my respondents, the *mashabe* spirit chooses its spiritual medium mostly in the family circle. In most of the cases they are transmitted matrilineally, from mother to daughter. The new coming spirit cannot manifest itself into other forms than those of a medium's affliction. At the beginning of the illness a set of symptomatic dreams such as flying, swimming under water, being chased or bitten by certain animals such as a lion, snake, monkey or dog usually occur. It needs to be stressed, that dreams play a much more important role in the process of diagnosis than the psychosomatic symptoms themselves which commonly consist of a persistent head-ache, tachyarrhythmia, dizziness, a loss of appetite, insomnia, infertility and weight fluctuation to name some of the most common.

An afflicted person receives various "spiritual demands" in his dreams that have the form of "rules" concerning the patient's behaviour. These must be respected if one wants to recover from his illness otherwise his health would worsen or even lead to his death. As already mentioned above, the rules that vary according to respective spirits, most often consist of prohibitions on adultery, promiscuity and the consumption of certain animals. The spirits of male and female ancestors choose the spiritual medium regardless of their sex. It may happen, that male *mashabe* spirits is jealous about a woman – healer's spouse, or even forbid her from getting married. When the marriage is respected, then extramarital sex is severely punished by the spirit with the disease – the same one as the healer had suffered at the beginning of his healer's career. In this case, the *ngoma* healing ceremony has to be organised again in order to remedy and restore the disturbed relations between a healer and his spirit.

The *ngoma* ritual organised for an afflicted person possessed by a *mashabe* spirit may be understood either at the individual level as a rite of passage (an initiation of a patient into the community of healers) or at the social level as a process of the patient's social integration into a group of spiritual healers. For analytical purposes I treat these levels separately, despite the fact that both levels are interconnected.

Ngoma as a form of initiation is performed for the patient who has been previously diagnosed by a spiritual healer as possessed, i.e. afflicted by *mashabe* according to the occurrence of a wide range of psychosomatic symptoms, culturally biased symptomatic dreams and preconditions based on family background. By undergoing the healing ritual that lasts optimally two or maximally four days a patient learns how to settle down and control the spirit in his body under the guidance of experienced healers possessed by the same type of spirit. The main aim of the ceremony is to appease and settle down a new coming spirit in the patient's body by practices of dancing, drumming and singing songs that were together with particular "spiritual demands" revealed to him in the dreams. By establishing an intimate relationship with the spirit a patient is expected to recover from his original illness and turns from a sufferer into a healer. As a result, the former afflicting spirit becomes the "healing spirit" i.e. the former "uncontrolled" possession becomes "controlled" possession through which the spiritual medium heals other members of the community afflicted by the same type of *mashabe*.

Ngoma is associated with a personal transformation, a reshaping of identity and the promotion of social status. Similarly to an initiation rite, it consists of several phases. Firstly a patient undergoes a several week long period of training before he passes through the final initiation ceremony. The whole treatment may vary in duration, from a few weeks to many years, depending on the nature of a given affliction and the particular external conditions. The effectiveness of *ngoma* therapy is not always assured, it might happen that a patient does not recover and therefore is not integrated into the *mashabe* community. For this reason it is problematic to conceive the *ngoma* as a rite of passage, in the terms as Victor Turner used. In some cases the clients could not complete the ceremony for financial reasons, or he decided to try another therapy option as the *ngoma* was simply ineffective. In one case I observed that the spirit of a patient did not cooperate with the healer's spirits, or became even more irritated because unsatisfied with its organisation.

Mashabe spirits are generally perceived as very capricious, redoubtable and the people feel awe and insecurity when dealing with them. As there is no assurance that the therapeutic enterprise will be effective, the spirits have to be approached with extreme caution. I noted that healers who organised the whole ceremony paid special attention not to violate the given conditions of the "ritual process" concerning choreography, the singing of songs, alternating drumming rhythms and the preparation of "traditional" food and beer. In a case where the *ngoma* therapy was ineffective they tended to explain it in terms of a violation of the ritual formulas i.e. the drummers did not play well, the beer was not prepared according to the traditional recipes; people went to sleep instead of staying awake, etc.

At the social level, *ngoma* therapy can be analysed, as Janzen (1992) proposed, from the point of view of social reproduction. The critical examination by his followers (Rijk van Dijk 2000; Reis 2000; Spierenburg 2000) has led to a wider delimitation of *ngoma* as a social, economic and political institution dealing with the issue of political power and reordering social relationships. In urban setting where traditional kinship networks became disturbed and fragmented, *ngoma* helps to create an alternative social solidarity network. In this respect, it helps in a similar way as prophet-healing church communities to release social tensions and to overcome everyday predicaments issuing from the common experience of social and economic marginalisation of its members.

My research disclosed that the social organisation of *mashabe* communities in Lusaka lack the corporate and hierarchical organisational structure typical for cults of affliction as reported in many parts of Bantu Africa. Rather than a cult, we can speak about an acephalous network of individual healers communicating and organising *ngoma* ceremonies through associations of traditional healers existing in Lusaka. During my fieldwork, I did not note any named *mashabe* associations or cultic office-holders as reported by Turner (1968) on Ndembu in Zambia. However, many spiritual healers were involved in diverse hierarchical social organisations such as prophet-healing churches or associations of traditional healers, where they have rank and maintain their positions. By means of the transmitting cultural heritage of traditional spiritual healing, the *ngoma* institution also helps to maintain cultural reproduction which is in contrast to other "traditional" religious events such as Kuomboka[4] not officially recognised by the Zambian government.

Holy Spirit Possession versus Demon Possession

In the prophet-healing churches the traditional ancestral and alien spirits are considered to be demons. "Demon possession" is thus seen as a manifestation of these spirits causing various afflictions. It is believed, that the invasion of demons in someone's body can strike without any reason. As a result, the spiritual afflictions are not interpreted in terms of God's punishment for inappropriate behaviour towards fellowman, or toward God. However there is a rule that those who don't have enough faith are considered to be more vulnerable than those who pray every day and regularly attend a church.

Demon possession can be categorised as "negative possession" (Bourguignon 1967), or "uncontrolled possession" (Lewis 1971). This means that a person possessed involuntarily by a spirit does not know how to master the state of trance, he is "knocked down". On the contrary, the Holy Spirit possession is conceived as a "positive" or "controlled possession" distinguished by the state of a trance evoked voluntarily by prayers and singing for the particular purpose such as healing or witchfinding. Those possessed by the Holy Spirit are publicly recognised as "Holy men" or "masters of spirits" (Lewis 1971), or "prophets".

During the main service in Mutumwa church the participants invoke the Holy Spirit by means of prayers, clapping hands and singing songs. This leads simultaneously to a trance manifestation of the power of the Holy Spirit in the bodies of prophets and of the power of evil spirits in

---

[4] Kuomboka is a traditional religious ceremony of the Lozi people in the Western province of Zambia which takes place at the end of the rain season. The festival celebrates the move of the Litunga, king of the Lozi people, from his compound at Lealui in the Barotse Floodplain of the Zambezi River to Limulunga on higher ground.

the bodies of patients.[5] However, the difference between these two spirit possessions is hardly visible at first sight. Thomas G. Kirsch who studied St. Moses God's Holy Spirit church in Zambia also noticed that, "for the participants in religious practice it is not possible to find definitively binding criteria to distinguish a medium of the Holy Spirit from the patient possessed by demons" (Kirsch 2002: 58).

According to my observations, both types of spirit possession can be distinguished by the different forms of trance manifestation. The Mutumwa prophets who experience the ecstatic Holy Spirit possession never fall down unless they do witch-finding operations. Those "touched" by the Holy Spirit start belching first, then bend forward hands joined behind their back and move quickly in all directions beating their ears and spinning. Turning around with speed thus symbolises that the Holy Spirit has entered the person.

On the contrary, trance experienced by patients possessed by *mashabe* spirits (demons) manifests itself by body shaking, from head to shoulders, by falling backwards down on the ground. Lying there the possessed person shakes and rolls in all directions, and letting loose *kumbiola* – the sound similar to hiccup combined with chattering of the teeth, sometimes even screaming. After being calmed, prophets assist the possessed patient who now sits up, by touching and massaging his hands, neck, legs and shoulders to relax tensed muscles, and praying over them.

On the basis of a closer investigation of this issue I came to a conclusion that the trance accompanying both *mashabe* and the Holy Spirit possession represents a culturally biased behaviour and sort of nonverbal bodily communication. The mediumistic qualities that represent symbolic capital are highly valued in Zambian society. Whoever who is publically possessed attempts to make himself visible in order to draw other church member's attention to his mediumistic qualities. Especially for illiterate members of society the possibility of becoming a prophet represents a way of raising their symbolic capital and thus acquiring higher social status and authority in the community. To become a prophet is

---

[5] It is believed that *mashabe* spirits got iritated by the Christian songs and prayers in the church.

equally attractive for these people as becoming a politician for the well educated, as both positions are intrinsically linked to power. As already mentioned above, the church represents the only place where many Zambians may find political self-fulfilment in the sense of gaining social prestige.

My research also disclosed the fact that the role of the patient and prophet is socially constructed (negotiated) and contextually conditioned on the basis of spirit possession. The meaning of the social label "possessed by demons" is undoubtedly negative, but at the same time it is "a promising" as it conceals the possibility of future healing career. The patient's affliction aetiologically attributed to demon possession is due to his trance behaviour being socially recognised. There is a large probability, that a sick who overcomes demons might become a prophet in the future. As there is no official procedure for the appointment of religious leaders, acquiring abilities as a spirit medium is viewed as a spiritually propelled phenomenon that has to be appreciated by other participants as it occurs (Kirsch 2002). This means that if a patient after being exorcised demonstrates loyalty to the church and a proper spiritual vigour, he has in principle good prospects to move to a higher rank of church membership. His mediumistic qualities, which were linked before to the "uncontrolled *mashabe* possession", are now cultivated in order to control the Holy Spirit's power entering his body. As it will be shown later, the social label "possessed by demons" serves also as a way of social stigmatization of the prophets whose popularity is on the decline in the church.

Possession as a Social Construction of a Healers Identity

As we argued, the prophet's charismatic identity is not shaped only by the personal experience of the spiritual calling but it is also socially constructed within the family, church community and through the institution of spirit possession. It has been repeatedly shown by many scholars (Sundkler 1961; Daneel 1987; Kirsch 2000; Tonda 2001) that charisma cannot be regarded as the only intrinsic characteristic of a person (Weber 1968) but that it is socially constructed, negotiated and maintained in the course of a ritual (a church service) by means of an interactional form of control over the performance.

As indicated above, the boundary between demon possession and Holy Spirit possession as manifested in Mutumwa church is thin and permeable. Its interpretation depends fully on its context and the community's social consensus. It is believed that the Holy Spirit who selects one as a medium might also cut this contact if one does not respect the moral code of the church. Apart from a serious infringement of the Commandments which leads directly to a prophet's degradation in his church function, other misdemeanours such as boasting, malignment, arrogance, promiscuity, alcohol consumption, over-materialism or involvement in traditional affairs, may lead to the deterioration of a prophets spiritual power.

The gradual transition from the status of a patient to the status of a spiritually endowed prophet might suddenly revert to his degradation and a return to the role of a sick again. This status transition goes hand in hand with a collective reinterpretation of the mediumistic activities of a prophet during the church service. The trance behaviour which was initially attributed to the manifestation of the Holy Spirit in a prophet's body is now degraded to the manifestation of demons blocking one on his way to God. *"He has lost his power"*, or *"demons are fighting for his heart"* was a common explanation of the church members. The fact, that the majority of prophets were in the past *mashabe* mediums, makes collective condemnation substantially easier.

To illustrate prophet's "fluctuational status" I draw on the example of prophet Dereck from the New Jesus Disciples church whose promotion and degradation in the church was inherently linked to the construction of his charismatic identity. Dereck was born in 1974 in Chipata in the Eastern province. When he was 18 years old he experienced his first spiritual calling. He started suffering from persistent headaches, dizziness and weakness accompanied by a set of strange dreams in which he was chased by lions. His parents decided to take him to different traditional healers who "beated drums" [organised *ngoma* ceremony] for him in order to settle down *nchota* – the spirit of the lion – that Dereck inherited from his mother who used to be a spiritual healer. As followed from Dereck's narration, he defied this spiritual calling as his life's dream was to become a "Holy man" and preach in a church. Since the time when the *nchota* possessed him, he had undergone several traditional cleansing rituals in order to get rid of that spirit. When doing an interview with Dereck in January 2009 he confessed: *"These two spirits could not live together. My spirit is Holy and doesn't like mashabe. Therefore there was a fight between nchota and the Holy Spirit, but now I am cleansed"*. However, as we will see further Dereck's "inner struggle" continued, as members of the Mutumwa church argued.

In 1994 he had a visionary dream about meeting Jesus on a hill which gave him power to strive for his life's dream. Dereck narrated: *"When the Spirit came for the first time into my body I felt sick, dizzy and weak. Since 1994 I have had a dream that I climbed the mountain and I cried. On the top there was a huge seat with a person sitting there shining as the brightest star. He was so bright (...) I woke up and I felt very surprised"*.

In 1996 he became a member of the Seventh Day Adventist Church in Chipata. After five years he said he *"became a real Christian"*. In 2003 he moved to Lusaka where he stayed with his uncle. He rented a house, got married and had a child. As he could not find work, living in the capital became extremely hard for him. Moreover, his wife with his only child abandoned him. Dereck recalled: *"She left me alone. 'When you get rich I will come back', she said to me. My spirit doesn't like women like this, she was quarrelling all the time, but my spirit likes calm and peace."* The situation got even worse since his relatives who lived in the next compound refused to help him when he was in need. *"They are stingy they all work on their own so we stopped communicating"*, he explained to me. It was in the background of this precarious situation that Dereck experienced another spiritual call. *"I had a terrible headache because I was thinking too much about my life. I went to the hospital where they gave me glasses so that I felt better, but just a little. In that time the spirit of Joseph* [mzimu – Biblical spirit] *came to me and he told me to do the work of God"*.

Soon after Dereck decided to join the Paradise church[6] in the Chawama compound where he stayed for the next five years and worked as

---

[6] The Paradise Spirit Church expanded at the end of the 1990s in many Lusaka compounds. Its members do not practice prophesying through the Holy Spirit, they do not use herbal medicine, or blessed water. Prophets heal spiritually through prayers and the laying on of hands on the patients. Its members dress in white clothes during their church service. As a religious symbol they use a big white cross instead of the *pidgika*.

a prophet and preacher. He told me that he had left this church and joined the New Jesus Disciple church in 2008 because he saw no advancement there. Moreover, he became unpopular there for the way he was preaching. *"There were many quarrels especially with elder pastors. You know, many people hate me because of my message, the way I preach. But what I know that I have to fight, I have to fight."*

Dereck joined the Kuku congregation during the period when I was doing my fieldwork there. I had therefore a unique opportunity to observe the development of his career and assertion of authority in the church from the beginning. His charismatic identity, as constituted by means of prophetic dreams and visions he identified with, was recognised also by other church members shortly after his arrival. Unlike other prophets, Dereck did not start as a patient there. The reason for his coming to the Mutumwa church was not linked to his health problems, but to a spiritual calling. He had a dream in which he was instructed to join this church in order to preach and heal people. Dereck's "strong spirit" [strong personality] in combination with his religious vigour immediately impressed the majority of the church leaders who therefore embraced him and made him feel welcome.

In a few months Dereck won over the authority, and Reverend Sikwefu conferred him with the power to prophesize and to heal patients. He was confided to the care of an elder, a prominent prophetess named Joane Mazumbe who had been teaching him. At the same time he regularly visited the Bible reading seminars in order to be able to preach in the church. Starting with the "comments" [preaching commentaries], he proved to be talented. The comments in his interpretation impressed everybody in the church.[7] Moreover he started to preach as well. He dedicated all his time to work in the church. As he showed an exceptional commitment to God, his promotion in the church came in a short time. His charismatic authority rose every day to that point that in a few months other church leaders started having a feeling that he was "boasting" and "attracting too much attention" during the church services.

---

[7] Dereck gave a stirring performance both in the form and the content which attracted attention to all attendees.

Dereck's quick promotion turned into his degradation – within a few weeks he was back in the role of a patient. The people in the church became negatively oriented toward him. At the same period, Dereck started attending to business, selling oil, to earn his living. Rumours about his new job and "dark past" gathered ground in the church. I was told that *"he became spiritually weak"* and as a result he cannot continue preaching and prophesying. All people in the church started spreading rumours about Dereck who stopped going there, which made the situation even worse. His business involvement and his boasting behaviour in the church were immediately attributed to the category of the hated traditional healers. *"He is weak. His mashabe came back on him, look at how he behaves when he is prophesying. He is like a monkey when he makes hy hy hy* [meaning a special sound when he got possessed. Joane started imitating Dereck's behaviour and other church members were laughing]. *He is interested more in getting money and prestige than going to the church! That's why you cannot see him here as often as before"*, said the church fellows on Dereck's account.

Dereck was also indirectly accused of having a bad temper. *"He makes too much noise"* church fellows said about him. As I could observe, Dereck became very stressed due to the strained relations in the church and as a result his headache came back again. He confided: *"I am moving up and down now, you know, these people* [church fellows] *are backbiting me, but my spirit does not like people who quarrel. He likes peace that's why I am not going there so often as before"*.

The last church services I attended I noted that Dereck took a back seat praying strongly and reaching the trance which was even stronger than before. This behaviour was however interpreted as proof of the internal fight between his spirit and the *mashabe* spirit. He was pressed to undergo prophesying in the same manner as other patients, during which he was said to become weak because of the demons manifesting in him. It was recommended to him that he get cleansed and submerge in deep prayer to gain more spiritual power.

It was not only with Dereck whose status fluctuation in the church was visible. At the beginning of my research in January 2008, I noticed another case, that of Agness one of the popular prophetesses in the church. This woman, with whom I used to meet every day, disappeared one day. When I asked other church members what happened to her I always received the same answer – *"she is ill"*. A few weeks later when they figured out that I was still insisting on visiting her in her house, I finally learnt that she had left Lusaka some weeks earlier to engage in farming. *"She did not belong to the church anymore because as she joined ng'angas. She drinks beer, smokes cigarettes and dances at night"*, her colleague told me. Drinking beer as well as smoking cigarettes is traditionally attributed to the *ngoma* healing ceremony during which the spiritual healers beat drums and dance several days and nights in order to settle down the ancestral spirits in their bodies. Moreover, smoking cigarettes and drinking alcohol are considered to be sinful acts and are strictly prohibited for church members. This rule is often emphasized during preaching. Similarly to Dereck, Agness was also accused of *"using more of her spirit of lion [mashabe] than the Holy Spirit"* and having a "bad temper". Unlike the case of Dereck I did not have an opportunity to follow her healing career from the beginning. As I learnt later, a sort of quarrel between Agness and the church leaders preceded her departure from the church. When I finally had an occasion to speak with Agness alone, she refuted the allegation of being *ng'anga* and claimed to work hard on the farm that she had inherited a few months earlier close to Lusaka. Her coming back to the church in January 2009 corresponded to the period of Dereck's eclipse.

7. Witchcraft

> *"Witchcraft is the highest science."*
> —Doctor Kasanda Sakukuwa, Lusaka

In this chapter I attempt to analyse the complex phenomenon of witchcraft as a theory, a system and praxis. My aim is to show how the local witchcraft discourse is socially and culturally constructed in specific situations and events. The first part of this chapter is focused on a general outline of the theories of witchcraft in both former and recent anthropological studies. Then I proceed to the historical, social and cultural context of witchcraft in Zambia. Special attention is paid to the symbolic representations of witchcraft in the context of actual socio-economic transformations. My interpretation of witchcraft in Lusaka requires the analysis of illustrative medical cases that will be carried out in the second part of the chapter.

Historical Context

The phenomenon of witchcraft in Africa has always aroused the curiosity of western observers depending on whether they were missionaries, travellers, colonizers or anthropologists. Belief in witches and ghosts pervading African religiosity has been traditionally attributed to the image of the Dark Continent – uncivilized Africa. Consequently witchcraft was perceived "as repugnant, baseless and even as diabolic superstitions which are deeply ingrained in the lives of 'primitive people' and will only disappear with the spread of western civilization, education and Christianity" (Niehaus 2001a: 186). This idea was reflected in the negative attitude of recurring colonial governments toward traditional healers. Endowed with authority and power, *ng'angas* enjoyed great respect in African communities at that time. For this reason they presented a serious challenge to the colonial authorities which strived to suppress them. Gradually, the traditional healers for whom the term witch-doctor became a common usage came under the same category as witches.

The proliferation of local trials with witches and the increasing power of witch-finders (*mchape*) were felt as a threat to peace in the colony by the British colonial administrators. As a result they decided to take away the chief's authority, to bring witches to court and put them on trial and assume a specific legal form imposed as the Witchcraft Ordinance in 1914[1] (Hinfelaar 2004). This law, which was also put into practice in neighbouring British colonies, prohibited any involvement in both witchcraft and traditional healing. As a result, witches, witch-finders and even diviners could be fined £50[2] and/or be imprisoned for three years. In this context Fields (1982) remarked that "in pre-colonial Africa, witchcraft was a crime. For colonial rulers, it was a superstition and the African judges and executioners of witches became murderers" (Fields 1985: 572). Prior to the legislation the British colonial regime in 1900 made an effort to prohibit the traditional witchcraft trials by outlawing the method of detecting witches known as *mwavi* or "poison ordeal"[3]. This technique commonly used throughout the whole of Africa in the pre-colonial era served to identify witches or better to test their innocence or guilt of an accused person by giving them a poisoned herbal drink, called *mwavi*[4] in Northern Rhodesia.

---

[1] The Witchcraft Ordinance of 1914 was renamed in 1967 as the Witchcraft Act. This version of the Witchcraft Act is amended. The last revision of the Witchcraft act occurred in 1995.

[2] The colonial British Pound.

[3] The "ordeal poison" called *mwavi* was widely used throughout the whole of Africa before the colonial era. This practice was documented not only in Zambia but also in Malawi, Tanzania, Congo and parts of Mozambique. *Mwavi* was commonly controlled by political leaders (chiefs, kings) in the region.

[4] *Mwavi* is obtained from Sassy bark (erythropholeum guineense). The bark of a dull red colour diversified by whitish spots, when used hypodermically, produces vomiting. In large doses it occasions a progressive stupefaction, when administered to animals, with complete muscular relaxation, paralysis of the heart's action, and death. During the progress of these effects there may also be observed a period of restlessness, succeeded by vomiting, quickened and laboured respiration, and finally convulsions. With man it is

... footnote continues on next page

However, the local population saw these restrictions as a British attempt to protect witches, a proof of their cooperation. As a protest against these restrictions, several anti-witchcraft eradication movements appeared. In spite of the ban on the *mwavi* poison ordeal the witch-finders continued their practice and replaced it with a non-poisonous concoction called *mchape*[5]. The name of this medicine gave rise to the famous witchcraft eradication movement that originated in Malawi in the 1930s from where it spread quickly to Northern Rhodesia (today Zambia) as well as to the neighbouring Southern Rhodesia (today Zimbabwe), southern Tanganyika (today Tanzania) and the Belgian Congo (today the Democratic Republic of Congo). The Mchape adherents, witch-finders and their helpers, were mostly young men, returned urban migrants dressed in western clothes claiming to be followers of a mythical leader Kamwende (Richards 1935, Marwick 1950a) that died and was resurrected to carry out the mission concerning the final eradication of the pervasive witchcraft from Africa. The witch-finders travelled from village to village at the request of the local chiefs[6] in order to detect, neutralise and destroy witchcraft through the use of special magical mirrors, and to cleanse all village dwellers by means of special non-poisonous

---

said to produce vomiting, vertigo, and muscular relaxation, gradual cessation of the heart's movements, with dyspnoea, convulsions, and death. The cause of its effects appear, according to investigators, to be owing to the fact that it contracts the blood vessels, thus occasioning increased blood pressure, resulting in the symptoms named.
(www.henriettes-herb.com/eclectic/kings/erythrophleum.html)

[5] *Mchape* is a chiNyanja word referring to a special non-poisonous medicine of red colour and soapy appearance that serve to detect witches. Local variations of this term include *mcapi, mcape, mucapi*. The same word is used for witch-finders. (in Bemba the *bamucapi*, in chiNyanja *mchape*)

[6] The so called "cleansing of villages" continues to be performed in Zambia even today. However witch-finders have to receive special permission from the local police and from the chief of a village to come and carry out their work.

medicinal herbs *mchape*[7] that would cause an alleged witch who returned to his evil practice to die (Marwick 1950a). This method was used together with the therapeutic techniques of body purification as well as for the detection and destroying of magical objects.

As Richards (1935) showed the emergence of the Mchape movement coincided with the rise of the world economic crisis that struck the entire world in the 1930s. As a result, a massive number of migrants returned to Northern Rhodesia as well as in other neighbouring countries at that time. The return of the young, independent and ambitious migrants back to their native villages brought along numerous problems. The returnees were pulled back to the traditional system of labour and social obligations which produced tension in the distribution of power in the village. This manifested in terms of generational (old versus young) and gender (young men versus old women) conflicts.

According to Marwick (1950a), this movement played an important role in the anti-colonial political struggles for three basic reasons. Firstly, witch-finders defied Europeans ban on the *mwavi* poison ordeal by giving their patients the drink *mchape*. Secondly, by using magical mirrors they made direct accusations of witchcraft, which again was bound to conflict with the requirements of the European administration whose main concern was to keep the peace in their colonies. Finally, they sold medicines and charms, a step that rendered them liable to prosecution for fraudulent dealing.

The witchcraft eradication movement is not a phenomenon of the past. We can still find them in many parts of Zambia, although today they are not collectively organised as Mark Auslander (1993) documented on the case of the Ngoni movement in Eastern Zambia in 1988–89 where young men, the witch-finders accused old men and women of blocking the womb of their women and thus causing their sterility. Nowadays, the ritual of "cleansing villages of witchcraft" is usually

---

[7] My informants defined *mchape* as "a medicine prepared by a witch-finder which is given to a patient to drink to prove if he is a witch or not. It is believed that if a person drinks it, the spirit enters his body and makes him speak and explains what he has done wrong".

carried out by individual witch-finders who are officially invited by the chief for this purpose.

Cosmological Context

When studying witchcraft in Africa it is necessary to take into consideration the broader context of African religiosity based on the experience of interrelationship between the terrestrial world and the world of invisible powers. The communication within these worlds is possible due to the omnipresent magical or vital power, which is accessible both to people and invisible powers. The idea that a person either living or deceased can directly influence by strengthening or weakening the vital power of another person or spiritual being (Tempels 1969) lies in the core of witchcraft imagination.

In terms of studying witchcraft, I find it necessary to mention the local conception of soul (*mzimu*) driven by the vital force (*moyo*). The soul as a spiritual entity consists of several components from which the double-soul or "shadow"[8] (*mthunzi*) plays the most important role in witchcraft beliefs. My informants acknowledged that the "shadow" is immortal and bound to the personality and character of a person. It is able to leave the body in the course of sleep and attack the soul of another sleeping person. During the period when the "twin-soul" leaves the body, it is considered to be particularly vulnerable and can therefore become an easy target for a witch. A witch may procure desirable shadows from their victims also by taking their footprints from the soil. It is believed that *mthunzi*, or rather its vital force might be magically manipulated, violated or "used" (*kusengela*) for diverse purposes. It holds generally that if a shadow of a man is attacked by a witch, one starts to suffer or can even die.

Witchcraft in Zambia is linked to unfortunate events that come either unexpectedly and suddenly or have a long and repetitive duration. Whereas the former concerns accidents, abrupt deaths, loss of work, money or a spouse, the later encompasses the long term or repetitive

---

[8] As my research revealed, people in Lusaka believe that a witch can enslave one's soul by capturing his shadow or footprint.

diseases such as epilepsy, sterility, madness, blindness, or a variety of symptoms such as sharp pain, circulating pain, weakness, loss of weight etc. Suspicion is usually aroused by a chaining of bad luck which does not have any rational explanation and which would be commonly interpreted in the West in terms of fate or misfortune. Lusaka dwellers attribute the notion of bad luck (*tsoka* or *mashamu*) to afflictions linked to the magical intervention of witches or due to magical contagion. The suspicion of witchcraft is often raised against those who have good luck, or get suddenly promoted in work, or gain fabulous wealth. The victimisation is in general aimed at those who are "different", extraordinary, or "stand out". A series of good luck and bad luck are conceived as interconnected situations folded in the mist of uncertainty that opens a space for a variety of explanations in which strong emotions mix with rich macabre symbolism.

The phenomenon of witchcraft refers to a broader frame of cosmological interpretation of the presence of evil in the world. There is no doubt that the personification of evil is a typical sign of African religiosity. Through accusation of a particular person the unarticulated shapeless evil is individualized, which enables it to be controlled and regulated. The process of accusation, searching for and finding the culprit, is always a matter of social consensus. The accused person rarely has any other option than to accept his status of scapegoat. As many anthropologists have already shown (Marwick 1965; Mitchell 1965; Douglas 1967; Colson 2000; Niehaus 2001a) witchcraft accusations and respective therapy can thus be interpreted as an allegoric form of catharsis of a social conflict created by tense social relations and at the same time a sort of effective group psychotherapy.

Anthropological Studies on Witchcraft

Anthropological research of the phenomenon of African witchcraft first appeared in Anglophone anthropological literature in the classical work of Evans-Pritchard *Witchcraft, oracle and magic among the Azande* (1937). Evans-Pritchard, a representative of British revised functionalism, promoted a cognitive approach to studying witchcraft belief systems. His main objective was therefore to capture the inherent logic of the "world view" of the Azande and reveal the meaning given to witchcraft by the local population.

Witchcraft, as viewed by him, is regarded as an ideational system providing explanations of unfortunate events. As he showed, the variety of possible explanations of "unjust fate" is positioned on an intellectual field that is composed of two different parallel causal planes that interweave and coexist within one socio-cultural system. It is a level of objective causality that explains *how* the unlucky event happened. However, it does not explain the reason *why* it happened – at that particular moment, particular place and to that particular person. This uncertainty opens a space for a level of interpretation based on religious or mystical causality[9] connecting the misfortune of an individual, or group, with either witchcraft, God's or ancestor's punishment for a transgression against binding social and religious norms. As Evans-Pritchard illustrated with the example of the collapse of an old granary among Azande[10],

---

[9] The notion of mystical causality was developed in the work of Lévi-Bruhl (1923).

[10] "In Zandeland sometimes an old granary collapses. There is nothing remarkable in this. Every Zande knows that termites eat the support in course of time and that even the hardest woods decay after years of service. Consequently it may happen that there are people sitting beneath the granary when it collapses and they are injured. Through years it might have collapsed but why should it fall just when certain people sought its kindly shelter? We say that the granary collapsed because its supports where eaten away by termites. (…) We also say that people were sitting under it at time because it was in the heat of the day and they thought that it would be a comfortable place to talk and work (…). To our minds the only relationship between these two independently caused facts is their coincidence in time and space. We have no explanation of *why these two chains of causation intersected in a certain time and place*. Zande philosophy can supply the missing fact. The Zande know that supports were undermined by termites and that people were sitting there in order to escape the heat of the sun. But he knows aside why these two events occurred at precisely similar moment in time and space. It was due to the action of witchcraft. Witchcraft explains the coincidence of these two happenings" (Evans-Pritchard 1938: 69–70).

witchcraft is one of the cultural aetiology thus supplies the "missing link" of coincidence between these two intersected chains of causation.

The terminology of witchcraft developed by Evans-Pritchard is based on the distinction between a *witch* (witchcraft) and *sorcerer* (sorcery). From his perspective, witchcraft is regarded basically as a psychic act. A witch harms others "by means of psychic emanation from an inherent physiological condition that is transmitted biologically" (Marwick 1965: 69). The status of a witch is based on an inherited principle given by a tangible substance (*mangu*) located in the witch's stomach. The status of a witch is thus genetically determined and their malefic practices are unconscious. A witch, according to Evans-Pritchard, neither performs rituals, nor uses magic or enchantments. In contrast, a sorcerer uses magical means such as enchantments and herbal medication. The abilities of a sorcerer are acquired during initiation through which they wilfully pass.

Evans-Pritchard's concept of witchcraft based on the principle of inherited and acquired ability was disputed by later anthropological researches that argued that this terminology cannot be universally employed as the difference between a *witch* and *sorcerer* is not present in all African communities. Moreover, the source of the ability to bewitch is not always so easy to identify. It is difficult to decide whether the magical physical properties or psychical negative powers are involved in witchcraft, as they often merge in many African societies.

The ambivalence of the roles of witch, sorcerer and *ng'anga* has been stressed by many anthropologists. In Lusaka, as in many other African societies, it is believed that a healer (in particular a witch-finder) who possesses the same magical power as a witch can manipulate it both positively and negatively. The fact that they both draw on the same occult power and use the same magical means to pursue their goals makes a healer a highly ambivalent figure. As one of my informant, witch-finder Samuel Mukanda concisely described, "*ng'anga has the same power as witches, because he manages to stop what they are doing and he uses the same medicine as they use. Ng'angas are even stronger than those witches. They can give back life to someone who had finished* [died as a result of being bewitched]. *If we manage to do this it simply means that we are chiefs of all witches.*"

The studies of the phenomenon of witchcraft continued in the second half of the twentieth century amongst members of the Manchester school[11] affiliated to the Rhodes-Livingstone Institute in Northern Rhodesia (now Zambia). The institute which was founded in 1938 represented the first local anthropological research facility to be set up in an African colony. It developed research projects of anthropological fieldwork in both urban and rural localities of British Central Africa that were carried out mostly in the 1950s and 1960s. At the base of this research, several new methodological and theoretical approaches were elaborated. Studies of the Manchester school represented a polemic within the dominant paradigm of English structural functionalism and its static vision of culture. Drawing on processual and situational perspective[12] prominent anthropologists such as Max Gluckman[13], Max Marwick, John Middleton, J. Clyde Mitchell, Victor V. Turner and Elisabeth Colson focused on themes encompassing issues of conflict and reconciliation within social structures. Furthermore the researchers highlighted the tension between individual agency and social structure in which the phenomenon of witchcraft was embedded. The emphasis was put on case studies of witchcraft in both rural communities and African complex societies undergoing a process of rapid urbanisation. Monographs of Marwick (1965), Middleton and Winter (1963), Mitchell (1956, 1965), Douglas (1963) focused primarily on the relationship of witchcraft, kinship organization and local political power. Witchcraft in its visible manifestations, i.e. in the processes of accusation, was supposed to serve as an indicator of the degree of social tension and conflicts in a given society. Witchcraft accusations were interpreted as an effective tool for the regulation of social conflicts in order to reproduce the social order. The

---

[11] The Department of Social Anthropology at the University of Manchester.

[12] By processual and situational perspective I mean in particular situational analysis (the notion of "social situation" and "trouble case") developed by Gluckman (1958) and processual analysis and the concept of social drama developed by Turner (1956).

[13] M. Gluckman (1911–1975) was a founder of the Manchester school and a director of the Rhodes-Livingstone Institute in 1941–1947. In 1949 he became the first professor of social anthropology at the University of Manchester.

attention of the scholars was primarily directed at the process of accusation within close social relationships, particularly those related to kinship organization, whereas neighbouring and working relationships were also taken into account.

Marwick's book: *Sorcery in its Social Setting. A Study of the Northern Rhodesian Chewa* (1965) was grounded on an analysis of witchcraft linked to the distinguished categories of kin, affine and neighbours amongst whom the accusations were the most frequent. Marwick argued that beliefs in witchcraft helped to exclude relations that have become redundant. This was based on the assumption that as a matrilineal family extends it becomes increasingly difficult to provide the subsistence for its members and identify leadership positions. According to Marwick, witchcraft accusations primarily have the function of discrediting rivals and thus enable segmentation of matrilineage (Marwick 1965). Furthermore, sorcery among Chewa also reflects polygyny tensions amongst co-wives who accuse each other of being involved in witchcraft. Fear of being accused of witchcraft or being attacked by a witch also plays an important role in the process of social control. As Marwick and his colleagues showed, witchcraft beliefs reinforce social norms and values and therefore preserve the traditions of a given society.

The Manchester scholars employed the concept of social mobility to explain the existence of witchcraft. From their point of view the tension arises particularly between members of a matrilineage who gained wealth by working in urban centres, and those who stayed at home and remained poor. The departure of the young male labour migrants from villages to towns not only resulted in the deepening social and economic differences between town and village, but it also brought the progressing disintegration of family structures in its wake. They noticed that the conflicts between the individual accumulation of funds and egalitarian norms of reciprocity are a breeding ground for witchcraft accusation among family members. As we will see later this assumption is valid even for contemporary forms of witchcraft in Lusaka.

Another famous representative of the Manchester school J. Clyde Mitchell (1965) contributed to the study of witchcraft[14] both in terms of methodology, by employing network analysis, and urban ethnography. Whereas witchcraft was primarily studied in rural areas, he drew his ethnographic data also from urban settings. The argument developed in his study *The Meaning of Misfortune for Urban Africans* (1965) is based on the assumption that belief in witchcraft decays in the urban setting more rapidly than the belief in the cult of ancestors (both as a source of affliction). He argues that the social relationships in towns, noted for having less intimacy and emotionality, thereby limit the catalytic function of witchcraft as it is primarily oriented on intimate kinship relationships. For this reason spirit possession as a form of cultural aetiology prevails in a town, in particular in the Salisbury townships where he did his research in the 1960s.

Even though the functionalist approach of Manchester school proved to be reductionist in many aspects it provided some of the arguments valid up today. For instance that witchcraft enhances the enforcement of moral codes in a society. This is even more apparent today in urban settings where witchcraft tends to proliferate in a vacuum that has followed the abandonment of traditional customary law. It is particularly the disrespect of moral obligations towards family members based on the system of shared reciprocity that is considered to be one of the main causes of witchcraft accusations in Lusaka today.

By emphasizing the significance of the political and economic processes, the authors however neglected the symbolic dimensions of witchcraft, as well as the context of power relations issuing out of colonial history. In this respect Isaac Niehaus (2001) criticises Marwick that "he did not explore sufficiently how claims of witchcraft are grounded in a structure of domination, may be shaped by political agendas and can perpetuate the subordination of certain categories of person" (Niehaus 2001: 84).

---

[14] Mitchell studied the phenomenon of witchcraft both in the rural and the urban settings, i.e. in Yao village and in Salisbury townships. See Mitchell 1956, 1965.

The phenomenon of witchcraft continued to be studied in the 1970's, when anthropological researches focused primarily on the inner logic of its symbolic representations (Turner 1957; Douglas 1970; Adler and Zempleni 1972).

As the neo-Marxist paradigm prevailed in this period, the authors analysed witchcraft within the broader context of political-economic development,. Scholars such as Van Binsbegen (1981) and Rowlands and Warnier (1988) put emphasis on the instrumentality of witchcraft within political economic struggles. In particular attention was paid to witchcraft eradication movements which they interpreted as a form of social resistance and protest (Ranger 1968; Willis 1968, 1970; Larson 1976).

Recent Anthropological Studies of Witchcraft

The assumptions of the initiators of the development projects in Africa that the "traditional magical superstitions" – ideas about witchcraft, the power of talismans and sorcerers – will disappear as a result of further political-economic development, and the growth of education in Africa, were soon rebutted after decolonization. The unprecedented proliferation of witchcraft, which anthropologists identified throughout Africa since the 1980s proved the contrary. The proliferation of witchcraft has been interpreted as a result of the failure of modernization efforts, as a response to the crisis of modernity and development accompanied by deepening social and economic differences between the inhabitants (in villages and towns) caused by an unequal attitude towards material resources, education and power.

Contrary to previous studies of witchcraft in the rural context, the recent anthropologists turn their attention to the "new forms of witchcraft" flourishing in the urban setting. These are interpreted in the context of socio-economic changes resulting from the penetration of international capitalism into the African societies and their consequent globalization. As a result, witchcraft is studied in connection with the accumulation of wealth[15], power, and modes of consumption, production

---

[15] Geschiere (1995) uses the term "the new witchcraft of wealth" in this respect.

and trade. At the same time they invite for abandoning moralizing concepts. The stress is placed on ambivalence of the term witchcraft, and the necessity of anchoring its discourse in everyday life where it is possible to uncover its real meaning and relevance.

The phenomenon of "modern" witchcraft is conceptualized from different points of view according to individual anthropologists. For some modernity and globalization as "non-local" provides a way to conceptualize "the local" (Comaroff and Comaroff 1993; Geschiere and Rowlands 1996; Geschiere 1997), others focus particularly on the emergence of the capitalist relations of production and new market opportunities (van Binsbergen 1981; Rowlands-Warnier 1988; Bond 1986; Ciekawy 1992; Parish 2001). The "modern forms of witchcraft" are also interpreted in relation to the political development of modern states in Africa. In particular, the process of democratization and the newly emerging independent Christian denominations are taken into account (Fisiy 1988; Ciekawy and Geschiere 1998; Niehaus 1993).

The prominent representative of the "new witchcraft paradigm" Peter Geschiere in his book *The Modernity of Witchcraft: Politics and the Occult in Postcolonial Africa* (1997) considers witchcraft as an effective political instrument, a mode of political action both at local and national level. According to Geschiere the variability of the political scene, its non-transparency, fast upswing and fall of political partakers typical for today's African states, represents a constellation which is inevitably associated with witchcraft. Inside the modern political arena, where rivalry and struggle for political posts mixed with various intrigues and machinations (very often hidden from the public) predominates, witchcraft represents a very effective means of internal political fight between the representatives of the key power positions who, despite their Western education voluntarily admit their belief in witchcraft. Notions of protective magic, powerful amulets, private marabou, regular consultations with oracles, which politicians seek and from which they want to get support in their political decisions, can be found all over sub-Saharan Africa.

On the other hand witchcraft also represents a tool of interpretation for political actions used by common citizens by means of spreading rumour, gossip and slander. The discourse of witchcraft entering the field of politics thus represents according to Geschiere "a two-edged weapon" justifying power on the one hand and powerlessness on the other. It the former case, witchcraft represents a means of grasping power within the struggle amongst the highest elites for access to power and wealth. In the latter case, witchcraft is used as a weapon of "ordinary" people against national projects and the elites of the powerful. In this sense Geschiere talks about dialectics of equality and ambition (or accumulation).

The new witchcraft paradigm embedded both in the colonial historical context and the processes of socio-political and economic transformation in contemporary Africa, does not count on "the theory of a return to traditions", i.e. the idea of revitalisation of magic-religious traditions as an effective weapon against advancing modernization. On the contrary, the adherents of this paradigm claim that the traditional concepts of witchcraft are no longer applicable in the changing socio-economic conditions. Rather than about revitalisation they speak about the process of "re-traditionalisation" of African societies that Patric Chabal (1999) defines as not simply a return to "traditions" but their adaptation to the modern society.[16]

Speaking about "tradition" and "modernity" as two opposite concepts entails the danger of falling into the ideological trap of classical modernisation theory that produced these categories as radically separated times from which the former was more advanced than the later and assumed that African's modern identification with the West is to be self-evidently distinct from African tradition (Horáková 2011). In this sense, the local discourse surrounding witchcraft integrates both "traditional" and "modern" elements and turns out to be exceptionally flexible and adjustable. It reflects not only the fascination of modernity, global processes of commodification and technologisation, but also the deprivation of ordinary African people from the economical marginalization.

Modernity's ambivalence encompassing both attraction and discontentment was critically studied by many anthropologists in Africa (Co-

---

[16] According to Chabal, it is not only the boom of witchcraft and African independent churches (especially Pentecostalism) in contemporary African cities, but also the resurgence of ethnicity and its attendant "tribal politics and violence that are involved in this process.

maroff and Comaroff 1993; Copper 2005; Ferguson 1994; Geschiere 1997; Meyer 1999 etc). These authors go beyond the optimistic model of unilinear modernization theory that proclaims the progress from tradition to modernity as symbolised by economic progress, technological achievement and the transformation of the African political system according to a Western model. They emphasize that modernity (or rather multiple modernities) should be studied following the genealogical principle as a historical phenomenon that is still developing in relation with the Other (Europe and the rest of the world). "This relational study of modernity in Africa takes into account the forms of globalisation, extraversion and appropriation by (temporary or permanent) inhabitants of the African continent and its 'others' and the creative recombination of elements of the modern package with its local or global alternatives"(Horáková 2011: 35).

The debate about the paradoxes of the processes of modernisation is interlinked to the process of globalization viewed as the specific global momentum generally associated with the development of a capitalist world market, western imperialism and modernity. From the point of view of culture, it is necessary to explore the impact of globalisation on everyday words, where the cultural local specifics mix and recombine with globalised, unified, modern cultural patterns which give rise to various forms of cultural syncretism. This process can be viewed as a part of a wider one – that of cultural hybridization. When talking about "cultural hybridity" in Africa, we should take into account on the one hand the experience of time, or better "mixed times" referring to the coexistence and interspersion of pre-modernity, modernity and post-modernity (Calderon 1988) and the process of migration where the cultural patterns of home culture and imported culture are mixed.

As Appadurai (1996) showed, the cultural aspects of globalisation are closely related to mass Media communication that impel the work of imagination that becomes a key component to the reshaping the cultural (rather than a culture as substance) through dissolving time and space. The imagination then becomes the metaphysical space in which dreams of equality, leisure, freedom, can be realized. It is in this space that society, and its individuals has imaginative agency to resist the homogenizing effects of globalization. The influence of mass Media is particularly noticeable in contemporary witchcraft discourse in African urban settings where the flow of information is greater than in villages. As a result, the ideas of witchcraft as presented on the radios, in the press and television spread more quickly and impact on a large amount of people. For instance the Zambian Media regularly informs audiences about "shocking" witchcraft cases which produces an effect that leads people to vividly discuss this topic and thus being vigilant of the danger of witchcraft. It is not only the Media, but also information technologies such as the internet or mobile phone that become an indispensable part of everyday communication and obtaining information in Africa.[17]

The ongoing process of global commodification (transformation of goods, services, people and ideas into a commodity) has been inscribed substantially in the appearance of African medicine. In Lusaka, medicinal herbs, magical charms, as well as healers' services are freely available at the Soweto market and have become commodified and commercionalised. The sale of love potions, diverse aphrodisiacs, "medicine for winning a court case", "getting back a run-away husband", or "lost money" are advertised and sold on every corner.[18] The progressing commercialisation of traditional medicine is represented by the healers' praxis of establishing a set dosage of herbal medicine for every disease, when pulverised herbs are labelled and packed in the small bottles and offered to clients as a ready product. Such medicines similarly to pharmaceuticals are able to compete on a national and global market. Similarly to "material" traditional medicine, also witchcraft has become an "invisible commodity" designated to purchase. As will be shown in the following chapter, the ideas about spiritual agents causing afflictions inherent in the local witchcraft narratives reflect primarily on the ongoing process of commodification of human life and people's anxieties over the social and economic contradictions introduced by capitalism.

---

[17] See Bruijn, Nyamnjohin 2009.
[18] Tanzania, in particular Zanzibar and the Pemba Islands, is a well-known place where the most powerful charms can be purchased.

Local Conceptualisation of Witchcraft in Lusaka

As for terminology I decided to employ the term "witch" and "witchcraft" firstly because they are commonly employed in recent anthropological studies and secondly because they correspond to the chiNyanja term *mfiti* (a witch) and *ufiti* (witchcraft) which is used by the local population for both witchcraft and a witch. Additionally, there is no difference between witchcraft and sorcery in chiNynaja language, both come under the term *ufiti*. Unlike the English usage of the term witch for women and wizard for men, the notion *mfiti* does not have any gender connotation.

Regarding the term witchcraft as a sort of affliction, the local population commonly employs the term *matenda yakubantu* "a disease caused by people" or *African disease* to indicate the afflictions attributed to witchcraft. In everyday discourse the term *kuzondewa* "to be heated", or *kusengela* "being used" often substitutes for the more general term *kulodza* "to be bewitched".

Local people conceive witchcraft as a magical attack against somebody's health and property by means of *wanga*. *Wanga* is the general term for all kinds of magic as well as harmful medicine employed by a witch. According to Dillon-Malone[19], *wanga* is "comprised of visible physical properties and invisible spirit-like ones which are not affected by the laws of matter, space and time" (Dillon-Malone 1988: 1163). From this follows that witchcraft in Lusaka may be defined in Evans-Pritchard's (1937) sense as "pure sorcery".

When defining what is witchcraft we need to specify what we understand by the term magic. Magic as a ritual act involves on the one hand the manipulation of material substances such as *mankhwala, chizimba*, magical objects *chinyanga* or *chitumwa*, and on the other hand the use of verbal spells or incantations, "all directed towards the influencing of forces conceived of as impersonals and subject to direct human control if correctly handled" (Pritchard 1937: 21). As ensued from the preceding

---

[19] Dillon-Malone is a British anthropologist, who carried out several studies about Mutumwa churches in Lusaka in the 1970s. In 2008–2009 he worked as a lecturer at the Department of Philosophy at the University of Zambia.

lines magic can be used either to the protective and curative purposes (by *ng'angas*) or to destructive purposes (by witches). However, both categories may overlap. What was used as protective magic can easily turn into destructive in its implication.

As we said, the general term for magic in chiNyanja is *wanga*. Whereas the term refers uniquely to the charms connected to witchcraft, the informants also use the anglicized term *magiki* which they interchange with the idiom "playing tricks" (*ndamupusitsa*). Whereas *wanga* is directly linked to witchcraft, the term *magiki* is conceived as a neutral term for charms and refers to both traditional healers and illusionists. When discussing what magic means to my informants I was told, that there is no real difference between an illusionist and *ng'anga* in the sense that both of them have to go through an apprenticeship to learn "*how make the visible things invisible to others*". As Doctor Bongo explained, "*magic is anything that science cannot prove, I can make a dove from a handkerchief that is magic, I can separate the body that is magic. But witchcraft is a specific magic of killing others that is what we call wanga*".

As noted, people in Lusaka believe that "magic is a proper African science" leading to advanced technologies such as the production of magical guns, trains or planes. A commonly shared opinion was that, "*these magical technical conveniences unfortunately cannot be marketable because they are invisible, otherwise Africans would become rich*". The same logic is applied when speaking about witchcraft. Witches are generally considered to be powerful because they are more "clever" than the others. According to Doctor Kasanda, "*witchcraft is the highest science*".

As the etymology of the English term witchcraft indicates, it is a *craft*, skill, art or practice carried out by a *witch*. This craft is based on the secret knowledge of *mankhwala* (herbal medicine) and *chizimba* (animal based medicine) as well as magical incantations in order to produce a desired effect. It is believed in Lusaka, that witches are not born as such and do not possess any inner essence that gives them special power. From this perspective, a witch is someone who in a quest for revenge and desire to hurt someone is driven by feelings of jealousy, envy and hate, and who intentionally procures *wanga* either by purchasing it from another witch specialist, or who is a witch specialist themselves.

From the point of view of "technique" (Augé 1982) there are two types of acquisition, and transmission of the occult power that can be distinguished in Lusaka. This corresponds to two different types of witches, firstly a "witch specialist" and secondly a "witch layman". The former acquires knowledge by a process of learning within the family in the same way as a herbalist. Witch specialists are considered to be particularly dangerous because they are able to generate the whole chain of magic through their own secret magical formula. Consequently, if they are well experienced they cannot be easily detected by a witch-finder. According to the quality of magic and the quantity of killed victims, a witch can advance in his career and gain a reputation among other witches in the same manner as a healer gains a reputation according to the quality of his medicine and quantity of cured patients.

On the other hand the witch-laymen do not need to pass through the process of apprenticeship because they buy or are given either intentionally or unknowingly relevant charms as a "finished product". However it should be stressed that its "working instructions" are especially important, if these are not followed, the charm can be easily turned against its owner. It can also happen that a purchased charm produces an effect other than intended. For instance the article *Love Charms* from Sunday Mail[20] deals with a case of a woman who bought a "love potion" from *ng'anga* to attract her husband. She was told to cut a chicken's throat and boil it together with the love potion in the form of herbal medicine in the pot while chanting her husband's name. Following these instructions, she saw the head of her husband in the boiling pot. A few minutes later she discovered that her husband had had his throat cut in the house. Subsequently she was accused of witchcraft and condemned.

The area of social chaos into which witchcraft undoubtedly falls is a source of rich macabre and sexual symbolism. Witches, who are in different cultures described in different ways, assume the characteristics of antisocial creatures. Abnormal behaviour, which is bound to the personality of a witch, represents more or less the inversion of social order, disruption of its moral norms of a particular society.

Witches and their activity are connected solely with darkness – night. It is believed that they are gifted with physical metamorphosis and the ability to become invisible. According to my informants, witches

---

[20] Sunday Mail. November 5, 2008: Love charms, p. 2.

may be even luminescent[21], however this can only be seen by a witch-finder or by another witch. Furthermore witches are also believed to dance naked on the roof of the house or on graves. When exposed by a witch-finder who has paralyzed them and made them visible by means of a special medicine, witches are "caught in the yard naked".

The ability of bi-location, commonly ascribed to witches, gives them the opportunity to penetrate unnoticed into a house and take possession of a person's double-soul in their sleep. It is believed that witches use the "magical aeroplanes" and "magical trains" to travel large distances.

There exists a wide spread idea both of an "astral exploitation" and anthropophagi in witchcraft imaginary in Lusaka. This means that a double soul (shadow) of a victim when attacked by a witch in the dream is caught, tamed and set working for them on an invisible plantation where the victim's body is consumed. A witch is also believed to eat parts of the body of its victim such as heart, tongue, sexual organs and drink blood. According to my informants witches gather on graveyards where they consume exhumed human bodies.

Another common negative stereotype is linked to the sexual behaviour of witches. They are described as sexually perverted and promiscuous. The opinion that witches gain power through incest practices and as a result a desire for human flesh is aroused was documented by Mitchell in *Yao* village in Malawi (Mitchell 1956). Lévi-Strauss in his study *Totemism* (1963) pointed out the connection between the idea of cannibalism and incest as a symbolic expression of sexual intercourse and consumption of food. In Lusaka, the image of a witch is usually linked to the adultery and sexual insatiability as we will demonstrate later on in the example of the *ilomba,* the magical snake.

Another idea involved in witchcraft imaginary concerns the social organization of witches. It is believed that witch specialists do not act on their own but operate in a coven. According to my informants, witches in a coven are hierarchically organized according to their occult power and credit. Witches are led by the most experienced and powerful witch who is called the "boss". The viability and productivity of the coven

---

[21] Even Evans-Pritchard mentions that Azande's witches are believed to be luminescent.

depends directly on his management. If the "boss" is killed by a witch-finder, the whole coven loses power because its members do not have anybody to coordinate their activities. *"They have meetings under a tree where they put their heads together in order to hatch a plot"*, said one of my informant's. Their cooperation is based on the regular supply of new victims. A hunt for new victims becomes soon a vicious circle in which a witch, who refuses to cooperate, automatically becomes the victim of their companions. Witches in covens are believed to share their victims in a sense of food supply and labour force and help each other with procuring new victims.

Witchcraft Techniques

As indicated above, a witch-finder when diagnosing a patient's illness focuses primarily on the identification of the "instrumental cause", in other words he tries to identify which magical technique was used by an alleged witch. As he is well acquainted with the symbolic repertoire of this domain, he draws on his knowledge to manipulate a client in order to convince him about the veracity of a diagnosis.

Among the most common instruments used by a witch that figure in the local witchcraft narratives belongs both material and immaterial entities that can be employed simultaneously. It is believed that a witch combines them gradually as his needs dictate. The instruments mentioned bellow are "invisible" and can become visible only after being neutralised by a witch-finder.

Instruments used by a witch are:

- *Chinyanga* – magical object
- *Chilubi* – voodoo doll representing a victim
- Dangerous *chizimba* (*wanga*)
- Witch familiars such as *ilomba* and *tuyobera*
- Magical guns and vehicles
- *Chivanda* – ghost

Witchcraft in Lusaka is essentially based on the use of "visible physical properties" (Dillon-Malone 1988) among which the *chizimba* figures predominantly. Knowledge of *chizimba* is an essential prerequisite for the manufacture of magical objects widely known under the general term *chinyanga*. A witch can either use *chinynaga* from a distance by "throwing" it or "sending" it via one of their associates. To make *chinyanga* move, a witch uses a special incantation in which the name of the victim figure or employs a magical object directly by planting it in a certain place, such as on a crossroads, under a tree or in a field. Usually the *chinyanga* is placed – hidden or buried – directly in the victim's house or workplace, in front of the door, under the bed, under the carpet, on the roof or in victim's clothes.

Paradoxically the *chingyanga* has to be concealed even though it is invisible. However, as my informants explained to me, it has to be hidden so that it cannot be easily found by a witch-finder. *"If somebody steps on this medicine, his legs start swelling until he dies as the heart is affected in the end"*, explained Doctor Kunda Kaleni. However, in most of the cases the *chinyanga* affects the victim directly without the necessity of touching it.

Apart from magical objects a witch also employs "spirit-like invisible properties" (Dillon-Malone 1988) to trouble their victims. For this purpose ghosts such as *chivanda* or *chipuku* of the dead bewitched people or of people who were not buried properly are exploited. Whereas *wanga* enters directly into one's body, *chivanda* is considered to "hang on someone" (*chivanda chamukwerera*). As a result, the victim is constantly troubled (*ali naziwanda*) or "hunted" by this malevolent ghost which causes him diverse psycho-physical problems. It is believed that a witch can even gain control over the spirit of the living person and use it for several purposes such as "carrying dead people", "working on invisible plantations or in a mill house". Being afflicted by *chivanda* is manifested by chronic weariness accompanied by the "loss of blood", experienced by an obsessive feeling of "being squeezed" or by losing weight. The patients hunted by *chivanda* also complain about having a heavy body as if they were "carrying dead people on their head all night long" and about having a variety of nightmares concerning snakes and dead people. Additionally, auditory hallucinations, such as someone walking on the roof of the house in the night, calling, or pulling one, are considered to be significant signs of this type of witchcraft attack. As I observed in individual medical cases, the employment both of *vivanda* and magical objects occurs concurrently within the same witchcraft attack. In this respect, a witch can simultaneously combine all the available techniques, for instance to manipulate *chivanda* in such a way that it brings *chinyanga* to someone in their sleep.

Witchcraft Aimed at Children

The victims of witchcraft, either dead or alive, are "used" by a witch for various purposes. They are valued mostly for their blood from which the *chizimba* as a fuel for "magical airplanes" is made. Informants also claimed that witches drank the blood of their victims in order to be more powerful. It is generally believed that witches will preferably attack the weak and unprotected group of people such as children, pregnant women, or old people. These are considered to be particularly vulnerable to a witch attack and must be properly protected.

As we will further see on example of medical cases, children are often designated as victims of witchcraft in Lusaka as they are considered to be very sensitive to witchcraft. *"They can easily recognize when a witch enters the house"*, explains one of my informants. Their high sensibility to detect "bad wind" (*mpepo oipa*) – an energy around the place regularly visited by witches, is linked to their inability to talk. The children as preferable victims of witchcraft are highly valued for their blood, because it is *"fresh, speed and vibrant and can easily speed up the witchcraft business. The process of a growing child is linked to the business of growing, that's why they* [witches] *prefer to do charms on children"*, explained Doctor Kasanda elucidating the problem. There are several different types of witchcraft aimed at children that can be recognised in Lusaka. The first type is a witchcraft attack by means of *tuyobera*, a witch familiar that helps an alleged witch to gain the blood of a child and enslave his shadow for business purposes.

The second type is *chibere* designating both the name of the illness that is caused by magic and a special medicinal herb that many Zambian mothers tie on their *chitenje*[22] to protect their children from witchcraft. *Chibere* as an originally protective charm can however become very offensive and kill every other child who the woman breastfeeds. As one of

---

[22] *Chitenje* is a traditional piece of cloth worn by Zambian women.

my informants explained, "*chibere kills babies when breastfeeding, it is a very common form of witchcraft amongst women (…) a baby after it stops suckling, starts instantly vomiting black things. It gets severe diarrhoea and it can even die*".

The last type of witchcraft illness which is said to be practiced on children is *tudoyo* which designates "*small magical creatures like magic worms*" sent by a witch in order to enter the child's body through his anus. It is believed, that *tudojo* feed on his intestines until the child dies.

Witchcraft Aimed at Women and Spouses

In Lusaka, there is a whole range of witchcraft aimed at destroying marital relationships. This type of *wanga*, employed mostly between jealous women or spouses, is primarily intended for getting rid of rivals in love. *Kavundula* is the most widespread charm easily available from every healer. It is primarily used by female rivals in love in order to attract a married man. The main objective of *kavundula* is to break up a marriage.[23] *Kavundula* is a sort of *chizimba* that can be applied either directly – by placing it in the victim's house, or at a distance – by means of sending it through a "bad smell". It is believed that if one of the spouses unknowingly touches the *kavundula* placed on the door of a house, the effect in the form of quarrelling or fighting is produced immediately. Another possible effect of *kavundula* is an immediate break-up of a married couple. "*When a women is sweeping dirt she is sweeping herself from the house and when she goes to the rubbish tip she throws away herself, so when her husband comes back home she says I am leaving you*", explained Doctor Mukanda. *Kavundula* burnt in a fire can be also sent from a distance by means of *mnunkho* – "a bad smell". An effect of this charm as described by Mukanda is that, "*a woman who is just cooking, smells the food, in that moment she becomes contaminated with that bad smell sent by a witch. Her body starts smelling like fish, faeces or septic tank*". Such afflicted women

---

[23] I was told, that *kavundula* can by implication affect any important mutual relationship such as that of an employer and employee. However, *kavundula* is most often employed between love rivals.

become repelling to their husbands. As a result, the witch, love rival, can easily attract him.

To my surprise, *kavundula* is not considered to be proper witchcraft by the majority of Lusaka people, simply because it does not kill. However, *kavundula* is surely one of the most sought after medicines among Lusaka's women. As one of my informants confirmed, *"this magic is very popular today, because there are many girls who want the husband of some other woman. That's why so many people are divorcing nowadays"*.

Another medicine aimed at love rivals is known under the name *of lukanko*. *Lukanko* is a charm used by men or women to protect their spouse from extramarital sex. Although it is a sort of protective medicine, *lukanko* is categorized as witchcraft by the majority of witch-finders in Lusaka. In most of the cases *lukanko* is applied on a husband's penis in order to "inject" it into his wife. If the wife has extramarital sex various problems may occur. The effects of *lukanko* are described in terms of the disappearance of the lover's sexual organs, or in the form of a fever *"coming from down and up his penis"*. Another possible way how a jealous husband can use *lukanko* is to apply it on a jack knife and "close it". Consequently, it is believed that the lover who has sexual intercourse with his wife is "stuck" in her vagina. The lovers cannot detach unless a witch-finder neutralizes the charm by opening the jack knife which in the meantime has become invisible to its owner (the husband).

Lukanko employed by women in order to "keep their husband at home" and prevent them from extramarital sex is effectuated by means of obstructing a man's potency. Most often, the charm has the form of *chinyanga*, a magical object made of a piece of *chitenje*, *lukanko* medicine and metal needles. All the ingredients are tied into a bundle and hidden in the house to the effect that a husband who would like to have extramarital sex simply cannot have an erection outside the house. His fidelity is thus secured.

Muito – love potion is employed by the majority of women living in Lusaka. It works on the same principle as *kavundula* but it is not offensive. When cooking *nshima*, traditional Zambian food a woman adds *muito* into the porridge in order to "call him back home" where ever he is at that moment. As previously stated, the increase in the use of "love potions" and *kavundula* charms by urban women reflects their marital and financial insecurity.

The last type of witchcraft employed amongst women in particular between a mother-in-law and her daughter-in-law is *mukunko*. This term refers to a disease occurring over prolonged periods. *"Mukunko is when you are bleeding* [menstruating] *maybe for one month, it never stops. Such a woman cannot have sex with her husband and she even smells like fish. Also, she cannot have children so her husband often chases her out of the house"*, explained Doctor Mukanda. As this charm is linked to women's menstruation and reproduction, it can never be employed by a man. *Mukunko* can be induced by means of a special *chizimba* made from the ash of the burnt shell and heart of a white snail (*kolokofo*), the footprint (*chidyakili*) of a victim and menstrual pads that she used. All these ingredients are mixed in the *chizimba*, tied with beads and sent by river. To produce the effect, an incantation and the mentioning of the name of the victim is crucial. As I was told the effect is immediate. *"When chizimba starts to flow on the water, the woman* [the victim] *starts bleeding"*, said Doctor Mukanda. In order to neutralize the charm, an afflicted woman has to visit a witch-finder who after carrying out a diagnosis employs the method of counter-magic by use of a similar medicine as the witch used. He applies the ash from the burnt snail shell directly inside the vagina of a patient.

Symbolism of Witch Helpmates

The following discussion will focus on the symbolism of three witch familiars, the magical snake *ilomba*, the magical orc *tuyobera* and enslaved dead people the *zombie*. My aim is to elucidate the meaning of these multivocal symbols emerging in the local witchcraft discourse in relation to the current socio-economical processes, in particular the economic exploitation and commodification of human beings, the individual accumulation of wealth, and socio-economic inequalities.

In Zambia, witches are believed to employ various familiars, in particular nocturnal animals such as snakes, hyenas, owls, bats or turtles, or monsters such as *tuyobera* and *ilomba*. These witch familiars become dominant symbols of witchcraft narratives in the period after 1960. They are mentioned in diverse monographs from Zambia (Turner 1968, 1957; Dillon-Malone 1988; Colson 2000). The same familiars were documented also in towns in the South Africa (Niehaus 2001), where they are known under the names *malambo* (magical snake) and *tokoloshi* (magical orc).

It is believed that these familiars are trapped, tamed and fed by a witch. Some of them are trained to carry out the witch's evil wishes such as stealing crops, money, or killing human victims. Some of the familiars possess human attributes such as the capability to communicate which is a necessary precondition for understanding the witch's instructions. According to my informants, the familiars are capable to ingest as well as reproduce themselves. "*Whereas a man eats nshima* [maize porridge] *and drinks water, they* [witch familiars] *feed on human flesh and drink blood*". *Ilomba* and *tuyobera* do not merely succumb to desires as an ordinary man, but rather represent a symbol of insatiability. According to Isaac Niehaus (2001), witch's familiars are "totally dominated by their cravings for food, sex, money and revenge" (Niehaus 2001: 49).

Ilomba and *tuyobera* are highly ambivalent creatures. They share both of the characteristics of an animal and human world they belong to the category of weird monsters. As Turner (1970) showed with the example of the Ndembu, monsters feature as multivocal symbols in male initiation rituals. "The exaggeration of a single feature is not irrational but thought-provoking (...) the grotesqueness and monstrosity of liminal sacra may be seen to be aimed not so much at terrorizing or bemusing neophytes into submission or out of their wits as to making them vividly and rapidly aware of what may be called the 'factors' of their culture" (Turner 1970: 106). As an example he uses a man-lion monster. This symbol encourages a novice to think about their empirical and metaphorical attributions such as force, courage and stature.

Ilomba – *The Symbol of Excessive Sexual Desire*

Ilomba represents a big invisible water snake-like creature which has the face of its owner – a witch[24] with whom it is essentially interconnected. It is believed that if the *ilomba* is killed by a witch-finder the witch dies too. The mystical interdependence of their lives is set by the fact that they share the same blood through the *ndembo* (tattoos) made on the body of

---

[24] Turner mentions *ilomba, tuyebela* and gigantic horned fresh-water crab *(nkala)* among the Ndembu of Zambia (Turner 1970: 95–98, 148–50); (Turner 1968:15, 41, 134, 138, 203–204).

the *ilomba*. Once created and summoned, the *ilomba* begins to grow and ask for human blood and meat. If an owner does not supply it with victims then he might become a victim himself, to be eaten by thesnake. According to Turner, "the human-faced snake-familiar which is believed gradually to swallow its victim, beginning with the legs, and proceeding upwards" (Turner 1970: 41). Marwick (1965) however showed that the *ilomba* likes mainly to eat eggs and its presence is attributed to the mysterious disappearance of eggs in the village. My research showed that the symbolism of the *ilomba* in Lusaka is intrinsically linked to the sexual harassment of women and the ideas of anthropophagi. According to the local narratives, witches are believed to set off at night as an invisible *ilomba* in order to rape married women. They possess an exceptional sexual prowess and a special medicine to lull their sexual victim and her husband into a deep sleep. Some informants claimed that the *ilomba* can transfigure into a woman's husband so that at night she may think she is having sexual intercourse with him while it is the witch's familiar. I did not encounter any mention of female *ilomba* who raped men. It is always described as male.

In the example of the two following medical cases, the symbolism of the *ilomba* will be further analysed and interpreted.

Witchcraf case 2: GRACE

Grace is a 24 year old married woman who lives with her only son, husband and his parents in a small house in the suburb of Kitwe. She got married six years ago, but only has one child. She does not have any regular work; she takes care of her child and the household. Her health problems started two years ago, when she miscarried for the first time. *"Soon after I felt a pitching inside my head and in my chest. I had sharp stomach pains, I felt it here and there… it was always changing, moving throughout the whole body"*, she recalled. During that two years Grace experienced two miscarriages and suffered from irregular menstruation. Within this time, she was also troubled by repetitive nightmares, in which the magical snake comes at night to rape her. *"I thought that I had sexual intercourse with my husband, but we did not do that that night. When I woke up I saw sperm on my body. My body was bleeding and I had tattoos all over my legs"*, depicted one of her frightening nightmares. *"The problems came soon after our first son was born. With my husband, we have been quarrelling all the time, once because of money, the next time because of his parents. My mother in law did not like me from the first moment she saw me. She was also against our marriage from the beginning. She reproached my husband that he married me and pressed him to leave me. My mother in-law wished to have a daughter-in-law Kalunda, but I am Luvale. She hates me for that. We quarrel often, last time she threw out my clothes from the house and ask her son to chase me away".*

As a first option, Grace tried Christian spiritual healing within the Pentecostal church in Kitwe that she had attended for more than one year. She underwent a prophesying there and was told that the *ndembo* (incisions) that she has got all over her body come from her mother-in-law who bewitched her. As therapy she received a series of prayers, underwent cleansing procedures by means of bathing in and drinking the Holy water. However, the final effect was not satisfactory and her problems still persist.

Soon after this event, I met Grace in Doctor Lukesha's clinics located in Lusaka downtown. At that time, Grace was very ill and forlorn. Her husband chased her from the house in Kitwe saying that he hated her. Grace had no place to go; she could not stay at her mother's house as she had a bad relationship with her step-father. She thus decided to move to Lusaka, to undergo a traditional treatment in Doctor Lukesha clinics and find a job there. She does not have any relatives in Lusaka, for this reason she was accommodated at the clinic for free.

When I met Grace at the clinic, she was fully convinced that she was bewitched by her mother-in-law and her father-in-law who both hate her for *"not being the right wife for their son"*. Grace further supposed that her mother-in-law was a dangerous witch who killed also her older sister who died recently under mysterious circumstances. At the clinics Grace had undergone the divination through mirrors that confirmed her suspicion about witchcraft from the side of her mother-in-law. Doctor Lukesha specified that Grace was bewitched when sleeping. *"Mother in law visited her in the form of a witch in the night. She made ndembo on her skin and rubbed the charmed medicine, so that the different parasite objects started circulating in her body and caused sharp migrating pain in the whole of her body. As a result, Grace suffered from viposo, and feels a persisting circulating pain in the whole of her body"*, explained Lukesha. Divination further disclosed that her mother in-law used another witchcraft charm called *mukunko*. She "put" this illness of prolonged periods on Grace in order to prevent her from having another child. The magical mirrors of Doctor Lukesha revealed that Grace's father-in-law was also involved in the whole case. According to the healer, he came regularly to Grace's bedroom and had sexual intercourse with her in the form of the *ilomba* magical snake. As a result, Grace had miscarried and could not conceive another child with her husband. He in turn thus hates her for this indisposition.

The therapy of Doctor Lukesha consisted in the prescription of medicinal herbs to bath and drink in order to protect Grace against another witchcraft attack. He also made *ndembo* incisions on her chest and legs, where protective medicine was rubbed. In order to get rid of *viposo*, Grace underwent surgery by means of *mulumiko* cupping horn that sucked out the blood with the parasitic objects in the form of wire braided small stones that as believed were circulating in her body. To heal Grace from the *mukunko* Doctor Lukesha employed the method of contra-magic. By means of burning a white snail shell and uttering an incantation he sent from a distance the same type of illness on the causer (the witch).

After three months of successive medication at Doctor's Lukesha clinics, Grace stopped dreaming about the *ilomba* and having no more incisions on her body when she woke up. She also claimed to get rid of the circulating sharp pain in her body and started having regular menstruation.

As follows from the medical cases no. 2 and no. 7 (no. 7 see in apendix Wicthcraft Cases), the *ilomba* as a symbol of uninhibited sexuality is principally regarded as the cause of female sterility. Both female patients, who complained of being repeatedly raped by the *ilomba* when sleeping, claimed to suffer from various reproductive disorders such as sterility, miscarriages, or emmeniopathy[25]. It is generally believed that a witch can afflict the reproductive system directly by "tying a woman's womb" in order to prevent conception, or by contamination through the

---

[25] Due to the involvement of the *ilomba* reproductive problems occur primarily among married women, whereas single women complain about having backache.

sperm of a male witch, or by stealing a baby from the womb to cause a miscarriage.

Doctor Lukesha's patient Irene describes her dream about the *ilomba* in the following words: "*After having three babies now I only miscarry. I started to have a weird experience when I was pregnant that some person comes into my house, starts following me and having copulation with me. When I look into his face I can see only a monster, it's like half a man and the second part of his body looks like a bird, or something. Then, when I woke up I realised that I had miscarried*".

Grace suffering from irregular menstruation that prevents her from conceiving a child she describes her experience with the *ilomba* in these words: "*I thought that I had sexual intercourse with my husband, but we did not do that that night. When I woke up I saw sperm on my body. My body was bleeding and I had tattoos all over my legs*".

Niehaus (2001), and Hammond-Tooke (1974), who draw on ethnographic data from South Africa, attribute similar characteristics to *tokoloshi* described as a hairy creature similar to a baboon with horrible teeth and an enormous penis. Hammond-Tooke (1974) interprets the sexual symbolism of the *tokoloshi* in the terms of the deprivation of Ngoni women. This explanation recalls Lewis, who in his study *Ecstatic religion* (1971) elucidated the occurrence of "*Bori* spirit possession" among Hausa women as a result of their deprivation due to their exclusion from the public and religious sphere where only men, Muslims, – have access. In a similar way Hammond-Tooke proposed that the belief in *tokoloshi* is linked to the fact that "the men view the crux of women's deprivation as sexual because it is here that manhood finds its most convenient expression" (Hammond-Tooke 1974: 212). As a result, Ngoni women are imagined to succumb to daemon lovers to fulfil their sexual needs and to wreak vengeance on men. This provides ex post facto rationalization for discrimination (Niehaus 2001: 52–53).

His colleague Niehaus (2001) comes with another interpretation of the *tokoloshi* symbolism which seems to be less controversial. In his opinion it was the system of labour migration which had a profound effect on conceptualisation of marital infidelity and thus produced the belief in the *tokoloshi*. Niehaus argues that young migrants were obliged to leave their wives in their home village, and as a consequence engage in long-term extramarital affairs with their lovers. This made the migrants project their guilt feelings on their spouses, and jealous anger to the elders or unemployed men who stayed in the village. As a result, this tension culminated in accusing the remaining male members in the village of witchcraft.

However, neither of these explanations fit with the situation of contemporary Lusaka as it is rather different from that of South Africa. Since the 1980's up to 85% of immigration has been between urban centres. Married men who moved to another town to search for a job migrate with the whole of their family. As a result they have no reason to suspect other men of seducing their wives. My interpretation of the frequent occurrence of *ilomba* symbolism in the local witchcraft narratives draws on the fact that reproductive problems (sterility) are prevalent amongst Lusaka women and are considered to be a serious threat for their marriage. The infertile woman is not only socially stigmatised but also devalued by her husband (and his family) who is not reluctant to abandon her without any remorse or mercy. As the marriage represents the only financial and existential security she has, the projection of her problems onto the accusation of affined male relative may provide her a sort of psychological relief.

Another possible interpretation does not draw exclusively on the two cases presented above but on the general belief in the *ilomba* that appears in every second witchcraft narrative. I suggest that this belief reflects the danger of sexual relations between men and women in the context of HIV/AIDS pandemic. In my opinion, *ilomba* symbolism might reflect the fear of women becoming HIV positive. As mentioned above, men in Lusaka have demonstrated more tendencies at promiscuity than women. This supposition is based on the fact that, on the one hand men in Lusaka have a tendency towards risky behaviour connected to excessive alcohol consumption and on the other they tend to maintain the cultural ideal and memory of polygyny despite their inability to financially support more than one spouse. This in turn leads man to the free-from-guilt attitude toward their wives. The promiscuity of men is often discussed and condemned by women in the Lusaka compounds. The changing of sexual partners is generally considered to be highly risky as the prevalence of HIV/AIDS in Lusaka is very high (estimates for Lusaka in 2008 reached almost 20%). Zambian men who are promiscuous represent in the eyes of their women the potential disseminator of this deadly disease. As a result, the *ilomba*, the magical snake, as an archetypal symbol of male sexuality thus might be inherently linked to the negative connotation of man's promiscuity linked with a danger of HIV/AIDS contagion. Moreover it is scientifically proven that the HIV disease appears to increase the risk of having menstrual disorders. These can include the cessation of bleeding for greater than three months (amenorrhea), excessive and irregular bleeding or an early menopause.

Tuyobera – The Symbol of Excessive Materialist Desire

Another symbol appearing in witchcraft narratives that I would like to analyse is *tuyobera*. This witch familiar seems to have been incorporated into the local belief system via South African migrant labourers where a similar belief in *tokoloshi* has been documented for a long time. Whereas the *tokoloshi* in South Africa are mostly connected to sexual symbolism, in Lusaka *tuyoberas* although similar in appearance have different attributes. The majority of my informants described it as an invisible small hairy being which looks like an innocent and peaceful child, whereas this image is regarded as a deception, because "in reality", *tuyoberas* are very wicked and violent. "*It is a funny little being with backward-facing feet, a big abdomen, several eyes and blond hair* [hair of white man]", depicted *tuyobera* one of my informants. It is believed that *tuyobera* uses a poisonous weed to chase away both its victims and enemies, in particular witch-finders. As I was told, these "little villains" do evil deeds on behalf of a particular owner (usually a witch) who had to either create them or purchase them in order to gain wealth.

As indicated above, the *tuyobera* attack mostly children and adolescents because of their need for fresh blood which is convenient for the growth of business. A witch can send this familiar to steal crops or money from people, or simply to cause financial difficulties for their victims. In return the *tuyobera* asks its owner for human blood and meat which is their staple food. Similarly to *ilomba*, this dwarf is considered to be greedy, possessive and insatiable. "*Tuyobera ask the owner to bring him more and more victims, otherwise it will destroy him. In order to get food* [enough victims] *the witch can even proceed to kill all the family, cause a big bus or train accident*", explained Doctor Mukanda.

Although *tuyoberas* are supposed to bring good luck to its owner in financial and business matters, there is a high risk that it becomes dangerous and uncontrollable to him. As they reproduce themselves very quickly, they can rapidly and easily dominate, enslave and destroy its owner. According to Doctor Mukanda, "*tuyobera can finish* [kill] *almost all your family. They will eat you if you produce no more victims*". In exchange for money a *tuyobera* asks for the blood of children. It is believed that if a witch (owner) fails to meet this demand the *tuyobera* will kill all their close relatives.

A witch driven by an insatiable desire to gain enormous wealth can manufacture their own *tuyobera* in the form of a *chilubi* (voodoo doll) made from the root of a tree to which the hair of a white man (*tsisi ya muzungu*) is added. By using special magical incantations and a "shadow" of its victim, the *chilubi* is given life and becomes a *tuyobera* which is however invisible to others. The witch-finders I interviewed claimed that whereas the fabrication of *tuyobera* is simple, its destruction is a very difficult task.

At the most general level of interpretation we can assume that the *tuyobera* is associated with the danger of the accumulation of wealth. The image of the *tuyobera* reflects the moral judgement on greediness and egoism of those who amass excessive wealth and hence do not respect the widely shared norm of egalitarian reciprocity. According to Niehaus, "*tuyobera* portrays the selfish lust for wealth as evil leading to death" (Niehaus 2001: 62). Its ambivalence embedded in its pleasing and peaceful appearance contrasting to its personal qualities, refers explicitly to the symbol of a white man (*tuyobera* looks like European). *Muzungu* – a white man – is generally considered to be both a symbol of wealth and power as well as a symbol of selfishness and greediness due to his obsession with money.

As can be concluded from the fieldwork, the imagery of the *tuyobera* plays an important part in the home education of children as well as in the psychology of motherhood. This small magic villain strikingly resembles the Czech folk witch fairies Polednice or Klekanice, with whom mothers use to frighten their children to come back home after sun-set (Klekanice) or not to bother them in the day (Polednice). In the same way Zambian mothers use the *tuyobera*. The children are told not to play too loudly and move too far away from the house otherwise the *tuyobera* comes and steals them away.

From the semantic point of view, *tuyobera* similarly to Polednice represents an ambivalent symbol of both loving mother fearing for the security of her child and the hated mother able to kill her child. The psychological projection of the former is particularly relevant when a mother expresses worries about her children who could become victims of the omnipresent human traffickers. In the same way as a witch uses *tuyobera* to gain the "blood of children" to speed up their business, the traffickers – most often kinsmen – exploit children by means of forced labour abroad in order to become wealthy.

This hypothesis draws on a well-known fact that Zambia is a transit point for the regional trafficking of women and children for the purposes of forced labour and sexual exploitation. We know that human traffic primarily occurs where migration flows are largest, and access to social networks relatively easy. Moreover, there is evidence that many women or children who are trafficked in Lusaka are recruited through personal relationships where, in particular, male relatives are intermediaries.

Human traffic is not a new problem in Zambia, but the government has only recently been willing to tackle the issue head on. The International organization of immigration (IOM) describes Zambia as a major battleground in the fight to disrupt the illegal movement of people, usually from countries like Mozambique and the Democratic Republic of Congo, who are abducted to South Africa and beyond.

The opposite of the image of anxious loving mother contained in the symbol of *tuyobera* is that of a hated stepmother driven by selfish needs. As we will see in the following medical case, the symbol of the *tuyobera* as a greedy monster devouring family members may also refer to the mother-witch who magically exploits her children in order to get rich. The symbol of *tuyobera* thus directly refers to the sphere of morality, i.e. points at the danger of the most socially condemned mode of behaviour, that of filicide.

Witchcraft case 3: DAVID AND HIS MOTHER

David is a 26 year old patient of the traditional healer Lukesha who suffers from epilepsy (a biomedical diagnosis)[26] and is believed to be bewitched by his mother (a traditional diagnosis). David is the youngest child in a family of eight children. He is single, childless and lives in Kitwe, a town 300 km to the north of Lusaka in the lodging house in the Central hospital with his older sister who works as a nurse. He moved there in 1999 from Luingu, his native village, in order to start a school.[27] Before his illness started he used to work in the biogas company in Kitwe and contributed money to the common household. David´s mother after the death of her husband sold the house in Luingu and moved to Kitwe to join David and his sister. She has not got any regular work, but sells beans at the market. However, she does not contribute any money to the common household. David´s elder brother Gabriel, who used to live in Kitwe with them, now lives in Livingstone alone. He suffers from "mood disorders", as David told me.

David's problem first occurred in 2007 when he started working in Kitwe. He experienced a series of fits during which he lost consciousness and in the period afterwards he felt dizziness and pain in his muscles. His mother took him to several *ng´angas* in surrounding villages but every time he started medication his health worsened. He had nightmares about a snake who tried to bite him and about a small scary villain *tuyobera* that were chasing him with a stick. He also dreamt that *"some man was sitting on him so that he could not breathe and when he looked into his eyes he became powerless"*. Despite being a Christian and belonging to the Seventh day Adventist church he has not tried to get help in any church. On the advice of his sister who learnt from the radio about Doctor Lukesha´s great healing qualities, David decided to visit him in Lusaka. During his first visit in September 2008 he experienced a strong complex seizure accompanied by aggressive behaviour during which he had to be transported to the Chainama psychiatric hospital where he was admitted,

---

[26] David Chamba was hospitalised at the Chainama psychiatric hospital for the first time in 2007.

[27] David´s sister paid for his education, he reached grade 7.

examined and given sedatives (phenobabitone). The provisional diagnosis in his medical file stated that he suffered from a "seizure disorder".

Following his release and return to Kitwe, he came back to Lusaka for a review at Doctor Lukesha's clinic and underwent the divination séance together with his mother, older sister and uncle. They all assisted in the "screening" divination and saw the "truth vision" in which David's mother was revealed as a witch. As they acknowledged, her reason for bewitching several family members, David, his sister's son and his elder brother from Livingstone, concerned money. According to David, she did not want to share the money she had obtained from the selling of the family house and moreover she wanted to get the bonus of David's elder sister. For this reason she bewitched her first born child who has been mentally ill since that time: *"He is 15 years old but is not going to school because he is mad. He talks about things that make no sense and laughs all the time. He is urinating in bed. We were told that he had taken some bad air* [he was bewitched]", explained David's sister. According to Doctor Lukesha, *"David's mother made a deal with the traditional healers in the village so that David could not be cured there. These ng'angas contaminated David with vivanda* [ghosts] *who were hunting him in the night. These vivanda were hung on the banana tree to make tuyobera. David's mother used this tuyobera to suck his blood, to use him, so that she could get money"*.

After the divination session all attendees sat down in Lukesha's office for a discussion. David's mother denied the accusation that had been shown "on the screen" and claimed her innocence by blaming David's step-brothers for witchcraft. After a long heated discussion Doctor Lukesha convinced her that she had bewitched David as well as other family members with the threat of contra-magic. He menaced her: *"If you will touch again* the magical objects you have hidden at home *you will become mad"*. David's mother finally gave in and pleaded guilty. She promised to get rid of these objects and apologized to the family. Doctor Lukesha prescribed a cleansing medicine for bathing and drinking for David as well as for his sister's son. David's mother underwent *ndembo* incisions where protective medicine was rubbed. Both were told to come back for a review in one month.

When I met them the next time David and his mother were still on the medication, however both admitted that, *"things were back on the rails"* and they felt healed. David also confessed that he forgave his mother. "*I am not afraid that she will start bewitching me again. Everybody in the family is aware now, she cannot do it! I have forgiven her. If she does it again I will not count her as my mother. I would not forgive her a second time*". This was the last time I met him. Two months later I met David´s sister who continued the medication of her son at Doctor Lukesha´s clinic. She told me that David´s brother from Livingstone died under mysterious conditions due to a fire in his house and that his body "disappeared". During the funeral David had several visions in which he saw the accident. As a consequence he also experienced another fit. Doctor Lukesha however admitted that this time David´s mother is not involved in the witchcraft. He concluded that, "*there has to be someone else playing tricks on him.*"

Zombie – A Symbol of Traumatic Human Exploitation

The symbolism of *chawe ya muzungu* "the white man's world" should also be taken into account when dealing with the symbolism of the *zombie* – exploited victims of magic forced labour. The stereotype attributes that Africans ascribe to the figure of a *muzungu* (white man) are abundantly expressed in the "moral geography" of witchcraft (Auslander 1993) all over Africa. As many anthropologists have shown (Auslander 1993; Comaroff Comaroff 1999a, 1999b; Niehaus 2001), the experience of colonial white dominance accompanied by the loss of property, labour exploitation and humiliation is inherently reflected in witchcraft symbolism, which is particularly connected to the image of *zombies* – the exploited dead victims. As follows from the local witchcraft discourse in Lusaka, the image of whites as "powerful outsiders" corresponds to the image of a witch in many aspects. A witch exploits and dehumanizes their victims in the same manner as white colonialists exploited the Africans. It is believed that a witch after capturing their victim and making him invisible "use" them as labour power for work at an invisible plantation in order to get rich. However, this image is today linked rather to the image of "powerful insiders" – the African *nouveau rich*.

With example of following illustrative case (and the case n. 8 available in the appendix Witchcraft Cases) I attempt to elucidate how the symbol of zombie refers to the phenomenon of labour migration, capitalist economic exploitation, processes of commodification of human body both in the past and today.

Witchcraft case 4: GERTRUDE

Gertrude is an 18 year old girl who lives together with her mother, father and three younger sisters in a rented house in the Kalingalinga compound in Lusaka. Her father works as a receptionist at a military hospital in Woodland (in Lusaka) where they also used to live before they moved to Kalingalinga. All her family members belong to the Jehovah Witness Church. They used to have a good relationship with their neighbours, also members of the same church, until Gertrude's father was promoted in his work and obtained a bonus which he used to run a business in the construction and renting of houses in the Mutendere compound (in Lusaka). From that time quarrels about money occurred between Gertrude's father and his best friend, a neighbour, who lives opposite his house. This neighbour X asked him for several loans which he could not pay back and started spreading rumours in the compound and in the church about Gertrude's father's rapidly gained money.

Apart from the neighbour, another two family members from Gertrude's mother's side – her elder sister with her son – figure in the whole case. The son lives in Kabwe and runs a business, which in the opinion of Gerhrude's parents *"made him rich at the same time as their daughter became ill."* Furthermore, his mother, the elder sister of Gerthurde's mother, lives in the Kalingalinga compound and makes her living by running bars and selling bananas in Soweto market in Lusaka. She is a very good friend of neighbour X and according to Gertrude's parents, *"she and her son are witches who use family members to run their business. That is why her husband is also blind."*

Gertrude's problem started six years ago, when her parents observed changes in her behaviour. *"She was seeing dead people and talking to them. She was laughing and dancing all the time. At night she was sleeping like a tree without moving or even bending her joints. During the day she was running in the street undressed and stealing bananas, she was also aggressive and wanted to kill us, she was completely insane"*, her father recalls. At the beginning her parents thought that she suffered from a sort of madness caused by cerebral malaria. As a consequence they decided to take her to the Chainama psychiatric hospital in Lusaka to let her be examined. Gertrude was admitted, observed and given some sedatives. During the admission her health condition was aggravated. She ran away from the hospital, had several paroxysms of rage and strong hallucinations. Her mother remembers that, "*she saw the people coming to visit her there which only increased her problem. That´s why we decided to take her back home from Chainama and search for a nganga*".

First the parents took her to Chongwe (30 km west of Lusaka) to visit a spiritual healer where they were told that witchcraft is involved. It was recommended that they visit another *mashabe* healer Doctor Chilango in Chazanga compound in Lusaka. The healer diagnosed with a help of spirit that several witches were involved in this case. She claimed that "*there is too much jealousy in the church* [the Jehovah Witness Church] *and in mother's family*". The reason for bewitching Gertrude was a jealousy about father´s property and about her intelligence. After the diagnosis, a cleansing ritual that consisted of shaving Gertrude's hair was carried out and a protective medicine to drink and a bath was prescribed. The house where the family lived was also protected.

Gertrude's father was convinced that his daughter was a victim of witchcraft from the side of the fellow church members who were jealous about his professional promotion from the post of a worker to a receptionist, as well as his election as a pastor in the church. His opinion supported the fact that Gertrude mentioned their names when she was hallucinating. At the same time Gertrude's father had to face diverse rumours in the compound, both in the neighbourhood and in the church, because he was given a bonus at work and started buying plots in Mtendere compound to build houses to rent. He explained to me, "*people did not know, they thought I stole that money or even that I am bewitching my child to grow the business, you know people here are judging instead of asking*." After some time the situation got even worse. Gertrude's memory was disturbed she could not recognize her own parents and also she lost her speech.

Subsequently the parents decided to take the advice of their friends and took her to the Mutumwa church in Kafue (30 km south of Lusaka) where relatives from the mother's side lived and could accommodate them. Gertrude was "prophesized" there and told that she was possessed by demons which made her unable to speak. Prophets from the church prescribed a treatment based on the use of Holy water and salt to drink, bath and sprinkle in the house for protection. Furthermore, Gertrude was taken to the mountains for some days to fast and pray. To bring back her voice a baptism in the river was recommended. Gertrude after having undergone all these procedures regained her voice. However, according to the parents her general health was even worse. Her father remembers that, *"she locked herself in the house and made a fire, she beat us. She became very dangerous"*. After these incidents, they went back to see the prophets from the Mutumwa church for a second time. The prophets pressured them into joining their church, the parents refused, finally fell out with them and never came back.

Following on from this experience they tried several *"brief case ng'angas"* who in their opinion *"were just eating money but do no work"*. They were also disappointed with the help they received at the Barrack church, a Pentecostal church in the centre of Lusaka, where *"they were using cooking oil to cure patients instead of anointing oil"* as the father told me. Gertrude's parents became desperate as they spent large amounts of money for the treatment of their daughter but to no advantage. Due to her illness, her father was forced to sell the plots he had bought and rent a house. *"It was like if all my money was siphoned and went to the illness of my daughter (...) every time I bought a new plot and started building, the problems were aggravated"*, he complained.

In 2008 when the parents were considering going to Congo to visit one reputable witch-finder, they suddenly came across Doctor Mukanda on the advice of their neighbour. They were told that *"a coffin is very near"* signifying the death of their daughter. Doctor Mukanda warned them not to go to Congo otherwise the witches would cause a bus accident to kill them – *"those witches are scanning you with their mirrors where ever you go"*, he said. Mukanda diagnosed that there was "a gang of witches" involved. During the divination séance parents were told that the witches used a kind of "bad smell" made by burning *chizimba* in a caldron and sent the smoke to Gertrude so that *"when that smell entered the house the sickness followed her"*. Additionally, the bad smell penetrated her body and caused that *"other people hate her"*. During the diagnosis Mukanda also specified that witches wanted to kill her by means of *chilubi* (voodoo doll) pierced with needles in order to make Gertrude mad. The healer explained to the family gathered for a divination that, "the *witches wanted to kill her to turn her body into a zombie which would working for them on an invisible plantation. For the moment they just abused her shadow by taking her footprints to enslave her as a part-time worker. They make her mute and insane so that she could not denunciate them"*, explained Mukanda.

The treatment itself consisted of several procedures. First of all the cleansing procedure in order to get rid of the "bad smell" was prescribed. Furthermore, the cleansing house ritual in order to detect and destroy the witches' mirrors hidden in the house was performed. Mukanda also carried out the contra-magic remedy aimed at detecting the *chilubi* from a distance and sending back needles in order to kill the boss of the gang of witches. The whole treatment, although it was very expensive, was successful and cured Gertrude within less than one year.

In her parent's opinion, Mukanda is the best witch-finder in the region. Gertrude's parents evaluated the whole treatment in words: "*Others ng'angas were just giving us medicine but Mukanda started from the beginning. He established a cause first, found and destroyed the magical objects, killed the witch boss and cured her* (Gertrude) *with his medicine. It is like when you construct a house, Mukanda started from the ground whereas all others we visited started from the roof"*.

Gertrude was definitively cured in October 2009 when the last consultation took place in the healer's house. By the time of my departure her father still had 700 000 Zambian Kwacha to pay back to Doctor Mukanda, but he was very happy to see his daughter recovered.

As it follows from the illustrative case n. 4 (and the case n. 8 available in the appendix) a witch can either kill his victim and use him as a "full time worker" (*zombie*) or just bewitch him at night by capturing his "shadow" and use him for "part-time night shifts". As a result, the victim when they wake up feels tired and overlaboured. The victim is usually treated as a mere object or a slave who loses his will, feelings, seated motionlessly in the corner of a house, or to uncritically serve a witch. As evident from the case of Gertrude, apathy and the loss of common sense refers to the total subordination of a victim (worker) to the witches.

The symbolism of *zombies* undoubtedly refers to the phenomenon of labour migration and economic exploitation of ordinary Zambians during the both colonial and post-colonial era. In accordance with the research of Jean and John Comaroff (1999a, 1999b) of the Tswana of South Africa, the symbol of the *zombie* (dead worker) corresponds to an image of a migrant, a labour worker deprived of their human attributes and alienated from fellowship with his kin. "He is in the state of eclipse affected by the essential selfhood of a living person, leaving behind a sentient shell as a mute witness to the erasure of the social being it once housed" (Comaroff 1999: 24).

The victims of witchcraft are often portrayed as insane, mute or blind as a witch cuts their tongues or pokes out their eyes so that they cannot criticize them or communicate with other people but being "useful" for a witch as showed example of Gertrude who became mute and insane. The *zombies* are depicted as pure "things" or a "commodities" as the following statement of an informant whose grand-daughter unexpectedly disappeared exemplifies: *"We thought that she was kidnapped or killed, but then when Doctor Kasanda came to our house and sprinkled his medicine in all corners, we could see that she was sitting naked and bounded in the corner of the house. We all started screaming and running away from the house."*[28]

As follows from witchcraft narratives, an alleged witch or a group of witches preferably chooses a victim who is intelligent so that he/she can siphon his intellectual capacity and use it for "kick-start the business". The idea of seizing the "life essence" in the form of blood, intellect, sight, sexual organs and converting it into money plays a crucial role in the imagination of the so-called occult economy. Comaroff and Comaroff (1999b) define it as the "deployment of magical means for material ends or, more expansively, the conjuring of wealth by resort to inherently mysterious techniques, whose principles of operation are neither transparent nor explicable in conventional terms" (Comaroff and Comaroff 1999b: 297).

The logic of witchcraft based on the principle of the "occult economy" corresponds to the logic of limited good (Foster 1965) that assumes

---

[28] The doctor Kasanda explained that victim was magically abused by her father who used her blood to make *chizimba* (magical object). According to him, *"the witch, a father of a girl, dug this chizimba in the pound, so that his cows produced more milk and young ones. He abused her shadow to make her work for him on plantations he owned together with other witches from the village."* (See Witchcraft case n. 8. in appendix)

that one cannot succeed in any other way than "at the expense" of others. This means that the occurrence of loss (illness, degradation in work, loss of husband, death of a close relative) on one side inherently implies the occurrence of gain (job promotion, gaining wealth, love) on the other. The idea that the growing material prosperity of a relative on the one hand, and the emergence of an illness in their offspring on the other is closely interconnected and figured in 80% of the medical cases recollected during the fieldwork.

The principle of "occult economy" is also closely linked to the conceptualisation of blood. Human blood as well as sperm which come under the same category is believed to contain a vital force *moyo* ("life" in chiNyanja). These bodily fluids generate, sustain, and invigorate life, while their diminishment leads to infertility and death" (Kaspin 1996: 569). Consequently the lack of sperm or amenorrhea is often linked to infertility. As I found out, the *moyo* changes throughout the course of life. Children and young people are considered the most vital as their blood is *"quick, fresh, powerful and abundant"*. As a person ages, blood becomes slow, weak and dries out which leads to death. The witches are supposed to choose their victims preferably among children and youths as their quick and powerful blood can figuratively kick start the business generating money.

The logic of witchcraft embodied in the symbol of *zombie* (but also *tuyobera*) thus implies the idea of socio-economic inequality and refers to people's endeavour to adopt, appropriate the symbolical capital in the form of the technology of power, the acquisition of wealth or participation in the global market. This socio-economic inequality is the most visible in urban settings where only a narrow range of inhabitants can enjoy this benefit whereas the majority of Lusaka dwellers are economically marginalised and stand at the edge of the global system.

The symbolism of *zombie* (as well as *tuyobera*) refers also to the process of commodification of human beings whose body serves as a commodity to be sold, exchanged or exploited. The modern capitalism thus may be seen as "bio-power" that focuses on the "body as a machine" that should be easily disciplined, manipulated and thus incorporated into effective economic systems of production.[29]

Another interesting finding issuing not solely from the presented case, is that people suspected of witchcraft rarely act independently, but on behalf of an organised group of witches that cooperate. According to my informants, witches are hierarchically organized according to their occult power and credit led by the most experienced and powerful witch called the "boss" who coordinates their activities. It is believed that "the boss" owns a special power to dominate the others by means of acquisition of unknown powerful medicine coming from abroad. The hierarchic organisation of witches' "coven", legitimisation of the authority of the boss and his compulsory measures strikingly reminds us of the organisation of English colonial power that used the tactics of bluffing and menacing those who refused to cooperate and awarding those who did.

According to collective narratives, the insatiate hunt for new victims under the dictate of *zombie* and *tuyobera* leads to vicious circle in which those who refuse to cooperate become automatically the victim of their companions. Witches in covens are believed to share their victims in a sense of food supply and labour force and help each other with procuring new dead. From this point of view, the imagery of witches does not strictly imply the idea of selfishness and individualism, as proclaimed by many anthropologists, but rather refers to the values of collective co-operation, reciprocity and interdependence as acknowledged in common interpersonal relationships.

Witchcraft Invisible Technologies

Another group of symbols which appear in the witchcraft discourse in Lusaka refer to the symbolical appropriation of European technology such as trains, airplanes and guns. In Lusaka, there is a widespread idea of magic trains (*tchima gamalele*) transporting victims to remote areas for work on a witch's invisible plantation. The trains visible only to other witches or witch-finders are depicted as huge with many coaches where people are crowded. It is believed that magic trains pass at night and

---

[29] See Foucault 1977.

ferry the *zombies* to their place of work.[30] Trains are made of human bones and stop only early in the morning, my informants say. Stories about magic trains vary according to individual informants who assert to have seen them. Doctor Kasanda for instance claims that he can recognize these trains at night by a noise such as jingling and people's shouting that wakes him up. Others claim to have seen magic trains illuminating their way from a distance, or spot them just for a second as they pass very quickly. For this reason it is also difficult for a witch-finder to catch and destroy them.

The explanation for this kind of symbolism might be found in the long term experience of labour migration in Zambia. Lusaka as well as other Zambian towns is located along the rail line which was extended in 1906 from South Africa through to Livingstone to the Broken Hill mines. Trains thus brought foreign labour migrants to the region as well as escorted local workers to South Africa and the Southern Rhodesian mines. Consequently, magic trains might reflect the collective memory of labour migration in the past. At the same time magical trains may refer to the fascination with increasing geographical mobility as experienced today. In this respect, Colson (2000) suggests that the magical technical conveniences reflect the awareness of a new technology that appeared in the 1990s. As she assumed, "the most feared witches are usually said to use horse, aeroplanes or guns, e.g. resources that obliterate the safeguard of distance and are associated with technology brought by Europeans but available since 1964 to an African elite that controls political power, monopolize much of Zambia's economic resources and is rich in a land of poverty" (Colson 2000: 341).

During my fieldwork I noted, that informants speak about magical guns (*kalilole*)[31] used by witches. *Kalilole* are believed to be lethal weapons whose manufacture is governed by a secret magical knowledge. Whereas the body of these weapons is said to be made of children's human bones, needles from porcupine spines are used instead of bullets in order to suck the blood from a victim. I was told that a witch uses *kalilole*

---

[30] Some witch-finders mentioned Mazabuka sugar plantations others did not specify the workplace.
[31] Other names are *katotola* or *kariroze*.

at night and shoots its victim three times[32] so that when he wakes up in the morning he starts suffering from chest pains, a strong cough, a headache and starts bleeding from the nose, eyes, ears and mouth. This is visible even after victim's death when the blood is still flowing out of his body. It is believed that as the needles pierce the victim's heart directly, he dies instantly, or in a few hours after being attacked or shot. If a special medicine from *ng'anga* is taken in time, a victim starts vomiting "black blood". Through this treatment the enchanted blood does not reach his heart and the victim is saved. The belief in *kalilole* refers on the one hand to the danger of violence executed by the means of guns, and on the other hand the symptoms of the disease caused by magical shooting are very similar to the symptoms of Ebola.

The magical aeroplane (*kalupe*) is another magical technology used by "progressive" witches to reach remote areas during their night travels. It is believed that they can construct it, or buy it at a specialized market. *Kalupe* is said to be made of a cow horn stuffed with special *chizimba* containing human blood and meat, or from human bones, basketry, a python and beads. It is believed that fresh human blood serves as fuel. The local narratives depict a witch as flying, sitting on the top of the *kalupe*, illuminating and making a noise. A newspaper article from the Times of Zambia (2007) describes a magical plane confiscated by a certain witch-finder as: *"Very small, but having the capacity to carry as many as fifty passengers"* (Times of Zambia. June 1, 2007, p. 3).

Doctor Mukanda explained that, *"magical planes land on a rubbish dump and they fly very quickly. From here to the Czech Republic, it can take a few seconds! When a witch flies over a house which is well protected with medicine, he simply falls down from the plane and gets exposed all naked in front of that house so that everybody can see him. People start railing and stick a banana in his ass."*

Isaac Niehaus assumes that "magical trains, planes and other witchcraft technologies do not only connote the power of mobility, but also convey the profound danger of speed and the unregulated movement of persons and objects" (Niehaus 2001: 76). At the same time, they are objects of fascination and the desired mobility and freedom of movement.

---

[32] Victim dreams about being shot by a normal gun.

As aforesaid, the majority of informants are convinced that these witchcraft technologies, if they were visible, would be highly marketable and would even outweigh European technical conveniences.

As we can see, the contemporary witchcraft discourse encompassing the symbol of *zombies*, *tuyobera*, *ilomba* and the magical means of transport proves to be exceptionally flexible and adjustable. It integrates a variety of symbols of modernity and mixes these with "traditional" specifics. Witchcraft symbolism as it appears in the urban narratives does not only reflect a fear and fascination with the processes of commodification, technologisation, mobility and the accumulation of wealth but primarily responds to the economical marginalization of ordinary people which "participate in the globalized world community not so much as consumers of manufactured material goods but as consumers and producers of mere images and ideas concerning the global world to which they seem to belong only marginally" (Binsbergen, van Dijk, Gewald 2003: 35).

The symbols we analysed proved to be ambivalent. They refer on one hand to people's fascination and *desire* for what is inaccessible and endowed with power (such as western technologies, biomedical science and material wealth) and on the other hand the *fear* of what is present, inexplicable and threatens life (such as human traffic, promiscuity leading to AIDS, sterility or poverty). Local witchcraft discourse expresses the endeavour to appropriate, assume and recast the symbols of power and powerlessness as matters of desire and the fear embedded in everyday reality of Lusaka people and thus incorporate them into comprehensible framework. As symbols are multivocal, several levels of historical and current experience intermingle at the same time. The conceptualisation of contemporary socio-economic problems in terms of witchcraft might thus resonate with the injustice and traumas embedded in the historical memory of colonialism.

Witchcraft as a Theory, System and Practice

For the purpose of analysis and interpretation of contemporary witchcraft in Lusaka with help of presented medical cases I employ Marc Augé's theoretical model of witchcraft as a theory, system and practice (Augé 1982).

Witchcraft as a *theory* represents an explanatory model that tries to clarify the existence of misfortune and evil in the world. According to Augé (1982) witchcraft as a theory can be interpreted at three permeable levels in terms of (1) "technique" that focuses on the modalities of acquisition and the transmission of occult powers, as well as its nature, (2) "interpretation" that focuses on diverse social actors involved in the processes of suspicions and witchcraft accusations and (3) "normativity" – belief in witchcraft functions as a socio-cultural mechanism supporting the desired model of behaviour. The fear of being accused and the effort to avoid this accusation represents an effective way of exercising social control in situations where practical forms of control are complicated or impossible.

Witchcraft analysed at the level of *system* explicitly refers to the social and political organization of a given society. The web of interrelations between social actors, their organization, hierarchy and power relations plays an important role in the processes of witchcraft accusation. As in other parts of Africa, even in Lusaka witchcraft is closely related to the family or the neighbourhood. Witchcraft accusations appear mostly in such relations that are, from the point of view of social stratification, complicated, conflicting or clearly ambivalent.

In *practice*, the phenomenon of witchcraft constituted at the level of theory and system reveals itself in practice as conditioned by a situation which "reveals itself in particular afflictions (medical cases) instigating suspicion, the searching for culprits and their accusations" (Augé 1982: 221). I suggest that this process as defined by Augé would be extendable to the process of conviction, punishment, or the potential treatment of an alleged witch. However, these complex processes composed of several separate events do not occur at random, but happen under predefined, culturally specific conditions which are, according to Augé, inherently linked to the distribution of power in a given society. Whereas the question "who accused whom" and "why" will be treated at the level of the social and normative system, the question "under which conditions" witchcraft accusations appear will be studied at the level of practice.

My interpretation of empiric data concerning witchcraft in Lusaka at the level of theory, system and practice as defined by Augé draws on the theoretic assumptions of the above outlined functionalistic tradition of the Manchester school and postmodern studies of modernity of witchcraft. Augé's triadic model employed here for analytical purposes presents the particular levels of interpretations of witchcraft as separated areas. However, the opposite is the case. In reality, the individual levels of interpretation are intermingled and inseparably interlinked.

I. Witchcraft as theory

Witchcraft as a theory represents a dynamic and malleable concept, one of a number of possible schemes of interpretation, which try to clarify the existence of misfortune and evil both at the level of the individual and his life and at more general level of theodicy or cosmodicy[33] in society. The later attempts to justify the fundamental goodness of the universe in the face of the occurrence of evil and suffering in the world.

Let us first focus on witchcraft from the perspective of an individual life where it represents as an interpretative aetiological model of misfortune referring to the disruption of social relations and the psychophysical integrity of an individual. Zambian, as many other African societies believe that adversities, inarticulate evil that occurs suddenly in their lives have its specific cause lying in the sphere of interpersonal relations. Such misfortune tends be personified, i.e. projected on a concrete person from the inner family circle or neighbourhood who is designated as an aetiological agent – a witch. By the process of social victimisation in the form of the accusation of witchcraft, the ambiguous affliction is possible to articulate, bundle and to physically control in the process of healing orchestrated by a witch-finder, the patient and his lay management therapy group. By the designation, accusation, punishment or rehabilitation of an alleged culprit the misty non-conscious conflict is resolved at the level of consciousness, which brings the patient's psychological catharsis and partial relief from his troublesome feelings. Witchcraft as an

---

[33] Term theodicy refers to general understanding of the suffering from the transcendent perspective of the belief in God (as defined by Gottfried Leibnitz in his work Théodicée), whereas cosmodicy refers in a general sense to the understanding of suffering from an immanent perspective, which is included in the relationship between man and nature (Ven, J. a ven Der 1998).

etiological model implies six distinctive but interrelated levels of interpretation of the affliction (illness).

1. *Psychological level*: The conscious and unconscious projection of a patient's problem; the accumulation of negative emotions such as envy, hate, jealousy; the repetitive occurrence of symptomatic dreams linked to witchcraft, belief in the efficacy of magic.

2. *Social level*: The existence of latent or manifest social conflict within the family, neighbourhood, which can be incited, reinforced or refuted through healer's mediation or by public opinion producing gossips and stereotypes.

3. *Physiological or biological level*: Illness in the form of physical or psychical ailment; a range of psychosomatic symptomatology.

4. *Socio-economic level*: A patient's economic destitution or social degradation versus gaining wealth, social prestige by promotion at work from the side of the patient's significant others.

5. *Environmental level:* Magical contamination of food, space, air; the use of material means (*mankwala, chizimba*, magical objects) for the purpose of witchcraft.

6. *Symbolic level:* Witchcraft multivocal symbols are anchored in local culture wrapping up the meanings of changing ideas about the world we inhabit. This last level is the most important as it represents the synthesis of all the above mentioned levels. This was illustrated in the example of the process of divination carried out by Lusaka healers who excel in their ability to first analyse, reorder and then unite the disparate levels of social reality, the patient's anamnesis in order to reorganise them into a comprehensive whole.

In the broader context, witchcraft represents an explanatory model of the world around intrinsically grounded in the local culture and its symbolic order. In this sense, witchcraft can be understood as a sort of logic, a specific way of conceptualising the contested reality, in particular evil. As I have shown in the examples of witch familiars and invisible technologies, witchcraft at the level of the symbolic system refers to the current social and economic transformation processes and creatively conceptualises the problems of the crises of modernity as well as the ongoing process of globalisation through a prism of "traditional" and Christian cosmology.

The logic of witchcraft based on the principle of the "occult economy" as defined by Comaroff and Comaroff (1999b) corresponds to the logic of illness that assumes that one cannot succeed in any other way than "at the expense" of others. This means that the occurrence of loss (illness, degradation in work, loss of husband, death of a close relative) on one side inherently implies the occurrence of gain (job promotion, gaining wealth, love) on the other. The logic of witchcraft thus implies the idea of socio-economic inequality and refers to people's endeavour to adopt, appropriate the symbolical capital in the form of the technology of power, the acquisition of wealth and participation in the global market. This socio-economic inequality is the most visible in urban settings where only a narrow range of inhabitants can enjoy this benefit whereas the majority of Lusaka dwellers are economically marginalised and stand at the edge of the global system.

The experienced contested reality conceptualised through the local prism of witchcraft is represents a sort of "myterium tremendum et fascinans" (Otto 1958). The symbols of welfare and social power inapproachable but longed-for by many ordinary Zambians pervades the local witchcraft discourse, as illustrated in the examples of the imagery of *tuyoberas* and *zombies*. These ambivalent symbols are multivocal, referring to different levels of historical and contemporary experience of socio-economic and political inequalities. The conceptualisation of urban predicaments such as (poverty, increasing promiscuity and HIV/AIDS, and human traffic) in terms of witchcraft resonate with the experience of oppression and the traumas from colonial era which is deep rooted in the historical collective memory of Zambians.

Witchcraft as a cultural idiom for distorted social relations is inherently linked with the field of normative order. It functions as a socio-cultural mechanism, supporting the desired model of behaviour. The fear of being accused and the effort to avoid this accusation represents an effective way of exercising social control in situations where practical forms of control are complicated or impossible. As the researchers from the Manchester school clearly demonstrated, witchcraft enhances the enforcement of moral codes in society. This is even more apparent today in urban settings where witchcraft tends to proliferate in the vacuum that has followed the abandonment of traditional customary law and disrespect of moral obligations towards family members based on the system of shared reciprocity. Refusing to provide necessary help to close relatives is generally regarded as anti-social behaviour and leads to witchcraft accusations amongst family members. Witchcraft thus becomes an expression of resistance to the erosion of traditional social values around family and community loyalty.

As we have already shown, in rapidly industrializing cities witchcraft accusation can express the anxieties over social contradiction introduced by capitalism. Hence, the accusations are directed at those individuals, who in the pursuit of economic success appeared most competitive, greedy and individualistic in their social relations. Witchcraft accusations thus represent a sort of social control and function in the sphere of morality as a levelling mechanism.

II. Witchcraft as system

Witchcraft at the level of system refers to social organization of a given society. The web of social relations between its participants, their organization and hierarchy plays an important role in the question of witchcraft. Apart from minor exceptions, witchcraft in Zambia is related to close relationships in a family or neighbourhood, and especially to those that are from the point of view of social stratification complicated, problematic, causing conflicts or easily accepting ambivalent features. Witchcraft is often understood by anthropologists as a socially constructed model of solutions for social anomies in the society (in the form of exclusion and rejection) resulting from dislocation or deformation of social, family, political and economic relations implicitly based on a certain form of inequality and therefore providing a fertile ground for feelings of tension, rivalry, envy and jealousy.

According to Mary Douglas, witchcraft serves as an indicator of an "unhealthy society" and represents a specific form of symbolic violence connected with people standing on the margins of a social system. The category of being different, which the witchcraft alone implies, is in the background of various forms of social exclusion or social control of "undesired" individuals or groups in process of creation of social borders and that both the outer or the inner ones. Witchcraft regularly acts as a stereotype at times of specific social crisis and thus enables the society community to change or amend its structure and to rid itself of certain moral obligations and unnecessary or excessive relationships (Douglas 1990).

Witchcraft as a metaphor of a social system is also employed by recent anthropologists (Mullings 1984; Geschiere 1995; Comaroff and Comaroff 1999a, 1999b; Niehaus 2001) who interpret it as a sort of social control of individual bodies intrinsically linked to politics and the economy (capitalism). These authors understand witchcraft accusation as expression of anxieties over social contradiction introduced by capitalism.

In the background of the social conflicts emerging from social stratification, the modes of accusations and victimisation are pursued. As the foregoing witchcraft cases showed, the accusations occur predominantly amongst family members. Although non kin members accused of witchcraft figure only in two of the presented medical cases (2 of the 8 cases), according to my observations, the accusations against neighbours, workmates or friends has the same frequency as quite frequent amongst kin members. In particular, relations with neighbours are considered to be especially difficult by the majority of people living in compounds where the high population density can easily lead to antagonism.

An interesting finding issuing from the presented cases is that relatives (or neighbours) suspected of witchcraft rarely act independently, but on behalf of an organised group of witches that cooperate. The organization of witches thus reflects the social order. According to my informants, witches are hierarchically organized according to their occult power and credit led by the most experienced and powerful witch called the "boss" who coordinates their activities. The insatiate hunt for new victims represents a vicious circle in which those who refuse to cooperate become automatically the victim of their companions. From this point of view, the imagery of witches does not strictly imply the idea of selfishness and individualism but rather refers to the values of collective cooperation, reciprocity and interdependence as acknowledged in common interpersonal relationships.

Every analysis of witchcraft imposes the question of gender and age. In the majority of African societies gender and age stereotypes derives from the social structure and distribution of power. From this perspective, vulnerable persons such as women, elders or children[34] are more prone to be designated as witches.[35] In Zambia, the situation is rather reverse. In all of the presented cases, the vulnerable, the weak and unprotected people such as children (3 of the 8 cases), women-mothers or women financially dependent on their husbands (3 of the 8 cases) were in position of victims of witchcraft.

From the point of view of gender, there is a general tendency to accuse a relative or a neighbour of a different sex. The only exceptions are two cases (2 of the 8 cases) where accusations emerge solely between women using the *kavundula* and *mukunko*. As seven of the eight cases concerned female patients, accusations of witchcraft were brought against men in seven of these cases. My inquiry further disclosed that, the relationship between a child and a parent of the opposite sex and his affine relatives is considered to be particularly conflicting and tense. In the five cases where women figured, the husbands and their family were accused of witchcraft (5 of the 8 cases).

Many anthropologists dealing with witchcraft have shown that differences between generations have been always a source of tension and rivalry and therefore the fertile ground for witchcraft accusations.[36] My research affirms this assumption as in all of the presented cases, the older were designated as witches whereas the younger as a victim. Unlike

---

[34] The phenomenon of witch-kids has come to light nowadays in some African urban cities. Since the nineties the testimonies of so-called cursed kids have been appearing in the Democratic Republic of Congo. This new form of witchcraft is known under the name of *ndoki* (in Lingala language). Anthropologists put this phenomenon into terms with the disintegration of family bonds, the problem of ever increasing poverty in the cities, the boom of AIDS and opportunism of independent denominations (inspired by the Pentecostal movement) in Kinshasa. (See Molina 2005). A similar phenomenon of child-boy witchcraft *gbati* appeared in the seventies in Cameroon (see Fisiy, Geschiere 2001).

[35] In many part sof Arica, especially old women are considered to be witches.

[36] There is anthropological evidence that, in segmental societies based on the hierarchy of age classes, the elder with their strong position posed a threat to the younger generation.

in the neighbouring Democratic Republic of Congo where children are considered to be witches causing harm to their parents (Molina 2004), in Lusaka children are mostly considered to be the victims of witchcraft from the side of their parents, or close relatives. As the sample of patients show, in four cases the victims were children or adolescents up to 18 years old (4 of the 8 cases), other cases concerned the young between 25 and 35 years old. The only exception was case 1 and 5, when the victim was more than 40 years old. We can thus conclude that in the majority of cases, parents have a tendency to accuse their affine relatives of bewitching their offspring.

The logic of witchcraft based on the assumption that one cannot succeed in any other way than "at the expense" of others is presented in all of the cases. The occurrence of loss in the form of an affliction, degradation in work, loss of husband on one side inherently implies the occurrence of gain such as promotion in work, gaining wealth, attracting love on the other. These findings imply the widespread idea that the process of healing is inherently linked to the process of afflicting. We may recall the father of Gertrude who complained that all of his money he received as a bonus in his work was "siphoned" in order to pay for the treatment of his daughter who suffered from a mental disorder. His awareness of the heavy price that he had to pay for his prosperity was clearly reflected in his statement: *"Every time I bought a new plot and started building the problems of my daughter aggravated"*.

The idea that the growing material prosperity of a relative on the one hand, and the emergence of an illness in their offspring on the other is closely interconnected and figured in 80% of the cases presented. This principle of "occult economy" is here closely linked to the conceptualisation of blood in terms of vital force. It is believed, that the blood of children is fresh, quick and vital and thus highly valued by older witches who use it to *"speed up their business affairs"*.

The reasons for accusations of witchcraft vary in every case. In the majority of the cases the reason for accusations was specified the growing business prosperity or social promotion of a close kin or neighbour (6 of the 8 cases). On the other side, the envy of money (7 of the 8 cases), intelligence and beauty of a patient (3 of the 8 cases) was stated as a reason why an alleged witch has chosen a given victim. The love rivalry and jealousy as a main motivation leading to witchcraft is mentioned in

2 of the 8 cases. In two of the cases the great distance of the kin accused of witchcraft was mentioned. The idea that, such kinsmen travels or live in the far-away country such as Tanzania where strong and efficient witchcraft may be procured, figures in the witchcraft narratives.

And what are the most common afflictions aetiologically linked to witchcraft? As the outline below shows, we can distinguish them into three main spheres:

1. Women's reproductive problems

The problem of sterility, abortions, amenorrhea and other gynaecological problems is symbolically linked to an intervention of a magical agent in the form of a snake the *ilomba* (wizard's familiar), or magical techniques such as *mukunko* – a magical disease over a prolonged period.

2. Marital problems

Lusaka women face the infidelity of their husbands which threatens their marital and thus economic security. The women then project their jealousy and insecurity onto the idea of a magical attack through *kavundula* – a charm employed by female love rivals to attract the attention of a married man. To secure the fidelity of her husband Lusaka woman use either an inoffensive charm – love portion (*muito*), or offensive (protective) charm *lukanko*. Although it is less frequent, a man can use *lukanko* against his spouse as well.

3. Economic destitution and social deprivation

The economic anxieties such as unemployment, the unexpected loss of work, living in poverty, failure in business or economic marginalisation in general are reflected in the symbolism of the *tuyobera* and the *zombie* which represent excessive materialist desire connected with an idea of magical exploitation of human labour power (especially those of children). The "principle of the occult economy" as it appears in the witchcraft narratives refers to the sphere of social stratification, normative order and power relations.

Schema 8: The Most Common Field of Afflictions Linked to Witchcraft

Sphere of affliction	Marital problems	*Header continues on next page*
Specification of the affliction	Infidelity of men Infidelity of women Quarrels among spouses	
Magical charm	*Kavundula*	*Lukanko*
Gender	Between women	Between man (W) and woman (B) Between women (W) and man (B)
Age	N/A	N/A
Social relations	Neighbours	Spouses

Notes: *W – witch, B – bewitched

Reproductive problems		Economic destitution and social deprivation	
Women's sterility Abortions Amenorrhea Gynaecologic problems		Financial shortcoming (loss of employment, bad luck in business, living in poverty) Social marginalisation.	
Ilomba	*Mukunko*	*Zombie*	*Tuyobera*
Between woman (B) and man (W)	Between woman (B) and woman (W)	Mostly between man and woman	N/A
N/A	Elder (W) Younger (B)	Elder (W) Child (B) Elder (W) Younger (B)	Elder (W) Child (B) Elder (W) Younger (B)
Between women (B) and her affine relatives (W)		Between child (B) and his parents (W) Between child-girl (B) and his patrilateral relatives (W) Between child-boy (B) and his matrilateral relatives (W)	Between child (B) and his parents (W) Between child-girl (B) and his patrilateral relatives (W) Between child-boy (B) and his matrilateral relatives (W)

Schema 9: Psycho-physiological Aspects of Illnesses Linked to Witchcraft

The physiological affected sphere	Eyesight	Speech	Intelligence	Locomotive organs
Instrumental cause	Poking eyes	Cutting tongue	Draining off brain	Laying magical objects underground; sending *chivanda*; working on invisible plantation
Objectives	The victim cannot see what a witch is doing	The victim cannot speak about what a witch is doing	The witch siphons the intellectual capacities of a victim for his own business promotion.	The victim starts suffering from painful swelling of the legs and thus cannot escape a witch. He is "knocked down".
Specification of an illness	Blindness Eye problems	Inability to speak	Psychosis	Epilepsy; Pain in legs; Backache

Respiratory organs	Reproductive organs	Digestive organs	Blood
Sending *chivanda*	The witch "ties the womb"; or afflicts the victim through sexual intercourse (*ilomba*)	Feeding the victim by human flesh	Siphoning of the "life essence" of the victim by means of *ndembo*; heating the victim
Suffering in general	The witch prevents a victim from having a child	Suffering in general	The Witch assures business promotion
Chronic respiratory diseases (TB)	Infertility; Abortions; Amenorrhea	Nausea; Sharp chronic pain in the stomach accompanied by regular vomiting; Ulcers	Weakness; Dizziness; Circulating sharp pain through the whole body (*viposo*)

III. Witchcraft as a practice

"The phenomenon of witchcraft constituted at the level of theory and system reveals itself in practice conditioned by a situation and context in which it reveals itself in particular types of afflictions instigating suspicion, searching for culprits and their accusations" (Augé 1982: 221). These complex processes composed of specific events do not occur at random, but happen under predefined, socially and culturally biased conditions.

As my research disclosed, there are five necessary conditions or circumstances in which witchcraft accusation can emerge. The most important is the dimension of chronological congruence of these apparently disparate experiences that plays a significant role in the process of divination.

1. The occurrence of psychical or physiological illness.

As mentioned earlier, witchcraft is generally linked to unlucky events that comes either unexpectedly and suddenly such as accidents, abrupt deaths, bad luck (such as loss of work, money or a spouse), or has a long or repetitive duration, like in the case of chronic diseases or sterility. The majority of medical cases related to witchcraft are multi-episodic and their treatment lasts several years. The average duration of individual medical cases related to witchcraft is 3.5 years (with the longest 9 years and the shortest 1year). Afflictions generally ascribed to the malefic activities of witches vary according to individual cases.

However, as the schema 9 shows, there are certain types of illness on level of biological body that tend to be interpreted in terms of witchcraft more than others. Such illnesses are believed to be caused by malevolent intrusion of both material and nonmaterial substances, into the being of the victim. This eclipses the self and affects the composition and flow of blood, temperature of the body, causes obstructions in digestive system, reproductive and respiratory system, or the immobilisation of the body in its locomotion functions (swelling of the legs, epilepsy, backache) and audio-visual functions (loss of sight, hearing, speech).

2. The occurrence of illness is always accompanied by symptomatic dreams

Kulodza, bewitching someone, is inherently linked to dreaming (*kulota*) as we showed in the chapter 4. Witches are generally believed to trouble people when they are asleep. By analysing the contents of the different dreams of 12 patients I have created the following survey of dreams related to witchcraft. With the intention of understanding dreams, a respective range of psycho-physical symptoms as described by the patients are attributed to each dream.

3. Occurrence of latent or manifest conflicts between an accuser and accused

What precedes an accusation is not only the occurrence of an illness but also the emergence of a certain social conflict or latent tension issuing either from the disrespect of a binding moral norm of reciprocity (refusing to provide help), or antipathy (I never liked him), or problems in communication (someone gains wealth, promoted at work and did not inform the others). As it follows from the medical cases, witchcraft accusations were mostly driven by emotions of jealousy, envy and hate. The symbolic violence is pointed against those who are "different", "extraordinary", "lucky" and "successful" (or beautiful, intelligent, fecund or rich). Their achievements and qualities incite jealousy as well as give offence to others, who therefore judge them. As I noted, witchcraft is a two-edged sword. Emotions of jealousy and hate that lead an accuser to accuse a significant Other are similar to those that are attributed to an accused (alleged witch). Any kind of "surpassing" such as success in work, business, school or even politics is thus conceptualised in terms of individualism and selfishness. In Lusaka, the individualism is considered to be a threat for collectively shared egalitarian norms of reciprocity and therefore implies the notion of witchcraft.

4. The gossip as an accelerant of strong negative emotions

Public opinion plays an important role in witchcraft accusations. By means of gossip, people in compounds, especially women control other people's behaviour. Although the phenomenon of gossip has not been systematically studied in anthropological literature, some authors such focused on it. For instance Max Gluckman (1963) considers gossip (or scandal) among the most important societal and cultural phenomena that has the function of unifying and affirming community values, control of aspiring individuals and cliques within the society, the selection of leaders and maintenance of group exclusiveness (Oakely 2005: 197). He analyses the relations of gossip and witchcraft on examples of ethnographic literature and analysis of African village life where gossips among lineages significantly contribute to witchcraft accusations.

By means of gossip the patients strengthen his personal view and negative emotions of hate, envy and jealousy against someone from the close environ. These animosities usually grow out of the initial problem that of communication – exchange of ideas. The obstruction in a flow of communication that often leads to exaggerated judgment, is expressed in the form of gossip that is spread around about someone's success as illustrated in the statement of Gertrude's father whose child was bewitched: "*People did not know, they thought I stole that money or even that I am bewitching my child to grow the business, you know people here are judging instead of asking.*" As collectivism is the basis of personal identity, one's opinion is significantly shaped by significant others, i.e. relatives and friends.

In Lusaka when talking about one who is suspected of being a witch, people do not explicitly use the term *mfiti* but rather have recourse to a number of euphemisms such as "being clever" (*kuchengela*) or "having something hidden in their pocket" (*kuziza mutumba*).[37]

5. The role of the healer as a mediator of the conflict

The patient influenced by the opinion of other family members as well as by public opinion in the form of gossip may have a certain suspicion about a witch in his surroundings. This assumption can be however affirmed or disproved by the healer in the process of diagnosis. As shown

---

[37] The collocation "he has something hidden in the pocket" means that "he is a witch" because of having some dangerous medicine on him.

in chapter 4, the healer significantly contributes to the construction of witchcraft accusations. It is precisely he/she who designated the cause of a patient's illness and who contextualises the patient's problem into a comprehensible whole. In the most general term, *ng'anga* represents a mediator of a social conflict, the negotiator among individual family members. Unlike in the past when witches had to undergone the poison ordeal to be detected and punished, today the main aim is to redress the balance between an afflicted person and an alleged witch.

As I observed, *ng'anga* ensures that an accused person is convicted in the majority of cases. Once proven to be a witch, the accused rarely has any other option than to accept this status. The optimal solution is, however, to make the witch undergo traditional treatment and thereby secure his remedy as it happen in the case of David and his mother. At other times, the culprit is publically designated but not explicitly named as the Witchcraft Act forbade healers to denounce the witches. In these cases, *ng'anga* combines the method of prescription of protective medicine for a patients, deactivation of magical objects, and destruction of an alleged witch or group of witches by means of contra-magic usually employed from a distance. In both cases, witchcraft accusations and its respective therapy represent an allegoric form of catharsis of a social conflict, mostly within the family. As witchcraft helps to explain inexplicable occurrences of misfortune, the therapy thus provides relief from anxieties, and can be thus interpreted as a sort of effective psychotherapy.[38]

---

[38] Many British anthropologists such as Marwick (1965); Douglas (1967); Colson (2000); Mitchell (1965) took this view as well.

Conclusion – Summary

In conclusion I would like to sum up the most important findings of my research and point out some of its general implications within the field of medical anthropology and African studies.

The first section of the book concerning the syncretic and pluralist medical culture in Lusaka disclosed that the continual questioning of the meaning of an illness leads people to experiment with different therapeutic options and employ the pragmatic therapy-seeking behaviour I call "therapy shopping". By analysing this phenomenon I found out that as a patients move from one medical sector to another, they deal with different beliefs and normative systems, whilst in each setting an illness is perceived, labelled and interpreted differently, and leads to a particular therapy. However, patients do not consider a different diagnosis to be contradictory, but rather complementary which enables them to undergo different treatments simultaneously. Patients tend to appropriate and creatively combine the elements from different healing systems in their lay medical knowledge. Their own interpretation of illness is thus socially constructed through the process of therapy itself and changes according to the situation and medical setting in which it is embedded. My inquiry further showed that the meaning of the illness is significantly conditioned by the patient's identification with the diagnosis. Which one will be final among others i.e. appropriate for him, depends on the effectiveness or ineffectiveness of the respective therapy the patient underwent. In this sense, my findings affirmed Whyte's (1989) argument that, the therapy itself establishes the diagnosis.

The analysis of the main decision-making factors involved in therapy shopping further showed that patients decide which medical option to choose according to recommendation of their kin, neighbours and friends. This finding supports Janzen's argument about the importance of the patient's "lay therapy management group" (Janzen 1978) in the therapy-seeking process. As personal health is never an individual but collective matter the patients' significant others represent a social decision-making body which helps to evaluate the treatment and search for an optimal solution for the future. The way how patients and their relatives interpret the illness and assess the therapy determines, not only the further process of therapy seeking, but the course of actual treatment independent of the symptomatic progress of the illness. As the kinship solidarity network seems to be in decline in Lusaka, others like neighbours, church communities and cult groups play an important role in the negotiation and maintenance of a patient's health.

As I pointed out, patient's identification with a particular diagnosis depends to a certain measure on consensus among family members, patient and healer, but is also conditioned by necessity of cognitive consensus, i.e. sharing the same ideas and symbols. This is not the case with biomedical treatment which although being the first medical option in more than half of the cases, is generally approached with distrust. It is precisely due to the incompatibility of both explanatory models that leads patients to label biomedicine as ineffective. In their eyes, biomedicine is unable to deal with the social, personal and spiritual context of an illness. The failure of biomedical treatment as stated by respondents is due to the fact that invisible forces are involved in the illness. As belief in "spiritual afflictions" (illness caused by witches, spirits, angry ancestors) pervades the minds of all Lusaka dwellers the option of indigenous or Christian therapy logically ensues.

As it has been demonstrated by many ethnographers, Africans conceive an illness in broader terms as a sort of misfortune, bad luck in business, school or marriage, the loss of property or job, or unreciprocated love. Contrary to the western fragmentised and dualistic conception of illness/disease that does not take into account the social and spiritual context and refer only to a dysfunction of the body, illness as conceived by Lusaka dwellers is "integrated" treating a number of apparently separated and non-overlapping fields as conjoined and continuous (Fabrega 1973: 233). The interpretation of illness caused by witchcraft refers to disturbed social relationship embodied both in the sphere of religiosity as of biology manifesting on symptmomatological level. As examples of medical cases showed, Lusaka dwellers conceptualise their illness as a comprehensive category embracing the social, spiritual, environmental, physiological and psychological aspects, that are all interrelated in an integral whole both at the level of diagnosis and treatment.

This holistic idea is also reflected in the local conceptualisation of the body that proved to be based on a metaphorical linkage between the physiology of a man and ecology (seasonal processes in nature) in terms of both temperature and fluidity. The local conceptualisation of male and female bodies in terms of hotness, coolness, wetness and dryness also plays an important role in the process of the symbolic construction of the notion of sterility and fertility as well as of spiritual illnesses, i.e. those caused by witchcraft or spirit possession. Drawing on the theory of "Minfull body" of Lock and Sheper-Hughes (1987), I further revealed how the health of an individual body is linked to the proper functioning of reproduction, digestion/secretion and blood circulation in terms of a smooth and obstructed flow on one hand and to the functioning of the social body in terms of smooth or obstructed communication and reciprocity in interpersonal relations, on the other.

The research of medical culture further disclosed that Lusaka dwellers understand illness/ health as a quantitative entity that imply the idea of a "limited good" (Foster 1965). In this view one cannot be healed unless his illness is transferred to someone else. As a result, the processes of healing and afflicting are interconnected and influence each other as I showed on examples of contra-magic and purgatory rituals. In this respect I argued that the logic of distribution of illness is the same as the logic of witchcraft, i.e. based on the assumption that one cannot succeed in any other way than "at the expense" of others.

Another theme I developed concerned the traditional healing and figures of traditional healers, in particular those involved in spiritual healing (i.e. healing through spirit). By focusing on the divinatory technique of "magical mirrors" used by diviners to identify witches, I proceeded to the interpretation of the social and cultural construction of illness in the course of divination and the creative role of the *ng´anga* in this respect. During a divination séance, the examination of a patient's history, his family and social background as well as the interpretation of his dreams plays an important role. The main task of a diviner is thus to arrange and interconnect the patient's separate experiences such as nightmares, social problems, actual health complications, fears and worries into a "comprehensible whole". I argued that whereas a patient's main interest is to discover the efficient cause, i.e. to know "who or what caused his illness", for the *ng´anga*, the interpretation of the instrumental cause, i.e. "magical technique used by a witch" is much more determining. The specification of this cause necessitates drawing on rich symbolism of witchcraft that provides the healer necessary source of rhetoric metaphors and flexible interpretative frame necessary for the construction of patient's diagnosis. By identifying with "his story", the patient finally comes to understand the causes of his illness which brings him relief from previous anxiety. The more a patient identifies with his story, i.e. diagnosis, the more there is a chance of effective treatment.

Another important part of the book is dedicated to the problems of Christian spiritual healing within the prophet-healing churches that have multiplied in poor Lusaka compounds since the 1960s. The increasing popularity of these churches lies in their ability to respond flexibly to the burning issues of low income populations that live in predicaments of ongoing economic and health crises. This target group represent the patients suffering from various health and socio-economic afflictions such as unemployment, poverty, alcohol abuse, promiscuity, marital and family problems as well as physiological and psychological disorders. Although *ng´anga* represents a negative point of reference for the prophets – Christian healers, their healing methods are strikingly similar. Shoffeleers (1994) speaks in this context about "the *ng´anga* paradigm" which means that a traditional healer provides a point of reference for the conceptualization of the role of Christ and the prophets and vice versa. This fact was proved when dealing with the biographies of Christian and traditional healers. The prophets from the Mutumwa church, where I did my extensive fieldwork, not only combined the Christian and traditional methods of healing, but also shared the same ontological and aetiological reality as their hated "friends" the *ng´angas*.

The detailed case community study of the Mutumwa church in the Kuku compound disclosed some basic facts about the composition of patients, their problems, personal attitudes and expectations towards spiritual healing provided in the church. The patients turned out to be an unstable shifting group preponderantly consisted of women (85%). More than half of them frequently wandered from one church centre to another in the quest of therapy. The closer investigation of "prophesying", i.e. the method of diagnosing illness through the Holy Spirit carried out by prophets in the church, disclosed that the most common problems that the women encountered were diverse socio-economic ailments within the household, family and marriage (such as runaway or a husbands fidelity), problems of cohabitation, financial insecurity, to mention some of the most common. Apart from that, the patients suffered from a whole range of diverse psychosomatic troubles such as anxiety, depression, heart palpitations, headaches, weakness, and bad moods that were traditionally attributed to capricious *mashabe* spirits, but in the Christian context interpreted as demon possession and treated by exorcism. Witchcraft mentioned in approximately 30% of the cases, was usually linked to close family members or neighbours involved in traditional medicine. The method of prophesying carried out by prophets in church showed to be strikingly similar to that of spirit divination of *ng'angas*. On the contrary, it was different to that of witch-finders, as it is based on the long narrative monolog of a prophet during which he/she proceeds through the analysis of disparate fields of a patient's life (family background, social problems, physical and psychical problems) to the level of synthesis and assigning the appropriate aetiology.

Another elaborated topic closely associated with both traditional and Christian spiritual healing concerned the spirit of possession. Regular observations of collective rituals such as Christian healing services in the Mutumwa church and "traditional" *ngoma* healing ceremonies brought a variety of comparative data. During the church service the participants invoke the Holy Spirit by means of prayers and the constant singing of hymns by which the sacred atmosphere is stimulated and culminating in the form of a "collective effervescence" suitable for manifestation of trance spirit possession. Similarly, the participants of the *ngoma* ceremony invoke the *mashabe* spirits in the appropriate sacred climate induced by drumming, singing traditional songs and all night dancing symbolising particular spirits. In both cases the trance is provoked on the side of patients (involuntarily possessed) as well as on the side of healers (voluntarily possessed). In Christian setting the trance of patients is interpreted as a manifestation of demons that get irritated and must be expelled, whereas the trance of prophets is linked to the manifestation of the healing power of the Holy Spirit. On the contrary, during the *ngoma* ritual patients and healers are believed to be possessed by the same type of spirit (*mashabe*) that must be calmed down, appeased and controlled under the guidance of experienced healers. It is then expected that by recovering from his original illness, the patient will become a healer and join the community of the *mashabe* healers. In the Christian setting, the role of a patient and prophet also turned out to be socially constructed on the basis of spirit possession. As there is no official procedure for the appointment of religious leaders, acquiring abilities as a spirit medium is viewed as a spiritually propelled phenomenon that has to be appreciated by others as it appears. This means that if a patient after being exorcised demonstrates loyalty to the church and a proper spiritual vigour, he has in principle a bright prospect to move to a higher rank of church membership or even to become a prophet in the future. His mediumistic qualities which were before linked to the "uncontrolled *mashabe* possession" are now cultivated in order to control the Holy Spirits power entering his body. As I demonstrated in the example of Prophet Dereck Kiri, the social label "possessed by a demon" serves also as a social stigmatization of prophets whose popularity is on decline in the church. The prophet's charismatic identity is thus not shaped only by the personal experience of the spiritual calling, but is also socially constructed and negotiated within the church community. As the boundary between demon possession and Holy Spirit possession is thin and permeable, its interpretation depends fully on the consensus of church community. On the basis of these findings I came to a conclusion that spirit possession in Lusaka represents a culturally biased behaviour, a sort of latent political strategy based on nonverbal bodily communication among the members of a given community that leads in a certain context to a position of power and authority. Spirit possession as a socially constructed phenomenon represents has a high symbolic value in Zambian society. I argued that for illiterate members of society the possibility to become a prophet or healer represents a sort of social lift, a way of raising their symbolic capital and acquiring the position of authority in the community. This position is equally attractive for uneducated, poor Lusaka dwellers as to become a politician is for those wealthy and well educated, as both of these positions are intrinsically linked to power.

In this book I engaged in polemics with social deprivation theories of traditional spirit possession that conceive this phenomenon as an instrument of the oppressed, frustrated and marginalised social groups (in particular women) having in strongly structured societies only limited possibilities to express their wish, and achieve the appropriate social status (Lewis 1971), or as a form of social and cultural adaptation to a rapid social change in town (Oosthuizen 1992), the political and social emancipation of women (Boddy 1989), or political cultural resistance (Stoller 1995). I took the view that spirit possession in today's Lusaka is primarily linked to reproductive problems believed to be caused by ancestral spirits who enter female bodies and bind their womb. The *ngoma* institution based on *mashabe* spirit possession helps to overcome the most profound insecurity that might be felt by women – being infertile. Such women are socially stigmatised and devalued by their husband and his family. As the majority of women are financially dependent on their husbands, his potential loss represents a serious danger for them. Entering the community of *mashabe* healers can be interpreted as a way that the Lusaka women gain psychological consolation, achieve social status and thus ameliorate their economic situation. In Lusaka, where traditional kinship networks became disturbed and fragmented, *mashabe* communities help to create an alternative social solidarity network. In this respect, it helps the people to release the social tensions and overcome everyday predicaments issuing from common experience of their social and economic marginalisation.

Traditional and Christian spirit possession was not analysed only from the social point of view but also from the point of identity formation of an individual in the background of "healer's syndrome". At the beginning there is the crisis of possession accompanied by ancestral calling, symptomatic dreams and the occurrence of serious illnesses that leads in better cases to his recovery with the help of the possessing spirit. The comparison of biographies of Christian and traditional spiritual healers has highlighted particular differences and similarities in their personal vocation. The occurrence of symptomatic dreams and visions that accompanies the initial crises plays a more important role in the process of diagnosis than the physical symptoms themselves. Whereas the symptomatic level is often emphasized by traditional healers complaining about persistent head-aches, tachyarrhythmia, dizziness, seizures, loss of appetite, and weight fluctuation or reproductive dysfunctions, in the case of prophetic possession it is not as clearly recognizable. The symptoms are rather vague, described in terms of mental confusion or madness, weakness or solitude. Unlike those afflicted by *mashabe* spirits have to undergo a sort of initiation, the prophetic vocation also affirmed by a social consensus usually lacks any institutional background. Contrary to spiritual healers, prophet's mediumistic qualities are never inherited but socially negotiated within the church community. Whereas the prophet's vocation is a self-imposed based on personal charisma and social affirmation, the vocation of traditional healers is conceived as a sacrifice, an involuntary fate. Unlike prophets who claim to be lucky to be chosen, to be gifted by God to serve people, all of the informants from the range of spiritual healers affirmed an initial resistance and defiance at becoming a healer.

The last topic I would like to conclude is the phenomenon of contemporary witchcraft in Lusaka. My interpretations were based on the analyses of witchcraft at the level of theory, system and practice (Augé 1982). On the one hand I draw on the functionalist tradition of the Manchester school that interpreted witchcraft as an indicator of the degree of social tension and conflicts in a given society, as well as an effective tool for the regulation of social conflict in order to reproduce the social order. On the other hand, I lean on the assumptions of modern scholars studying witchcraft in connection within the crises of modernity and globalisation encompassing different forms of socio-political and economic transformations. I treat witchcraft from two main perspectives. Firstly in the more narrow sense as an individual illness aetiology and secondly in the wider sense as a philosophical world view, local discourse reflecting the occurrence of evil, misfortune and inequalities in the world and the way the local people conceive and experience the contested reality.

Witchcraft as an aetiology is linked to particular afflictions that refers to concrete social tensions and conflict within the family or neighbourhood. Amongst those most common is women's sterility symbolically associated to the intervention of the magical snake *ilomba* that reflects the women's fear about the infidelity of their men that threatens not only their marital and economic security, but also health (a high risk of HIV/AIDS). Further it is the economic destitution and social deprivation reflected in the narratives of *zombies* and *tuyoberas* – symbols of excessive materialist desire connected with magical exploitation of youth and children. In my research I focused also on patterns of witchcraft accusation. I found out that that it occurs the mostly between women themselves, further between women and their children on the one side and their older affine relatives of the opposite sex.

Witchcraft as a cultural idiom for distorted social relations is inherently linked with the field of normative order. It functions as a sociocultural mechanism, supporting the desired model of behaviour. The fear of being accused and the effort to avoid this social stigmatisation represents an effective way of exercising social control in situations where practical forms of control are complicated or impossible. This is even more apparent today in urban settings where witchcraft tends to proliferate in a vacuum that has followed the abandonment of traditional customary law and the disrespect of moral obligations towards family members based on the system of shared reciprocity. Refusing to provide necessary help to close relatives is generally regarded as anti-social behaviour and leads to witchcraft accusations amongst family members. Witchcraft thus becomes an expression of resistance to the erosion of traditional social values around family and community loyalty. As have been shown by many anthropologists, in rapidly industrializing cities witchcraft accusation can express the anxieties over the social contradiction introduced by capitalism. Hence, the accusations are directed at those individuals, who in the pursuit of economic success appeared most competitive, greedy and individualistic in their social relations. The being accused of witchcraft thus functions in the sphere of morality as a sort of levelling mechanism.

By analysing the symbolism of contemporary witchcraft pervading the mind of Lusaka dwellers, I realised that witchcraft is linked to many aspects of human life and do not represent only illness aetiology. It is the sophisticated symbolic system that proves to be exceptionally flexible and adjustable as it integrates the variety of symbols of modernity and mixes these with traditional specifics. As I have shown in the example of witchcraft familiars and technologies, the contemporary local discourse reflects primarily the people's ambivalent feelings of fear and fascination with the processes of commodification, technologisation and economical marginalization. In this sense, witchcraft represents a specific way, that people conceptualise the local precariousness of their everyday life (here and now) in relation to the far-away, blurred and unattainable global world (there, in future or past).

In conclusion we can say, that witchcraft as an aetiology and cultural explanatory model refers to the deepest existential uncertainties of the local population expressed in three main registers: biological (death, disease, infertility), economic (poverty, economic marginalisation) and social (decomposition of the family, marriage). These findings correspond to my informants' universal basic life expectations, expressed in the simple but all-inclusive statement that, *"a full value life is to get married, have a lot of children and live nicely"*.

Bibliography

Adler, A.; Zempléni, A. (1972): *Le bâton de l'Aveugle. Divination, Maladie et Pouvoir chez les Moundang du Tchad.* Paris: Herman.

Aguilar Molina, J. (2006): *The Invention of Child Witches in the Democratic Republic of Congo. Social Cleansing, Religious Commerce and the Difficulties of Being a Parent in an Urban Culture.* London: Save the Children.

Anderson, A. (1995): Challenges and Prospects for Research into African Initiated Churches in Southern Africa. *Missionalia* 23: (3): 283–294.

Appadurai, A. (1996): *Modernity at Large. Cultural Dimension of Globalisation.* Minneapolis: The University of Minnesota Press.

Ashforth, A. (2005): *AIDS, Witchcraft and the Problem of Power in Post-apartheid South Africa.* Chicago: University of Chicago Press.

Augé, M. (1986): L'Anthropologie de la Maladie. *L'Homme* 26: (97): 81–90.

Augé, M. (1982): *Génie du paganisme.* Paris: Gallimard.

Augé, M; Zémpleni, A. (1984): *Le Sens du Mal.* Paris: Editions des Archives Contemporaines.

Auslander, M. (1993): "Open the Wombs!" The Symbolic Politics of Modern Ngoni Witchfinding. In: Comaroff, J.; Comaroff, J. (eds.): *Modernity and its Malcontents. Ritual and Power in the Postcolonial Africa*, pp. 167–192. Chicago: University of Chicago Press.

Austen, A. R. (1993): The Moral Economy of Witchcraft: An Essay in Comparative History. In: Comaroff, J.; Comaroff J. (eds.): Modernity and its Malcontents. Ritual and Power in the Postcolonial Africa, pp. 12–23. Chicago: University of Chicago Press.

Berger, H. S.; Luckman, T. (1967): *The Social Construction of Reality*. Harmondsworth: Penguin.

Bettison, G. D. (1959): *Numerical Data on African Dwellers in Lusaka, Northern Rhodesia*. Livingstone: Rhodes-Livingstone Institute.

Boddy, J. (1989): *Wombs and Alien Spirits. Women, Man and the Zar Cult in Northern Sudan*. University of Wisconsin Press: Milwaukee.

Bond, G. C. (2001): Ancestors and Witches. Explanation and the Ideology of Individual Power in Northern Zambia. In: Bond G. C.; Ciekawy D. M. (eds.): *Witchcraft Dialogues. Anthropological and Philosophical Exchanges*, pp. 131–157. Ohio: Ohio University Center for International Studies.

Bourdieu, P. (1992): *The Logic of Practice*. Stanford: Stanford University Press.

Bourdieu, P. (1977): Cultural Reproduction and Social Reproduction. In: Karabel J.; Halsey A. H. (eds.): *Power and Ideology in Education*, pp. 487–511. New York: Oxford University Press.

Burgess, S. M. (2006): *Encyclopedia of Pentecostal and Charismatic Christianity*. New York/London: Routledge.

Bourguignon, E. (1976): *Possession*. San Francisco: Chandler.

Brain, J. L. (1982): Witchcraft and Development. *African Affairs* 81: (324): 371–384.

Bromley, D. B. (1990): Academic Contributions to Psychological Counselling: A Philosophy of Science for the Study of Individual Cases. *Counselling Psychology Quarterly* 3: (3): 299–300.

Bruijn, M.; Nyamnjohin, F. (2009): *Mobile Phones: The New Talking Drums of Everyday Africa*. Leiden.

Büchner, H. (1980): *Spirits and Power: an Analysis of Shona Cosmology*. Cape Town: Oxford University Press.

Budil, I. (2003) : *Mýtus, jazyk a kulturní antropologie*. Praha: Triton.

Burgess, A.; Dean, R. F. A. (1962): *Malnutrition and Food Habits.* London: Tavistock Publications.

Chabal, P. (2009): *Africa. The Politics of Suffering and Smiling.* South Africa: University of KwaZulu Natal Press.

Chabal, P.; Daloz, J.-P. (1999): *Africa Works. Disorder as Political Instrument.* James Currey Publisher.

Charsley, S. (1992): Dreams in African Churches. In: Jedrej, M. C.; Shaw, R. (eds.): *Dreaming, Religion and Society in Africa,* pp. 153–177. Leiden: Brill.

Charsley, S. R. (1987): Dreams and Purposes: An Analysis of Dream Narratives in an Independent African Church. *Africa* 57: (3): 281–296.

Charsley, S. R. (1973): Dreams in an Independent African Church. *Africa* 43: 224–257.

Cheyeka, A. M. (2008): Towards a History of Charismatic Churches in Postcolonial Zambia. In: Gewald, J.-B.; Hinfelaar, M.; Macola, G. (eds.): *One Zambia, Many Histories. Towards a History of Post-colonial Zambia,* pp. 144–164. Leiden: Brill.

Ciekawy, D. M. (2001): Utsai as Ethical Discourse. A Critique of Power from Mijikenda in Coastal Kenya. In: Bond, G. C.; Ciekawy, D. M. (eds.): *Witchcraft Dialogues. Anthropological and Philosophical Exchanges,* pp. 158–189. Ohio: Ohio University Center for International Studies.

Ciekawy, D.; Geschiere, P. (1998): Containing Witchcraft: Conflicting Scenarios in Postcolonial Africa. *African Studies Review* 41: (3): 1–14.

Clifford, J.; Marcus, G. E. (eds.) (1986): *Writing Culture: the Poetics and Politics of Ethnography.* Berkeley: University of California Press.

Clifford, J. (1988): *The Predicament of Culture: Twentieth-Century Ethnography, Literature and Art.* Cambridge: Harvard University Press.

Colson, E. (2000): The Father as a Witch. *Africa, Journal of International African Institute* 70: (3): 333–358.

Colson, E. (1969): Spirit Possession among the Tonga of Zambia. In: Beattie, J.; Middleton, J. (eds.): *Spirit Mediumship and Society*, pp. 82–85 and 94–96. London: Routledge.

Comaroff, J.; Comaroff, J. (1999a): Alien-Nation: Zombies, Immigrants, and Millennial Capitalism. *Codesria Bulletin* 3: (4): 17–28.

Comaroff, J.; Comaroff, J. (1999b): Occult Economies and the Violence of Abstraction: Notes from the South African Post-Colony. *American Ethnologist* 26: (2): 279–303.

Comaroff, J.; Comaroff J. (1993): Introduction. In: Comaroff, J.; Comaroff, J. (eds.): *Modernity and Its Malcontents. Ritual and Power in the Postcolonial Africa*, pp. 1–25. Chicago: University of Chicago Press.

Comaroff, J. (1985): *Body of Power, Spirit of Resistance: The Culture and History of a South African People*. Chicago: University of Chicago Press.

Comaroff, J. (1980): Healing and the Cultural Order: The Case of the Barolong Boo Ratshidi of Southern Africa. *American Ethnologist* 7: (4): 637–657.

Copper, F. (2005): *Colonialism in Question. Theory, Knowledge, History*. Berkeley and Los Angeles: The University of California Press.

Cornwall, A. (ed.) (2005): *Readings in Gender in Africa*. International African Institute.

Daneel. I. (1974): *Old and New in Southern Shona Independent Churches. Vol. 2, Church Growth: Causative Factors and Recruitment Techniques*. The Hague: Mouton. Daneel, I. (1987): *Quest for Belonging*. Gweru: Mambo Press.

Daneel, I. (1970): *Zionism and Faith Healing in Rhodesia – Aspects of African Independent Churches*. The Hague: Mouton.

de Heusch, L. (1987): Heat, Physiology and Cosmology: Rites de Passage among the Thonga. In: Karp, I.; Charles, S. B. (eds.): *Explorations in African Systems of Thought*, pp. 27–43. Washington DC: Smithsonian Institute.

de Heusch, L. (1962): Culte de Possession et Religions Initiatiques de Salut en Afrique. In: *Religions de Salut*, pp. 127–167. Bruxelles: Université Libre de Bruxelles, Institut de Sociologie.

de Rosny, E. (1992): *Afrique des Guérisons*. Paris: Karthala.

de Sardan, O. J.-P. (1995): La Politique du Terrain. Sur la Production des Données en Anthropologie. *Les Terrains de l'Enquête* 1: 71–109.

Devauges, R. (1974): Croyance et Cérification: Les pratiques Magico-Religieuses en Milieu Urbain Africain. *Cahiers d´Études Africaines* 66 –67 (XVII (2–3)): 299–306.

Devisch, R. (2001): Sorcery Forces of Life and Death among Yaka of Congo. In: Bond, G.; Ciekawy, D. M. (eds.): *Witchcraft Dialogues. Anthropological and Philosophical Exchanges* pp. 101–130. Ohio: Ohio University Center for International Studies.

Devisch, R. (1993): *Weaving the Threads of Life: The Khita Gyn-Eco-Logical Healing Cult among the Yaka*. Chicago: University of Chicago Press.

Devisch, R. (1979): *Perspectives on Mediumistic Divination in Contemporary Subsaharan Africa*. Leiden: Afrika-Studiecentrum.

Dillon-Malone, C. (1988): Mutumwa Nchimi Healers and Wizardry Beliefs in Zambia. *Social Science and Medicine* 26: (11): 1159–1172.

Dillon-Malone, C. (1983a): The Mutumwa Churches of Zambia: An Indigenous African Religious Healing Movement. *Journal of Religion in Africa* 14: (3): 204–222.

Dillon-Malone, C. (1983b): Indigenous Medico-Religious Movement in Zambia: A Study of Nchimi and Mutumwa Churches. *African Social Research* 36: 455–474.

Donald, D. R.; Hlongwane N. M. (1989): Issues in the Integration of Traditional African Healing and Western Counselling in School Psychological Praxis. Three Case studies. *School Psychology International* 10: 243–249.

Douglas, M. (1970): *Natural Symbols: Explorations in Cosmology.* London: Barrie & Rockliff.

Douglas, M. (1966): *Purity and Danger: An Analysis of the Concepts of Pollution and Taboo.* London: Routledge & Kegan Paul.

Drewal, H. J. (2008): *Mami Wata: Arts for Water Spirits in Africa and Its Diasporas.* Los Angeles: University of California Los Angeles.

Durkheim, E. (1965) (c1915): *The Elementary Forms of the Religious Life.* New York: Free Press.

Eisenberg, L. (1977): Disease and illness Distinctions between Professional and Popular Ideas of Sickness. *Culture, Medicine and Psychiatry* 1: (1): 9–23.

Evans-Pritchard, E. E. (1937): *Witchcraft, Oracles and Magic among the Azande.* Oxford: Oxford University Press.

Fabrega, H.; Manning, P. K. (1973): An Integrated Theory of Disease: Ladino-Mestizo. Views of Disease in the Chiapas Highlands. *Psychosomatic Medicine* 35: (3): 223–239.

Fainzang, S. (1995): *Pour une Anthropologie de la Maladie en France. Un Regard Africaniste.* Paris: Editions de l'EHESS.

Fairclough, N. (1992): *Discourse and Social Change.* Cambridge: Polity Press.

Fassin, D. (1992): *Pouvoir et Maladie en Afrique.* Paris: PUF.

Favret-Saada, J. (1977): *Les Mots, la Mort, les Sorts.* Paris: Gallimard.

Ferguson, J. (1999a): *Expectations of Modernity. Myths and Meanings of Urban Life on Zambian Copperbelt.* Berkeley and Los Angeles: University of California Press.

Ferguson, J. (1999b): *Global disconnect. Abjection and the Aftermath of Modernism.* Unpublished paper.

Fernandez, J. W. (1982): *Bwiti: Ethnography of the Religious Imagination in Africa.* Princeton: Princeton University Press.

Fields, K. E. (1985): *Revival and Rebellion in Colonial Central Africa.* Princeton: Princeton University Press.

Fisher, H. J. (1978): Dreams and Conversion in Black Africa. In: Levtzion, N. (ed.): *Conversion to Islam*, pp. 217–235. New York: Holmes and Meier.

Fisiy, F. C.; Geschiere, P. (2001): Witchcraft, Development and Paranoia in Cameroon. In: Moore, H. L.; Sanders, T. (eds.): *Magical Interpretation, Material Realities: Modernity, Witchcraft and the Occult in Postcolonial Africa*, pp. 226-247. Routledge: Oxon.

Fisiy, F. C. (1988): Containing Occult Practices: Witchcraft Trials in Cameroon. *African Studies Review* 41: (3): 143–163.

Foster, G. M. (1976): Disease Aetiologies in Non-Western Medical Systems. *American Anthropologist* 78: (4): 773–782.

Foster, G. M. (1965): Peasant Society and the Image of Limited Good. *American Anthropologist* 67: 293–315.

Frankenberg, R. (1969): Man, Society and Health: Towards the Definition of the Role of Sociology in the Development of Zambian Medicine. *African Social Research* 8: 573–587.

Frankenberg, R.; Leeson, J. (1977): The Patients of Traditional Doctors in Lusaka. *African Social Research* 23: 217–234.

Frankenberg, R.; Leeson, J. (1976): Disease and Sickness: Social Aspects of the Choice of Healers in Lusaka Suburbs. In: Loudon, J. B. (ed.): *Social Anthropology and Medicine*, pp. 573–587. New York: Academic Press.

Frazer, J. (1922): *Golden Bough. Study in Magic and Religion.* New York: Macmillan.

Geertz, C. (1973): *The Interpretation of Cultures.* New York: Basic Books.

Geschiere, P. (2000): Sorcellerie et Modernité: Retour sur une Étrange Complicité. *Politique Africaine* 79: 17–32.

Geschiere, P. (1995): *Sorcellerie et Politique en Afrique. La viande des Autres.* Karthala: Paris.

Gewald, J.-B. (2011): Fears and Fantasies in Northern Rhodesia, 1950–1960. In: Jan-Bart Gewald, Marja Hinfelaar and Giacomo Macola (eds.): *Living the End of Empire: Politics and Society in Late Colonial Zambia*, pp. 207–228. Leiden: Brill.

Gifford, P. (1998): *African Christianity. Its Public Role.* London: Hurst.

Gluckman, M. (1945): Seven-year Research Plan of the Rhodes-Livingstone Institute. Human Problems in British Central Africa. *Rhodes-Livingstone Journal* 4: 1–32.

Good, B. (1984): *Medicine, Racionality and Experience. An Anthropological Perspective.* Cambridge: Cambridge University Press.

Good, B. (1977): The Heart of What's the Matter. The Semantics of Illness in Iran. *Culture, Medicine and Psychiatry* 1: 25–58.

Gupta, A.; Ferguson, J. (1992): Beyond Culture: Space, Identity and the Politics of Difference. *Cultural Anthropology* 7: (1): 6–23.

Hahn, R. A. (ed.) (1995): *Sickness and Healing. An Anthropological Perspective.* New Heaven and London: Yale University Press.

Hammond-Tooke, W. D. (1974): The Cape Nguni Witch-familiar as a Mediatory Construct. *Man* 9: (1): 25–39.

Hansen, T. K. (2008): The Informalisation of Lusaka's Economy: Regime Change, Ultra Modern Markets and Street Vending, 1972–2004. In: Gewald, J.-B.; Hinfelaar, M.; Macola, G. (eds.): *One Zambia, Many Histories*, pp. 213–239. Leiden: Brill.

Hansen, T. K. (2005): Getting Stuck in the Compound: Some Odds against Social Adulthood in Lusaka, Zambia. *Africa Today* 51: (4): 3–16.

Hansen, T. K. (1992): Gender and Housing. The Case of Domestic Service in Lusaka, Zambia. *Journal of International African Institute* 62: (2): 248–265.

Hansen, T. K. (1984): Negotiating Sex and Gender in Urban Zambia. *Journal of Southern African Studies* 10: (2): 219–238.

Hansen, T. K. (1982): Lusaka's Squatters: Past and Present. *African Studies Review* 25: (2/3): 117–136.

Héritier, F. (1985): Le Sperme et le Sang. *Nouvelle Revue de Psychanalyse* 32: 111–122.

Héritier, F. (1979): Symbolique de l'inceste et sa prohibition. In: Izard, M.; Smith, P. (eds.): *La fonction symbolique*, pp. 209 –243 Paris: Gallimard.

Hinfelaar, H. (2004): *History of the Catholic Church in Zambia*. Lusaka: Bookworld Publisher.

Horáková, H. (2011): *Antropologie Moderní Afriky*. Studijní texty. Pardubice: Univerzita Pardubice, Katedra Sociálních Věd.

Horton, R. (1967): African Traditional Thought and Western Science. *Africa* 28: (1): 50–71.

Hulec, O.; Olša, J. (2008): *Dějiny Zimbabwe, Zambie a Malawi*. Praha: Nakladatelství Lidové Noviny.

Janzen, J. M. (1992): *Ngoma: Discourses of Healing in Central and Southern Africa*. Berkley: University of California Press.

Janzen, J. M. (1985): Changing Concepts of African Therapeutics. A Historical Perspective. In: du Toit, B.; Abdala, I. H. (eds.): *African Healing Strategies*, pp. 61–81. New York: Trado-Medic books.

Janzen, J. M. (1981): *The Quest for Therapy in Lower Zaire*. Berkeley: University of California Press.

Jedrej, CH. M.; Show, R. (eds.) (1992): *Dreaming, religion and society in Africa*. Leiden: Brill.

Jonker, C. (2000): The Politics of Therapeutic Ngoma. The Zionist Churches in Urban Zambia. In: van Dijk, R.; Reis, R.; Spierenburg, M. (eds.): *The Quest for Fruition through Ngoma: Political Aspects of Healing in Southern Africa*, pp. 117–131. Oxford: James Currey.

Jules-Rosette, B. (1981): *Symbols of Change. Urban Transition in Urban Community.* London: Ablex.

Jules-Rosette, B. (1978): The Veil of Objectivity: Prophecy, Divination, and Social Inquiry. *American Anthropologist*, New Series 80: (3): 549–570.

Jules-Rosette, B. (1975): Song and Spirit: The Use of Songs in the Management of Ritual Contexts. *Africa* 45: (2): 150–165.

Kambou, S. D.; Shaw, M. K.; Gladys N.; Nkhama, G. (1998): For a Pencil: Sex and Adolescence in Peri-Urban Lusaka. In: Guijt, I.; Shaw, M. K. (eds.): *The Myth of Community: Gender Issues in Participatory Development*, pp. 110–120. London: Intermediate Technology Publications.

Kandert, J. (2009): *Podoby duchů a předků v Západní Africe.* http://www.antropologie.zcu.cz/clanek/podoby-duchu-a-predku-v-zapadni-africe (retrieved 26. 7. 2009).

Kaspin, D. (1996): A Chewa Cosmology of the Body. *American Ethnologist* 23: (3): 561–578.

Kaspin, D. (1993): Chewa Visions and Revisions of Power: Transformation of the Nyau Dance in Central Malawi. In: Comaroff, J.; Comaroff, J. (eds.): *Modernity and Its Malcontents. Ritual and Power in the Postcolonial Africa*, pp. 34–57. Chicago: University of Chicago Press.

Kay, G. (1967): *Social Geography of Zambia.* London: University of London Press.

Keller, B. (1978): Marriage and Medicine: Women's Search for Love and Luck. *African Social Research* 26: 489–505.

Kiernan, J. P. (1990): The Canticles of Zion. Song as Word and Action in Zulu Zionist Discourse. *Journal of Religion in Africa* 20 (2): 188–204.

Kiernan, J. P. (1985): The Social Stuff of Revelation: Pattern and Purpose in Zionist Dreams and Visions. *Africa* 55: 304–318.

Kiernan, J. P. (1976a): Prophet and Preacher. An Essential Partnership in the Work of Zion. *Man*, New Series 11: (3): 356–366.

Kiernan, J. P. (1976b): The Work of Zion: an Analysis of a Zulu Zionist Ritual. *Africa* 46: (4): 340–356.

Kirsch, T. G. (2002): Performance and the Negotiation of Charismatic Authority in an African Indigenous Church in Zambia. *Paideuma* 48: 57–76.

Kleinman, A. (1995): *Writing at the Margin. Discourse between Anthropology and Medicine*. Berkeley: University of California Press.

Kleinman, A. (1980): *Patients and Healers in the Context of Culture. An Exploration of the Boarders between Anthropology, Medicine and Psychiatry*. Barkley: University of California Press.

Kramer, F. (1993): *The Red Fez. Art and Spirit Possession in Africa*. London: Verso.

Lambeck, M. (1993): *Knowledge and Practice in Mayotte. Local Discourse of Islam, Sorcery and Spirit Possession*. Toronto: University of Toronto Press.

Laplantine, F. (1993): *Anthropologie de la M aladie*. Paris: Payot.

Larson, L. E. (1973): *Witchcraft Eradication Sequences Among the People of the Ulanga District, Tanzania*. Dar es Salaam: University of Dar es Salaam, History Research Center.

Last, M. (1976): The Presentation of Sickness in a Community of Non-Muslim Hausa. In: Loudon, J. B. (ed.): *Social Anthropology and Medicine*, pp. 104–149. London and New York: Academic Press.

Last, M.; Chavunduka, G. L. (1986): *The Professionalization of African Medicine*. Manchester: Manchester University Press and International African Institute.

Lévi-Bruhl, L. (1923): *Primitive Mentality*. London: Allen & Unwin.

Lévi-Strauss, C. (1976): *Structural anthropology*. Chicago: Chicago University Press.

Lévi-Strauss, C. (1966): *The Savage Mind*. Chicago: University of Chicago Press.

Lévi-Strauss, C. (1963): *Totemism*. London: Beacon Press.

Lewis, I. M. (2009): The Social Roots and Meaning of Trance and Possession. In: Clarke, B. P. (ed.): *The Oxford Handbook of the Sociology of Religion*, pp. 375–390. Oxford: University Press.

Lewis, I. M. (1971): *Ecstatic Religion. A Study of Shamanism and Spirit Possession*. London: Routledge.

Lock, M.; Sheper-Hughes, N. (1987): The Mindful Body. A Prolegomenon to Future Work in Medical Anthropology. In: Whitaker, E. D. (ed.): *Health and Healing in Comparative Perspectives*, pp. 296–315. Upper Saddle River: Pearson: Prentice Hall.

Logan, M. H. (1975): Selected References on the Hot–Cold Theory of Disease. *Medical Anthropology Newsletter* 6: (2): 8–14.

Luig, U. (1999): Construction Local Words: Spirit Possession in Gwembe Valey, Zambia. In: Behrend, H.; Luig, U. (eds.): *Spirit Possession, Modernity and Power in Africa*, pp. 124–141. Oxford: James Currey Publishers.

Malina, J. a kol. (ed.) (2009): Antropologický Slovník. Brno: CERM.

Marcus, E. G. (1994): On Ideologies of Reflexivity in Contemporary Efforts to Remake the Human Sciences. *Poetics Today* 15: (3): 383–404.

Marie, A. (1997): Avatars de la Dette Communautaire. Crise des Solidarités, Sorcellerie et Proces d'Individualisation. In: Marie, A. (ed.): *Afrique des individus*, pp. 249–327. Paris: Karthala.

Marwick, M. G. (1965): *Sorcery in its Social Setting: A Study of the Northern Rhodesian Chewa*. Manchester: Manchester University Press.

Marwick, M. G. (1950a): Another Modern Anti-witchcraft Movement in East Central Africa. *Africa* 20: (2): 100–112.

Marwick, M. G. (1950b): The Bwanali-Mpulutmutsi antiwitchcraft movement. In: Marwick, M. G. (ed.): *Witchcraft and Sorcery: Selected readings*. Harmondsworth: Penguin Books.

Mauss, M. (1973) (c1938): Techniques of the Body. *Economy and Society* 2: (1): 70–88.

Mbiti, J. S. (1976): God, Dreams, and African Militancy. In: Pobee, J. (ed.): *Religion in a Pluralistic Society*, pp. 38–47. Leiden: E. J. Brill.

Meyer, B. (1999): *Translating the Devil Religion and Modernity Among the Ewe in Ghana*. Edingurg: Edinburg University Press.

Meyer, B. (1993): If You Are a Devil, You Are a Witch and if You Are a Witch, You Are a Devil: The Integration of Pagan Ideas into Conceptual Universe of Ewe Christians in South-Eastern Ghana. In: Bax, M.; Koster, A. (eds.): *Power and Prayer*, pp. 159–189. Amsterdam: VU University Press.

Middleton, J.; Winter, E. H. (eds.) (1963): *Witchcraft and Sorcery in East Africa*. London: Routledge and Kegan Paul.

Mitchell, J. C. (1965): The Meaning of Misfortune for Urban Africans. In: Fortes, M.; Dieterlin, G. (eds.): *African System of Thought*, pp. 192–203. Oxford: Claredon Press for International African Institute.

Mitchell, J. C. (1956a): *The Yao village. A Study of a Nyasaland Tribe*. Manchester: Manchester University Press.

Mitchell, J. C. (1956b): The Tribes in the Towns. In: Brelsford, W. V. (ed.): *The Tribes of Northern Rhodesia*, pp. 109–120. Lusaka: Government Printer.

Moore, L. H.; Sanders, T. (eds.) (2001): *Magical Interpretations, Material Realities: Modernity, Witchcraft and the Occult in Postcolonial Africa*. London: Routledge.

Mphande, L.; James-Myers, L. (1993): Traditional African Medicine and the Optimal Theory. Universal Insights for Health and Healing. *Journal of Black Psychology* 19: (25): 25–47.

Mulenga, L. CH. (2003): Urban Slums Report: The Case of Zambia, Lusaka. In: *Understanding Slums: Case Studies for the Global Report 2003*. Lusaka.

Mulenga, S.; Campenhout, van B. (2003): Decomposing Poverty Change in Zambia. Growth, Inequality and Population Dynamics. *African Development Review* 20: (2): 284 – 303.

Mullings, L. (1984): *Therapy, Ideology and Social Change*. Barkley: University of California Press.

Muuka, N. G. (1997): Too Rich to Be Poor? A Glimpse of the Poverty Situation in Zambia in the 1990s. *Scandinavian Journal of Development Alternatives and Area Studies* 16: (1): 139–156.

Niehaus, I. (2001a): *Witchcraft, Power and Politics. Exploring the Occult in the South African Lowveld*. South Africa: David Philip Publishers.

Niehaus, I. (2001b): Witchcraft in the New South Africa: From Colonial Superstition to Postcolonial Reality. In: Moore, H. L.; Sanders, T. (eds.): *Magical Interpretation, Material Realities: Modernity, Witchcraft and the Occult in Postcolonial Africa*, pp. 184–205. Routledge: Oxon.

Niehaus, I. (1993): Witch-Hunting and Political Legitimacy: Continuity and Change in Green Valley, Lebowa 1930–91. *Africa* 64: (3): 498–529.

Oakely, A. (2005): *The Ann Oakley Reader: Gender, Women and Social Science*. Bristol: Policy Press.

Ogura, M. (1991): Rural-Urban Migration in Zambia and Migrant Ties to Home Villages. *Developing Economies* 29: (2): 145–165.

Ojo, M. A. (1988): The Contextualisation and the Significance of the Charismatic Movement in Independent Nigeria. *Africa* 58: 175–190.

Oosthuizen, G. C. (1991a): *The Healer-Prophet in Afro-Christian Churches*. Leiden: E. J. Brill.

Oosthuizen, G. C. (1991b): Indigenous Healing within the Context of the African Independent Churches. In: Oosthuizen, G. C. (ed.): *Afro-Christian Religion and Healing in Southern Africa*, pp. 73–90. New York: The Edwin Mellen Press.

Otto, R. (1958): *The Idea of Holy*. Oxford: Oxford University Press (2 edition).

Parish, J. (2000): From the Body to the Wallet: Conceptualizing Akan Witchcraft at Home and Abroad. *J. Royal Anthropological Institute* (N. S.) 6: 487–500.

Parrinder, E. G. S. (1969): *Religion in Africa*. Harmondsworth: Penguin Books.

Patton, M. Q. (1990): *Qualitative Evaluation and Research Methods*. London: Sage.

Pfeifer, J. (2006): Money, Modernity, and Morality: Traditional Healing and Expansion of the Holy Spirit in Mozambique. In: Luedke, T. J.; West, H. G. (eds.): *Borders & Healers. Brokering Therapeutic Resources in Southeast Africa*, pp. 81–100. Bloomington: Indiana University Press.

Redfield, R. (1960): *The Little Community and Peasant Society and Culture*. Chicago: University of Chicago Press.

Redfield, R. (1952): The Primitive World View. *Proceedings of the American Philosophical Society* 96: 30–36.

Redmayne, A. (1970): Chikanga: an African Diviner with an International Reputation. In: Douglas, M. (ed.): *Witchcraft Confession and Accusation*, pp. 103–128. London: Tavistock.

Reynolds, P. (1992): Dreams and the Constitution of Self among the Zezuru. In: Jedrej, M. C.; Shaw, R. (eds.): *Dreaming, Religion and Society in Africa*, pp. 21–36. Leiden: Brill.

Řezáčová, V. (2011): *Not So Traditional Healing: Constructions of Illness reality and Spirit Possession in a Rapidly Changing Society in Venda, South Africa*. Prague: The Charles University in Prague. Unpublished Dissertation.

Řezáčová, V. (2007): Healing and the Problem of Resistance. The Case of Spirit Possession in the Venda-speaking Region of South Africa. In: Machalík, T.; Záhořík, J. (eds.): *Viva Africa: Proceedings of the Second International Conference on African Studies*, pp. 107–112. Pilsen: Dryada.

Richards, A. I. (1935): A Modern Movement of Witch-finders. *Africa* 8: 448–461.

Roberts, A. (1972): *The Lumpa Church of Alice Lenshina*. Lusaka: Oxford University Press.

Rowlands, M.; Warnier, J.-P. (1996): Witchcraft, Modernity and the Person: The morality of Accumulation in Central Malawi. *Critique of Anthropology* 16: 257–279.

Sanjek, R. (ed.) (1990): *Fieldnotes: the Makings of Anthropology*. Ithaca: Cornell University Press.

Schmitt, J.-C. (1994): *Les Revenants: Les Vivants et les Morts Dans la Société Médiévale*. Paris: Gallimard.

Schoffeleers, M. (1994): Christ in African Folk Theology: The Nganga Paradigm. In: Blakely, T. D.; van Dijk, W. E. A.; Thomson, D. L. (eds.): *Religion in Africa. Experience & Expression*, pp. 73–88. London: James Currey.

Schoffeleers, M. (1978): *Guardians of the Land. Essays on Central African Territorial Cults*. Gwello: Mambo Press.

Scotch, N. (1963): Medical Anthropology. In: Siegel, B. J. (ed.): *Stanford CA Biennial Review of Anthropology*. Stanford: Stanford University Press.

Sembereka, G. (1996): The Place of Gule Wamkulu in Dreams Attributed to Spirits, Nominal Reincarnation and Spirit Possession: The Nankumba Experience. The *Society of Malawi Journal* 49: (1): 1–32.

Shoko, T. (2007): Karanga Religious Perception of Health and Well-being. *Journal for the Study of Religion* 20: (1): 31–41.

Sindzingre, N. (1995): The Anthropology of Misfortune and Cognitive Science. Examples from the Ivory Coast Senufo. *Science in Context* 8: 509–529.

Sindzingre, N.; Zempleni, A. (1981): Modele et Pragmatique Activation et Répétition. Réflexion sur la Causalité de la Maladie chez les Senoufo de Côte d'Ivoire. *Social Science Medicine* 15: 279–293.

Spradley, J. P. (1990): *Participant Observation*. New York: Holt, Rinehart and Wilson.

Spradley, J. P. (1989): *The Ethnographic Interview*. New York: Holt, Rinehart and Wilson.

Stake, R. E. (1995): *The Art of Case Study Research*. London: Sage.

Stoller, P. (1995): *Embodying Colonial Memories: Spirit Possession, Power and the Hauka in West Africa*. London: Routledge.

Sugishita, K. (2009): Traditional Medicine, Biomedicine and Christianity in Modern Zambia. In: *Africa. International African Institute* 79: (3): 435–454.

Sundkler, B. (1961): *Bantu Prophets in South Africa*. London: Oxford University Press.

Taylor, Ch. C. (2012): Sacrifice as Terror: The Rwandan Genocide of 1994. In: Grinker, R. R;

Lubkemann, S. C.; Steiner, C. B. (eds.): *Perspectives on Africa. A Reader in Culture, History and Representation*, pp. 555–569. Oxford: Willey-Blackwell.

Tempels, P. (1969): *Bantu Philosophy*. Paris: Présence Africaine.

Ter Haar, G.; Ellis, S. (1988): Spirit Possession and Healing in Modern Zambia. An Analysis of Letters to Archbishop Milingo. *African Affaires* 87: (357): 185–206.

Tonda, J. (2001): Le Syndrome du Prophète: Médicines Africaines et Précarités Identitaires. *Cahier d'Études Africaines* 161: (XLI 1): 139–162.

Turner, V. W. (1970): *The Forest of Symbols: Aspects of Ndembu Ritual*. Ithaca N. Y.: Cornell University Press.

Turner, V. W. (1969): *The Ritual Process. Structure and Anti-structure.* London: Routledge & Kegan Paul.

Turner, V. W. (1968): *The Drums of Affliction.* Oxford: Clanderon Press.

Turner, V. W. (1964): Witchcraft and Sorcery: Taxonomy versus Dynamics. *Africa* 34: (4): 314–325.

Turner, V. W. (1957): *Schism and Continuity in an African Society: A Study of Ndembu Village Life.* Manchester: Manchester University Press.

van Binsbergen (2006): Religious Change in Zambia. In: Morris, B. (ed.): *Religion and Anthropology. A Critical Introduction,* pp. 164–177. Cambridge: Cambridge University Press.

van Binsbergen, W. M. J. (1981): *Religious Change in Zambia. Exploratory Studies.* London: Kegan Paul International.

van Binsbergen, W. M. J.; van Dijk, R.; Gewald, J.-B. (2003): Situating Globality: African Agency in the Appropriation of Global Culture. An Introduction. In: van Binsbergen, W. M. J.; van Dijk, R.; Gewald, J.-B. (eds.): *Situating Globality: African Agency in the Appropriation of Global Culture. An Introduction,* pp. 3–56. Leiden: Brill.

van Dijk, R. A. (1995): Fundamentalism and its Moral Geography in Malawi. The Representation of the Diasporic and the Diabolical. *Critique of Anthropology* 15: (2): 171–191.

van Gennep, A. (1960): *The rites of passage.* London: Routledge de Kegan Paul Lid.

Ven, J. a ven Der (1989): Theodicy or Cosmodicy: a False Dilemma? *Journal of Empirical Theology* 2: (1): 5–27.

Vidal, L. (1988): Possession et Sorcellerie. *Cahiers d'Études Africaines* 111–112: (XXVIII – 34): 541–542.

Waite, G. (1992): Public Health in Pre-colonial East-Central Africa. In: Feierman, J.; Janzen, J. M. (eds.): *The Social Basis of Health and Healing in Africa,* pp. 212–234. California: University of California Press.

Weber, M. (1968) (c1921): *Economy and Society. An Outline of Interpretative Sociology.* N. J.: Bedminster Press.

Werbner, R. P. (1989): *Ritual passage, Sacred Journey: the Process and Organization of Religious Movement.* Washington, D. C.: Smithsonian Institution Press.

West, H. G.; Luedke T. J. (2006): Introduction. Healing Divides. Therapeutic Border Work in Southeast Africa. In: West, H. G.; Luedke T. J. (eds.): *Borders & Healers. Brokering Therapeutic Resources in Southeast Africa*, pp. 1–21. Bloomington: Indiana University Press.

Westerlund, D. (1989): Pluralism and Change. A Comparative and Historical Approach to African Disease Aetiologies. In: Jacobson-Widding, A.; Westerlund, D. (eds): *Culture, Experience and Pluralism. Essays on African Ideas of Illness and Healing*, pp. 177–218. Uppsala: Department of Cultural Anthropology.

Whyte, S. R. (1989): Anthropological Approaches to African Misfortune. From Religion to Medicine. In: In: Jacobson-Widding, A.; Westerlund, D. (eds.): *Culture, Experience and Pluralism. Essays on African Ideas of Illness and Healing*, pp. 289–301. Uppsala: Department of Cultural Anthropology.

Whyte, S. R. (1981): Men, Women and Misfortune in Bunyole. *Man*, New Series 16: (3): 350–366.

Willis, R. G. (1999): *Some Spirits Heal, Others Only Dance: A Journey into Human Selfhood in an African Village.* Oxford: Berg Publishers.

Willis, R. G. (1968): Kamchape: An Anti-Sorcery Movement in the South-West Tanzania. *Africa* 30: (1): 1–15.

Wilson, M. (1951): Witch-Beliefs and Social Structure. *American Journal of Sociology* 56: (4): 307–313.

Young, N. (1982): Anthropologies of Illness and Sickness. *Annual Review of Anthropology* 11: 257–289.

Zempléni, A. (1982): Ancien et Nouveaux Usages Sociaux de la Maladie en Afrique. *Archives des Science Socials des Religions* 54: (1): 5–19.

The Sources

Central Statistical Office (2011): *Living Conditions Monitoring Survey Report 2006–2010*. Lusaka: CSO.

Central Statistical Office (2009a): *Zambia Demographic and Health Survey 2007*. Lusaka: CSO, Ministry of Health.

Central Statistical Office (2009b): *Living Conditions, Poverty in Zambia 1991 – 2006*. Lusaka: CSO.

Central Statistical Office (2001): *Census of Population and Housing*. Lusaka: CSO.

Central Statistical Office (1994): *The Social Dimensions of Adjustment Priority Survey I*. Lusaka: CSO.

International Labour Office (2008): *Investigation Forced Labour and Trafficking in Zambia*. Lusaka: International Labour Office.

Registrar of Societies (2004): *The Church Constitution of the New Jesus Disciples Church* Lusaka: Registrar of Societies.

Republic of Zambia (2010): *National Health Strategic Plan 2011–2015*. Lusaka: Ministry of Health.

Republic of Zambia (1995): Witchcraft Act. In: *Penal Code,* Chapter 90. Lusaka: Government Printers.

Traditional Health Practitioners Association of Zambia (2001): *Constitution. Code of Ethics. Policy Guidelines*. Lusaka: Traditional Health Practitioners Association of Zambia.

World Health Organisation (2006): *Constitution of the World Health Organization – Basic Documents, 44. Edition, Supplement*. Geneva: WHO.

World Health Organisation (2001): *Legal Status of Traditional Medicine and Complementary/Alternative Medicine. A Worldwide Review*. Geneva: WHO.

From Where Does the Bad Wind Blow? 269

United Nations Development Programme (2010): *Human Development Report 2010*. New York: UNDP.

The Newspapers

Times of Zambia. November 21, 2006: *Court Jails Witch-finder for Causing Man's Death*, p. 2.

Times of Zambia. June 1, 2007: *Copperbelt Museum, Cultural Services Confiscate "Magical Plane"*, p. 3.

Times of Zambia. September 27, 2007: *Kitwe Shocker*, p. 1.

Times of Zambia. November 22, 2007: *Copperbelt Tortoise Shocker*, p. 6.

Sunday Mail. November 5, 2008: *Love charms*, p. 2.

The Internet Sources

http://www.henriettesherbal.com/eclectic/usdisp/erythrophleum.html (retrieved 20. 10. 2009)

http://www.humantrafficking.org/updates/448 (retrieved 30. 9. 2009)

http://www.moh.gov.zm/docs/nhsp.pdf (retrieved 1. 10. 2014)

http://www.state.gov/g/tip/rls/tiprpt/2008/105389.htm (retrieved 30. 9. 2009)

http://ww.o-bible.com

http://www.britannica.com

http: www.chichewadictionary.org

http://hdr.undp.org/en

http://www.indexmundi.com

http://www.populationmondiale.com

http://www.thefeedictionary.com

https://en.wikipedia.org

Appendix I: Additional Illustrative Witchcraft Cases

Witchcraft case 5: Anna, Iris and Catherine

Anna is a 45 year old mother of six children who lives in the Ngombe compound in Lusaka in a house together with four of her children. Her husband died in 2005 and she has not married again. She works as cleaning woman at the swimming pool in the centre of Lusaka. She used to go to the Zion church in the Ngombe compound and she believes to be possessed by the *muzimu* (Christian spirit) of Maria and Moses. At the same time Anna claims to have ancestral spirit that she inherited from her elder sister who was a spiritual healer and died some years ago. Because the doctrine of the Zion church does not acknowledge *mashabe* spirits, Anna keeps them concealed. As she has not passed *ngoma* ceremony, her spirit remains "inactive". As a result she does not use them for protection or healing. However, she claimed to be able *"to feel as if witchcraft is around because the spirit starts to manifest itself – like electricity in my heart"*. Apart from Anna, other family members have *mashabe* spirits as well.

I met Anna's family in January 2009 through Doctor Mukanda. In that time Anna had been suffering from advanced herpes for almost two years. She had festering blisters all over her waist. At the beginning she used to visit the University Teaching Hospital in Lusaka (UTH) where she received some injections. However, the problem continued to persist. Anna also visited several healers where she was told that, *"there is something at her place"*, meaning there was a witchcraft object in her house. Nevertheless *"these small ng'angas were too scared to come to her house and get rid of those magical objects"* she added. She also tried to find help at several church congregations such as the Zion Church of which she was a member, but every time she had a meeting with a pastor he did not come. As a result, she decided to visit "Go centre church" and undergo the overnight prayers as well as receive blessings. But neither there, she didn't see any progress. Following the advice of her friend from Kalingalinga compound whose daughter Gertrude was healed of witchcraft by Doctor Mukanda, she went to consult him with her problem as well.

The first healing session I assisted in consisted of mediumistic divination and purgatory healing procedures. Anna was told that her problem and problems of her grand-daughter Catherine (11 years old) were related because caused by witchcraft, in particular by a magical object planted in her house. She was advised to come again together with Catherine and Iris (Catherine's mother) and undergo the cleansing house ritual (*kutchotsaziwanda*).

Iris (24 years old), the daughter of Anna and her first born child Catherine both figure prominently in the whole case. Iris[1] told me that Catherine had been suffering from a stomach-ache since she was two years old. First she brought her to the hospital where they were told that Catherine was suffering from ulcers and they were given pills. Anna who received a sign from her *mashabe* spirits, that Catherine was not ill from natural causes, forbade Iris returning to the hospital. Instead she arranged consultations with several *ng'anga*s (within three years they tried eight). I was informed that Catherine was given *ngezo* medicine and vomited "human fingers and nails". One day after she collapsed and was transported to a private clinic in Kabulonga (wealthy neighbourhood in Lusaka) where Iris worked as a maid in the house of a white businessman who also arranged Catherine's hospitalization. However it was too late – a medical doctor after having ineffectually tried to resuscitate her certified that a death had occurred. Anna ignored doctor's instruction to wait for an ambulance and transport Catherine to the mortuary and decided to take Catherine immediately to *ng'anga*.

The healer named Chezera, was known by Anna as someone who is able to bring back people to life by means of special anti-witchcraft medicine applied into the nose. Astonishingly Catherine's life was saved by this medicine. Doctor Chezera diagnosed through means of divination with mirrors that *"there are some people jealous about Catherine's beauty"*. The Doctor Chezera also confirmed Anna's suspicion that they both were victims of witchcraft from the side of parents of Iris's ex boyfriend.

---

[1] Iris rents a house in Kalingalinga compound where she lives with her 3 children and husband who she has got married recently. Her younger sister Catherine and her children live in the same house too. Iris works as a made at Kabulonga (wealthy neighbourhood next to Kalingalinga).

Anna was then convinced about the truthfulness of the divination because, as she said she personally *"saw face to face those witches"* during Doctor Chezera's "screening" divination because she also took the visionary medicine *mwavi*.

By interviewing Iris I found out that the relationship between her family and the family of her ex-boyfriend Samuel[2] was tense because of Catherine who had been the object of disputation for years. Iris became pregnant with Samuel when she was still attending secondary school and therefore she could not get married. Samuel's family however refused to pay compensation to Iris family but staked a claim to the child. Iris and Anna both refused to give them Catherine, but after several quarrels they finally consented to leave Catherine in trust with her father for several days. Samuel took Catherine to Tanzania without telling Iris about his plans and did not bring the child back as agreed and did not answer her calls. Iris decided to go to the central police at Lusaka and file a complaint. Due to police corruption nothing could have happened without paying a big amount of money. She thus paid and received her daughter back. Soon afterwards Samuel received summons. From that time Catherine started suffering again from severe stomach-ache accompanied by nightmares and hallucinations. *"She is sleeping in the sitting room and starts screaming in the middle of the night, 'mum mum' I saw some old women sitting next to me and when I switched on the light there was no one"*, Iris recollects. She was convinced that all of Samuel's family, in particular those living in Tanzania, are witches because of their growing business and wealth they possess. Doctor Mukanda shared the same opinion convinced that Catherine was bewitched in Tanzania by powerful *chizimba* made of the heart of a sheep. At the same time she was fed by the meat of dead people in her dreams so that now *"things growing in her stomach and make her suffering"*. After the "cleansing house ritual" during which a *chitumwa*, magical object in the form of horn, was destroyed, Anna and Catherine were given *mankhwala ya kusamba* "medicine to cleanse" and were told to come back with a sheep that had to be sacrificed for Catherine near the river.

---

[2] Samuel's parents live in the same compound as Anna, they make thein living as farmers.

During another divination séance that I assisted in, the spirit of Doctor Mukanda´s grandfather instructed the people gathered: *"The heart of the sheep has to be mixed a chicken and other medicine and she* [Catherine] *has to drink it so that things in her stomach die and she will be protected."* After all these therapeutic procedures the health condition of both Anna and Catherine significantly improved. Anna's herpes subsequently visibly disappeared, and Catherine, according to her mother, *"feels much better now then ever before"*. At the time of my departure they were still taking medicine to bathe and drink as prescribed by Doctor Mukanda.

Witchcraft case 6: Rebecca and Hope

1. General information about the patient

Patient's name: Hope and her mother Rebecca
Sex: female
Age: Hope – 12 year old, Rebecca – 45 year old
Tribe: Nsenga
Religion: the Croma Catholic Church
Status: Rebecca is divorced, Hope is single.
Children: Rebecca has six children (three boys and three girls).
Residence: Chingilisano compound (Lusaka province)
Household pattern: Rebecca lives alone with her children.
Occupation: Rebecca sells vegetables and *capenta* (fish) at the market in the George Compound.

2. Aspects of affliction

Duration: two years
Symptoms: the patient Hope cannot speak properly, runs away from house, eats a glass and her faeces, she has bad dreams as well.
Specification: Hope has got problems with her speech since she was a child. The Hope's mother claims that *"her voice is tied up because of witchcraft"* coming from the husband side. Hope often dreams about animals chasing her and about a tall man who wants to kill her. Consequently, she runs away from the house, she eats glass and her faeces. Rebecca believes that Hope was bewitched by her father who used to beat her

before he left them to live with another woman. Rebecca has also a suspicion that Hope's paternal grandfather is involved in witchcraft as he lives in Tanzania.
Pt provisional diagnosis: witchcraft in the family

3. Previous medication (chronologically)

Rebecca and Hope consulted four *ngan'gas* in Lusaka where they were told that witchcraft is involved. They also tried a medical hospital at the place where they live. According to Rebecca, they were given pills without any proper examination and told to come back for check up. However, they have not come back as they have no trust in the biomedicine. They have not tried any church consultancy with their problem.

4. Other patient's relatives afflicted

None

5. Social problem

Description: Rebecca used to live with her husband and her children in the George compound in Lusaka. Her husband used to drink and beat her and her children. One year ago, they had a quarrel over the family business affairs. Rebecca told me, "*That day he ran away from us as we quarrelled about our business* (selling small fish capenta). *I sold capenta to one woman on credit because she did not have any money. My husband was so angry, he said, that woman is a problem… Then, he beat me and he was also arrested by the police that day. He made a clear break with us from day to day.*" Since that time, Rebecca's husband does not contribute any money to feed his children and he lives with another woman with whom he used to have a love affair since long time. According to Rebecca, the husband never liked his children, but only the business. Rebecca suspects him and his father (who lives in Chipata) of witchcraft against Hope. She adds, "*Husband's father is jealous and he hates us. He was never interested in my children. When he came to Lusaka it was just for visiting his son.*"

6. Current traditional medication

Reason for current medication: suspicion of witchcraft, ineffective therapy of others *ngan'gas*.
Traditional healer: Lukesha
Duration of medication: two months
Way of diagnosing: divination through mirrors
Diagnosis: witchcraft from Rebecca's husband's side. The witches – Hope's father and grand-father – used Hope's "shadow" by collecting it from the soil to bewitch her. They also tied her voice so that she cannot speak properly.
Therapy: protective medicine to drink and bath
Effect: not observed

Witchcraft case 7: Irene

General information about the patient

Patient's name: Irene
Sex: female
Age: 35
Ethnic origin: father Tonga, mother Bemba
Religion: the Seventh day Adventist
Marital status: married
Children: three
Residence: Kabwe
Household pattern: living together with her children and husband
Occupation: farming cassava together with her husband

2. Aspects of affliction (specified by patient)

Duration: Two years.
Symptoms: bad dreams, two miscarriages after having two children, pain under the ribs, a bad cough, deep depression – "not laughing, not speaking and sitting at home".
Specification: since bad dreams about a monster *ilomba* having sexual intercourse with her had occurred, the patient experienced a miscarriage.

She also dreamt about an old woman with whom she fought over her children and about a very tall person in the forest who carried a coffin and told her, *"you lie down in the coffin so that people can bury you"*. When she woke up she felt sharp pain in her ribs.
The Patient's provisional diagnosis: witchcraft from the husband's family side because of jealousy about the client's business success.

3. Previous medication

a) Biomedical medication
Place: Kabwe main hospital
Duration: one-off
Diagnosis: kidney problems
Therapy: antibiotics
Effects: none

b) Traditional medication
Place: Kabwe
Duration: in two years she visited three herbalists
Diagnosis: only symptomatological – pain in the ribs
Therapy: medicinal herbs for drinking
Effect: temporary relief from pain

c) Christian spiritual healing
None

4. Other patient's relatives afflicted

Specification: the patient's father died suddenly in 2007.
Diagnosis provided by traditional healers: witchcraft (diagnosed by a local witch-finder during the funeral, she was told that her father had been killed by *kalupe* (magical gun).
Biomedical diagnosis: tuberculosis
Relation to the patient's problem: the patient claims that the death of her father is linked to her problems. She has a suspicion that the relatives of her husband are involved in witchcraft.

5. Social problem

Description: parents from Irene's husband side (father, step mothers and the youngest brother) live together in the household and cultivate guava and maize. They live close to Irene and their relations are not good. Irene's husband's family is jealous of their success. In particular, her step mothers complained to her husband that Irene's family has stopped giving them loans. According to Irene they do not work properly, only when a famine is brewing. As a result, they are not able to meet their needs.

6. Current traditional medication

Reason for current medication: the patient believes that her affliction is caused by witchcraft; herbalists and biomedical doctors are not able to find the cause of her illness, they just heal the symptoms.
Traditional healer: witch-finder Lukesha, Lusaka.
Duration of medication: two months, second consultation.
Way of diagnosing: divination through mirrors, patient assisted in the divination séance and took *mwavi* medicine (a visionary medicinal herb).
Diagnosis: witchcraft in the family due to economical tensions. A young kinsman (a wizard) in the family used an *ilomba* to bewitch her, to cause her miscarriage. He is greedy and wants to do Irene's job himself to gain wealth. He is cooperating with other female witches from the family (probably Irene's steps-mothers). They made *ndembo* incisions on her chest to afflict her with respiratory problems.
Therapy: medicinal herb to bathe and drink and to protect patient's house.
Effect: the patient claims to have got rid of the pain in her ribs.

Notes: this medical case was not completed.

Witchcraft case 8: Alice

1. General information about the patient

Patient's name: Alice
Sex: female
Age: 19
Ethnic origin: Bemba
Religion: Apostolic church
Status: single
Children: none
Residence: Mtendere compound, Lusaka
Household pattern: living together with her mother, father and her two brothers
Occupation: student

2. Aspects of affliction (specified by patient)

Duration: three years
Symptoms: persistent headache at the beginning, sharp pain in the eyes, blindness, bad dreams, loss of menstruation.
Specification: at the beginning she experienced a persistent headache and sharp pain in her eyes, within one month she lost her sight. In 2005 she underwent an operation for the removal of a tumour in the UTH hospital in Lusaka. Furthermore, 14 strange dreams occurred in which she dreamt that her uncle (the oldest brother of her father) wanted to kill her with a knife and burn her. She also dreamt about a skeleton and a two metres tall person.
The patient's provisional diagnosis: witchcraft from her patrilateral uncle (the oldest brother of her father). Her family is also convinced that the uncle bewitched her because he needed her blood in order to get promoted in his job as army commandant and to increase his business. According to Alice's mother, *"Alice has good blood for business, because she is very intelligent"*.

3. Previous medication (chronologically)

a) Christian spiritual healing
Place: the Zion Christian church (in the Mtendere compound Lusaka)
Duration: one month
Diagnosis: after she was "prophesied", she was told that *"she had something in her head"* [tumour].
Therapy: herbal treatment and regular praying. She was recommended to go to the hospital by prophets in the church.
Effects: none

b) Western medication
Place: UTG Lusaka
Duration: two months
Diagnosis: brain tumour
Therapy: surgical removal of the tumour
Effects: soon after the operation Alice became completely blind. In hospital she started having bad dreams. As a result her mother took her directly to *ng´angas*.

c) Christian spiritual healing
Place: the Pentecostal church in Lusaka
Duration: two years
Diagnosis: witchcraft (without specification who is a witch)
Therapy: anointing oil rubbed in the eyes and face, overnight prayers, fasting
Effects: None

d) Traditional medication
Place: Lusaka
Duration: she visited four traditional healers within one year
Diagnosis: witchcraft from her father's side
Therapy: herbal concoction to drink to be protected
Effect: relief from pain in the head and eyes

4. Other patient's relatives afflicted

Specification: wife of Alice's uncle is blind as well
Diagnosis provided by traditional healers: none
Biomedical diagnosis: blindness
Relation to the patient's problem: Alice's mother claims that the uncle uses his wife in the same manner as he does with Alice.

5. Social problem

Description: when Alice and her parents used to live in Ndola, they had a good relationship with the uncle and his wife; they lived nearby and helped each other. Alice's father and his brother used to work together. The problems started when they moved to Lusaka. Alice's uncle was promoted in his new job as an army commandant and he promised Alice's mother to lend her money so that she could open a shop. "*Instead of it, he was just blinding us and using us* [bewitching]", said Alice's mother. According to her, the blindness of her daughter is directly linked to the job promotion of the uncle. Alice's family believes that the uncle procured a special medicine from Tanzania to achieve his promotion. They stated that he goes there often to visit his older brother, a reputable witch.

6. Current traditional medication

Reason for current medication: the patient believes that her affliction is caused by witchcraft.
Traditional healer: witch-finder Lukesha, Lusaka
Duration of medication: three months
Way of diagnosing: (a) divination through mirrors, Alice and her mother assisted in the divination séance and took *mwavi* medicine; (b) divination through writing, Alice was given a plain piece of paper by Doctor Lukesha and told to put it under her pillow when she goes to sleep. The name of an alleged witch was revealed on the paper within three days.
Diagnosis: witchcraft comes from Alice's patrilateral uncle. According to Lukesha, another two witches cooperate with the uncle, but they could not be recognised during the divination, because they hide their faces

with masks. The uncle used Alice's footprints and her blood to get a powerful *chizimba* for promotion. With the help of the other two witches he enslaved her soul and uses it to speed up his business.

Therapy: *mankhwala* (medicinal herbs) for bathing eyes, a protective *mankhwala* to drink. Doctor Lukesha removed several objects from the patient's head such as bones, small stones and copper wires by using a cupping horn several times.

Effect: Alice and her mother claim that her health has ameliorated. Alice stopped having bad dreams and started seeing colours and shapes.

Note: this medical case was not completed.

Appendix II: Witchcraft Act

The Laws of Zambia

CHAPTER 90

THE WITCHCRAFT ACT

ARRANGEMENT OF SECTIONS

Section
1. Short title
2. Interpretation
3. Penalty for naming or imputing witchcraft
4. Penalty on professional witch doctors
5. Penalty for professing knowledge of witchcraft
6. Acts constituting witchcraft
7. Employment or solicitation of persons in matters of witchcraft
8. Presence at tests
9. Carrying out advice in matters of witchcraft
10. Deceiving or imposing by means of witchcraft
11. Possessing charms, etc.
12. Penalty on chief or headman encouraging witchcraft
13. Obtaining goods, etc., by false pretences

CHAPTER 90
WITCHCRAFT

5 o/1914
47 o/1948
31 o/1952
47 o/1963
Government Notice 493 o/1964
24 o/1977
26 o/1993
Act No. 13 o/1994

An Act to provide for penalties for the practice of witchcraft; and to provide for matters incidental to or connected therewith.

[9th May, 1914]

1. This Act may be cited as the Witchcraft Act. *Short title*

2. In this Act, unless the context otherwise requires— *Interpretation*

    "act complained of" includes any death, injury, damage, disease or calamity, whether of an accidental or of a tortious character;

    "boiling water test" means the dipping into boiling water of the limbs or any portion of the body of a person;

    "property" includes animals;

    "witchcraft" includes the throwing of bones, the use of charms and any other means, process or device adopted in the practice of witchcraft or sorcery.

3. Whoever— *Penalty for naming or imputing witchcraft*

    (a) names or indicates or accuses or threatens to accuse any person as being a wizard or witch; or

    (b) imputes to any person the use of non-natural means in causing any death, injury, damage or calamity; or

    (c) asserts that any person has, by committing adultery, caused in some non-natural way death, injury, damage or calamity;

shall be liable upon conviction to a fine not exceeding seven hundred and fifty penalty units or to imprisonment with or without hard labour for any term not exceeding one year, or to both:

Provided that this section shall not apply to any person who makes a report to a police officer of or above the rank of Sub Inspector or,

where there is no such police officer, to a District Secretary or an Assistant District Secretary.
(As amended by No. 47 o/1948, No. 31 o/1952, No. 47 o/1963 G.N. No. 493 o/1964), No. 24 of 1977, No. 26 of 1993 and Act No. 13 of 1994)

4. Whoever shall be proved to be by habit or profession a witch doctor or witch finder shall be liable upon conviction to a fine of not more than one thousand five hundred penalty units or to imprisonment with or without hard labour for any term not exceeding two years, or to both. *Penalty on professional witch doctors*

(As amended by No. 47 o/1948, No. 31 o/1952, No. 26 o/1993 and Act No. 13 of 1994)

5. Any person who— *Penalty for professing knowledge of witchcraft*

(a) represents himself as able by supernatural means to cause fear, annoyance, or injury to another in mind, person or property; or

(b) pretends to exercise any kind of supernatural power, witchcraft, sorcery or enchantment calculated to cau; e such fear, annoyance or injury;

shall be liable to a fine of not more than one thousand five hundred penalty units or to imprisonment with or without hard labour for any term not exceeding two years.

(No. 47 o/1948 as amended by Act No. 26 of 1993 and Act No. 13 of 1994)

6. Whoever shall— *Acts constituting witchcraft*

(a) by the exercise of any witchcraft or any non-natural means whatsoever, pretend or attempt to discover where and in what manner any property supposed or alleged to have been stolen or lost may be found or to name or indicate any person as a thief or as the perpetrator of any crime or any other act complained of; or

(b) in the pretence of discovering or in the attemptto discover whether or not any person has committed any crime or any other act complained of, administer or cause to be administered to any person with or without his consent any emetic or purgative or apply or cause to be applied to any person with or without his consent the boiling water test or any other test whatsoever; or

(c) instigate, direct, control or preside at the doing of any act specified in the foregoing part of this section;

shall be liable upon conviction to the punishments provided by section four .

7. Whoever employs or solicits any person—
    (a) to name or indicate any person as being a wizard or witch;
    (b) to name or indicate by means of witchcraft or by the use of any non-natural means or by the administration of any emetic or purgative or by the application of any test whatsoever any person as the perpetrator of any alleged crime or other act complained of;
    (c) to advise him or any person how by means of witchcraft or by the use of any non-natural means or by means of any emetic or purgative or test whatsoever the perpetrator of any alleged crime or other act complained of may be discovered;
    (d) to advise him on any matter or for any purpose whatsoever by means of witchcraft or non-natural means;
shall be liable upon conviction to the punishments provided in section three.

Employment or solicitation of persons in matters of witchcraft

8. Any person who is present at the administration to any person of any test, the administration of which is punishable under the provisions of this Act, shall be liable upon conviction to a fine not exceeding two hundred penalty units or to imprisonment with or without hard labour for any term not exceeding one year, or to both.

Carrying out advice in matters of witchcraft

Provided that no person called as a witness to prove the administration of any test as aforesaid shall be deemed to be an accomplice or to need corroboration as such by reason only that he was present at the administration of any test as aforesaid.

(As amended by No. 31 o/1952, No. 26 o/1993 and Act No. 13 o/1994)

9. Whoever, on the advice of any person pretending to have the knowledge of witchcraft or of any non-natural processes or in the exercise of anywitchcraft or of any non-natural means, shall use or cause to be put into operation such means or processes as he may have been advised or may believe to be calculated to injure any person or any property shall be liable upon conviction to the punishments provided by section four

Deceiving or imposing by means of witchcraft

10. Every person professing to be able to control by non-natural means the course of nature or using any subtle craft, means or device by means of witchcraft, charms or otherwise to deceive or impose upon any other person shall be liable upon conviction to a fine not ex-

ceeding two hundred penalty units or to imprisonment with or without hard labour for any term not exceeding one year, or to both.

(As amended by No, 31 of 1952, No. 26 of 1993 and Act No. 13 of 1994)

11. (1) Any person who collects, makes, sells or uses or assists or takes part in collecting, selling , marking or using any charm or poison or thing which he intends for use Either by himself or by some other person for the purpose of any act punishable by this Act shall be liable upon conviction to a fine not exceeding two hundred penalty units or to imprisonment with or without hard labour for apy term not exceeding one year, or to both. *Possessing charms, etc.*

(2) Any person who has in his possession any charm or poison or thing which he intends for use either by himself or by some · other person for the purpose of any act punishable by this Act shall be liable upon conviction to a fine of not more than one hundred penalty units or to imprisonment with or without hard labour for any term not exceeding six months, or to both.

(3) A person found in possession of anything commonly used for the purpose of an act punishable by this Act shall be deemed to have intended such thing for use for the purpose of an act punishable by this Act unless and until the contrary be proved.

(As amended by No. 31 of 1952, No. 26 of 1993 and Act No. 13 of 1994)

12. Any chief or headman who directly or indirectly permits, promotes, encourages or facilitates the commission of any act punishable by this Act or who knowing of such act or intended act does not forthwith report the same to a police officer of or above the rank of Sub Inspector or, where there is no such police officer, to a District Secretary or an Assistant District Secretary, shall be liable upon conviction to a fine or to imprisonment with or without hard labour for any term not exceeding three years. *Penalty on chief or headman encouraging witchcraft*

(As amended by G.N. No. 493 of 1964, No. 24 of 1977, No. 26 of 1993 and Act No. 13 of 1994)

13. (1) Any person who shall receive or obtain any consideration whatsoever or the promise thereof for or in respect of the doing by such person of any act punishable by this Act shall, if he has actually received such consideration, be deemed guilty of the of- *Obtaining goods, etc., by false pretences*

fence of obtaining by false pretences and, if he has not actually received such consideration but only the promise thereof, be deemed guilty of the offence of attempting to obtain by false pretences and shall be liable upon conviction to punishment accordingly.

(2) Any agreement for the giving of. any consideration for or in respect of the doing of any act punishable by this Act shall be null and void.

REPUBLIC OF ZAMBIA
Copyright Ministry of Legal Affairs,
Government of the Republic of Zambia

Source: The Laws of Zambia

Appendix III: Zambia Statistical Figures and Maps

Statistical Figures about Zambia
(In the time of the research 2008–2009)[1]

Total area: 752 614 km²
Total population: 11.5 (estimate 2007)[2]
Lusaka population: 10.7% of the total population
Average age: 16.8 years
Life expectancy: 38.4 years

HDP: 1400 USD/ per person (estimate 2007)
HDI: 0.453 (low), 164th (estimate 2009)[3]
Incidence of Poverty: Increase from 49% in 1991 to 53% in 2006 Zambia
Unemployment: officially 40% of the total population, 65% "self-employed" in the informal economic sector.

Official language: English
Local languages: Nyanja, Bemba, Lunda, Tonga, Lozi, Luvale, Kaonde.
Literacy: 80.6% (estimate 2003)
Religion: Christianity 75% (Protestant, Roman Catholic, African Independent Churches); Islam 5–10%; Traditional Religion 15%

Independence date: 24. October 1964
Governement: Republic
Presidents: Lévy Mwanawasa (2. 1. 2006 – 19. 8. 2008[†])
Rupiah Banda (2. 11. 2008 – 23. 9. 2011)
Currency: Zambian kwacha (ZMK)

---

[1] Hulec, Olša 2009.
[2] Hulec, Olša 2009.
[3] *Human development indices*. United Nations Development Programme. http://hdr.undp.org/en/media/HDR_2009_EN_Complete.pdf. (Retrieved 05-10-2009).

List of Coumpounds in Lusaka

Bauleni compound (South-West)
Garden compound (North)
George compound (North-West)
Chaisa compound (North)
Chawama compound (South)
Chazanga compound
Chelston compound (North- West)
Chilenje compound (South-west)
Chipata compound (North)
Chunga compound (North-West)
Jack compound
John Howard compound
John Lenge compound (South-West)
Kabanana compound
Kamwala (centre)
Kabwata (centre-East)
Kalingalinga (East)
Kalundu (Nort-East)
Kanyama (West)
Libala (South-West)
Lilanda (North-West)
Mandevu (North)
Marapodi (North)
Matero (North-West)
Mississi (South-West)
Mutendere (East)
Ngombe (North-East)
Woodland (West)
Chibolya (centre)
Chinika (centre)

Geographical Map of Zambia

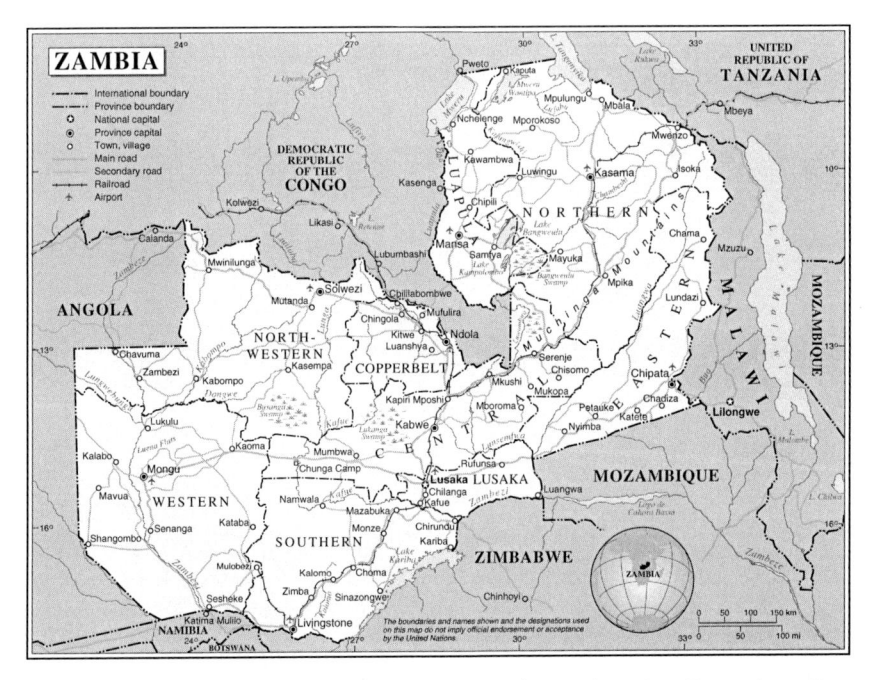

Source: UNITED NATIONS, Department of Peacekeeping Operations Cartographic Section; Map No. 3731 Rev. 4 January 2004.

Map of Lusaka

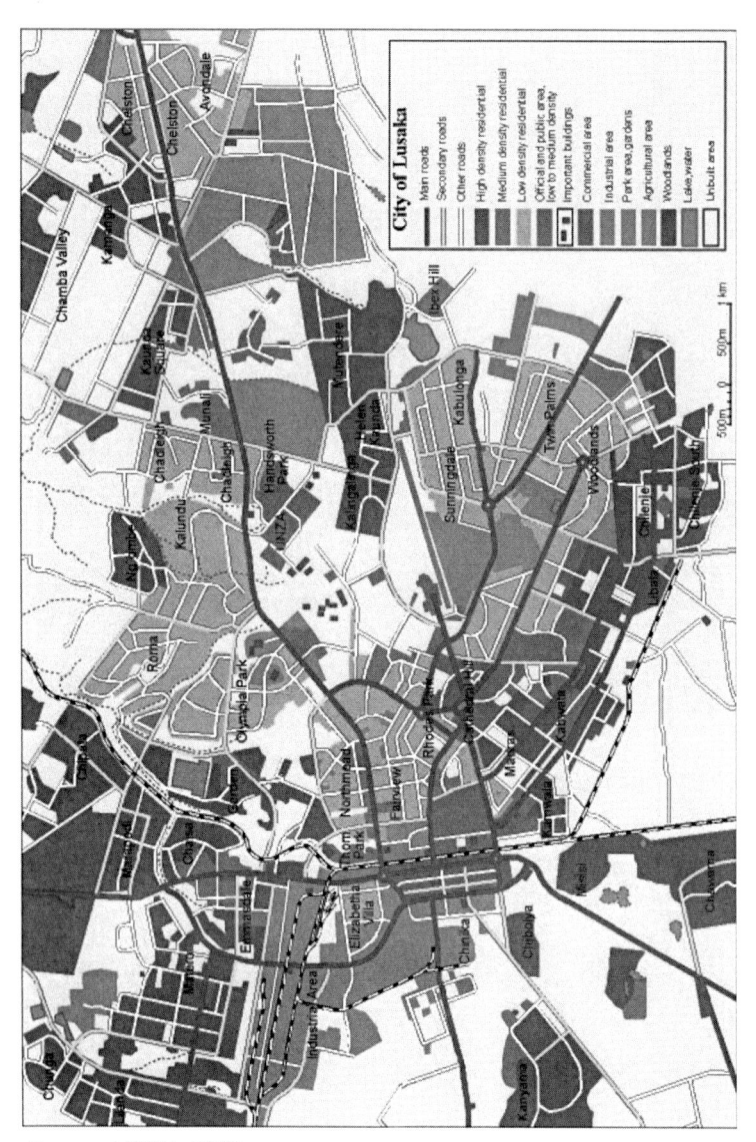

Source: LWZA, 1999.

Appendix IV: Languages Spoken in Zambia

Language of Communication in Lusaka (in percentage)[1]

Bemba	14.5	Luvale	0.2	Nyanja	52.8
Lala	0.2	Lunda	0.2	Mambwe	0.6
Bisa	0.1	Kaonde	0.8	Namwanga	0.4
Lamba	0.2	Nsenga	3.1	Tumbuka	0.9
Tonga	4.6	Lozi	1.4	Senga	0.1
Lenje	0.8	Chewa	2.4	English	6.6
Ila	0.2	Ngoni	1.0	Others	8.8

Total Population: 1,259,258

ChiNyanja Language[2]

Population	803,000 in Zambia (Johnstone and Mandryk 2001). 196,640 Chewa, 256,588 Ngoni, 8,032 Kunda (1969 census).
Region	Eastern and Central provinces.
Language map	Reference number 25
Alternate names	ChiNyanja
Dialects	Chewa (Cewa), Peta (Cipeta, Chipeta, Malawi, Maravi, Marave), Chingoni (Ngoni), Manganja (Waganga), Nyasa, Kunda.
Language use	Official language of police and Zambia regiment. Language of education, administration.
Language development	Taught in primary and secondary schools.

---

[1] *Language and ethnicity.* Available at: www.zamstats.gov.zm, retrieved 10.12.2008

[2] www.ethnologue.com (retrieved in June 2009)

Bemba Language

Population	3,300,000 in Zambia (Johnstone and Mandryk 2001), decreasing. 741,114 Bemba, 32,022 Luunda, 5,190 Shila, 26,429 Tabwa, 16,833 Cishinga, 28,172 Kabende, 6,706 Mukulu, 42,298 Ng'umbo, 14,040 Twa–Unga (1969 census). Population total all countries: 3,602,000.
Region	North, Copperbelt, and Luampula provinces. Also in Botswana, Democratic Republic of the Congo, Malawi.
Language map	Reference number 2
Alternate names	Chibemba, Chiwemba, Ichibemba, Wemba
Dialects	Lembue, Lomotua (Lomotwa), Ngoma, Nwesi, Town Bemba, Luunda (Luapula), Chishinga, Kabende, Mukulu, Ng'umbo, Twa of Bangweulu, Unga. Town Bemba has a Bemba base with heavy code mixing with English and neighbouring Bantu languages
Classification	*Niger–Congo, Atlantic–Congo, Volta–Congo, Benue–Congo, Bantoid, Southern, Narrow Bantu, Central, M, Bemba (M.40)*
Language usage	Language of wider communication. Town Bemba is a widely used lingua franca in urban areas, and has higher social status than other languages except English. Bemba is recognized for educational and administrative purposes. All ages. Positive attitude
Language development	Newspapers. Radio programs. Dictionary. Bible: 1956–1983.
Writing system	Latin script.

Language Map of Zambia

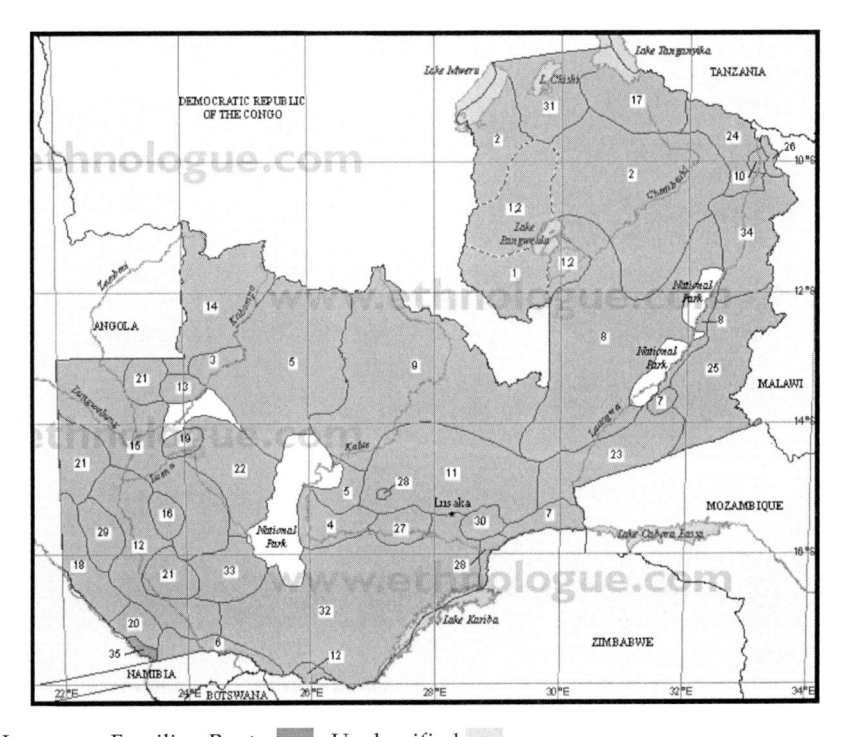

Language Families: Bantu ▨, Unclassified ▨

1 Aushi (3)
2 Bemba (4)
3 Chikwe
5 Kaonde (2)
6 Kuhane
7 Kunda (2)
8 Lala–Bisa (2)
9 Lamba
10 Lambya
11 Lenje
12 Lozi (2)
13 Luchazi
14 Lunda
15 Luvale
16 Luyana
17 Mambwe–Lungu
18 Mashi
19 Mbowe
20 Mbukushu
21 Mbunda (3)
22 Nkoya
23 Nsenga
24 Nyamwanga
25 Nyanja
26 Nyiha
27 Sala
28 Shona (2)
29 Simaa
30 Soli
31 Taabwa
32 Tonga
33 Totela
34 Tumbuka
35 Yauma

National Language: English   Widespread Language: Afrikaans

Notes: 1. White areas are sparsely populated or uninhabited; 2. Dashed lines show overlap of language areas; 3. Brackets show the number of times a language's number appears on map, if more than once.

Source: www.ethnologue.com; © 2009 SIL International

ChiNynanja (Bemba) – English Glossary

bamucapi – cleanser, witch-finder (in Bemba)
Buku laMulungu – the Bible
capenta – small fish
chamukwerera – to hang on
chibalala – ritual rattles for calling spirits
chibere – medicine used by mother to protect her child
chibola – sterility for men
chidyakili – footprint
chikoka – medicine to attract people, love, business
chilansengo – witch-finder in the Mutumwa church (etym. poison collector)
chilubi – toy, voodoo doll
chimba – pelt from leopard used for healing of skin problems (Bemba)
chinyanga – witchcraft magical object in general
chipali – polygamie
chipuku – ghost, revenant
chironda – sore, disease
chisokonezo – confusion
chitambala – headscarf
chitenje – traditional cloth worn by women around the hips as a long skirt
chitumwa – witchcraft magical object in the form of horn
chivanda – see *vivanda*
chizenguzengu – dizziness
chizimba – medicine made from animal stuffed in the horn or in other vessels wrapped in black cloth or in the skin of a python and entangled in the string of colourful mostly red beads
choka – to leave
chubu – tube
chumba – sterility for women
dalitso twa Mulungu – spiritual blessings
demoni – demon
foka (wofoka) – weak
fuaka – cigarette
ilomba – magical snake, a familiar of witch
Itchipingo – the Bible (in Bemba)
jikalangue – plant with thorns used for protection of space against witchcraft
kalilole – magical gun used by a witch
kalindula – popular musical style in southern-central Africa, type of a bass guitar
kalupe – magical airplane used by witches
kamboma – money power oil used for chizimba
kasesema – prophet (in Bemba)
kavundula – magic to separate the couple
kolokofo – white snail, medicine from white snail
kolwe – baboon
kubwina – to dance
kubweza mtendere – to restore peace
kudwala – to be sick
kufoka – weakness
kukamba za musogolo – to prophesize
kukulodza – to bewitch
kukunena – to become possessed by spirit
kuluka – to vomit
kumbiola – strange sound similar to a loud hiccup, one makes it when possess by spirit

kupeza – to find
kuponda pa wanga – to step on bad charm
kupya – hot, hotness
kusamba – to cleanse
kusecha – to search, to prophesize
kusengela – to be used
kusewera ndi wanga – to play with bad charm
kutchinjirizo – to protect
kutchoza ziwanda – the house cleansing ritual
kuvutika – to suffer, to be troubled
kuzondewa – to be heated, to be bewitched
kwasila – I have finished (at the end of the sentence)
lubani – aromatic yellow stone used for protection of space against witchcraft
lukanko – medicine to protect women from adultery
magiki – magic
mahule – prostitute
maloto – dream
maloto oipa – nightmare
mankhwala – herbal medicine
mankhwala ya chinjiriza – protective medicine
mankwala ku mulilo – "fire medicine"
mansalamba – water spirit
manzi – water
mashabe – ancestral spirit
mashamu – bad luck (in Bemba)
matenda – illness
matenda yakubantu – illness coming from people, witchcraft
matulo – "faster asleep", deep dreaming
mavuto – problem

mbojo – herbal medicine from tree called *mbojo*
mbosha – herbal medicine, aromatic fresh leaves used for cleansing body and space from witchcraft
mbuzi – goat
Mchape – witchcraft eradication movement in 1930′s
mchape – witch-finder
mdula – strange disease
mfiti – witch
mkanko – lion
mneneri – prophet
mnunkho – bad smell, the illness
moyo – vital force, life
mpemba – white clay
mpepo – air
mpepo oipa – bad wind, a space regularly visited by witches
mphaso yakwa Mulungu – gift from God
msana ku wava – back ache
mtendere – peace
mtendere mu mtima – peace in the heart
mtengo – tree
mthunzi – shadow, a double soul
muchezo – magical contagion by unintentional contact with a magical object
mugezo – medicine to vomit
muito – love portion
mukunko – witchcraft charm, disease of prolonged periods
mulumiko – cupping horn
munda – field
musanga – friend
musikonezo – confusion
mutototo – stimulating aphrodisiacal medicine for man
mutu ku wava – headache
Mutumwa – prophet-healing church in Zambia

mutumwa – sent by God
muzungu – white man
mwavi – visionary medicine
muzimu woyera – the Holy Spirit
muzimu woyipa – bad spirit
muzimu/ mizimu – spirit/ spirits
napieyne – I am burning (in Bemba)
nchimi – Christian healer (in Tumbuca)
Nchota – name for *mashabe* spirit of lion
ndalama – money
ndalama ya maliro – money for funeral
ndapusitsa – playing tricks
ndembo – tattoos, traditional skin incision where herbal medicine is rubbed.
ndili nchito – to do work
ngan´ga – traditional healer
ngoma – drum, traditional healing ceremony
ngulu – ancestral spirit (in Bemba)
njoka – snake
nkholombe – ritual calabash
nkoli – stick
nsengo – horn
nsima – traditional Zambian food, maize porridge
nyama ya muntu – human meat
nyang´anya – aphrodisiacal medicine for women
nyanja – local language, lingua franca in Lusaka
nyumba – house

ofunta – mad, madness
oipa – bad
pemphera – to pray
pidgika – prophet's divine stick (etym. "the light from Jesus")
propheti – prophet
sandawana – bush rat
sanga luenge – medicine to sneeze
shabinda – hunter (in Bemba)
tchima gamalele – magic train (in Bemba)
tokoloshi – invisible grotesque small being, a witch familiar
tsisi ya muzungu – white man's hairs
tsoka – bad luck
tsopani – now (in Chewa)
tuyobera – invisible grotesque small being, witch familiar
ubatizo – baptism
ufiti – witchcraft
ukukowesha – to be contaminated (in Bemba)
umoyo – health
unga – maize flour
viposo/chiposo – circulating object(s) in the blood
vivanda/chivanda – ghost/ ghosts
wanga – bad charm
zikomo – thank you
zombie – enslaved soul, dead worker
zunguluka – to wander

Appendix V: Photos and Images

1. Healer (Kalingalinga compound, Lusaka)

2. Healer (Chazanga compound, Lusaka)

From Where Does the Bad Wind Blow?   301

3. Healer (Ngombe compound, Lusaka)

4. Healer (Lusaka centrum)

5. Healer with his wife (Mtendere compound, Lusaka)

6. Christian prophet Dereck Kiri
(The New Jesus Disciple Church in the Kuku compound, Lusaka)

7. Pastor
(The New Jesus Disciple Church in the Kuku compound, Lusaka)

306   Appendix V: Photos and Images

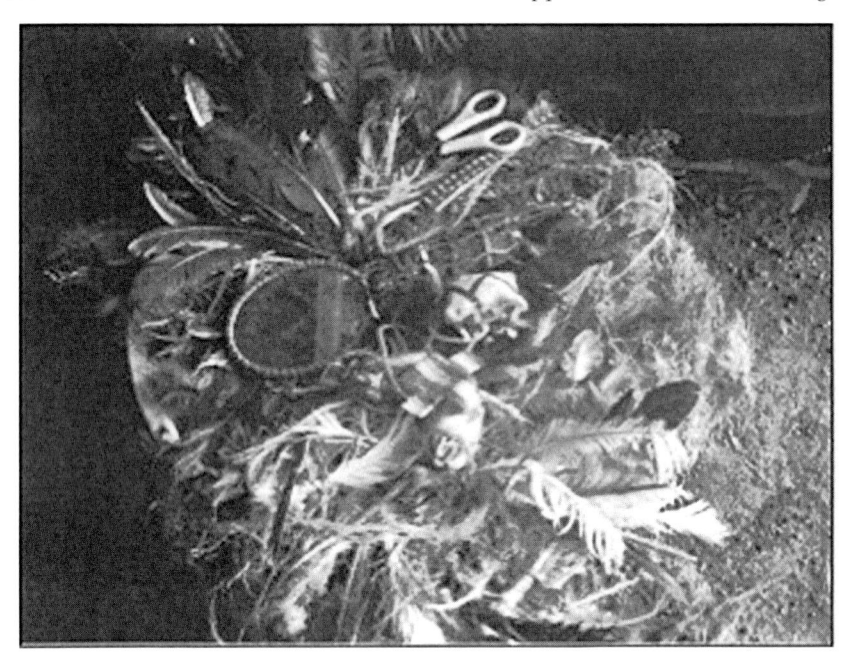

8. Divinatory paraphernalia – "magic mirrors"

From Where Does the Bad Wind Blow?

1. Wodden bird (symbol of the spirit of grand father)
2. Can with unga (as an offering to the spirit)
3. Magical mirror (for divining)
4. White beads (symbol of spirit)
5. Ritual kalebas (for destroying witches at distance)
6 Pelt from tiger (to heal skin rash)

9. Ritual paraphernalia of Doctor Kasanda

10. Mankhwala– medicinal herbs used by traditional healers

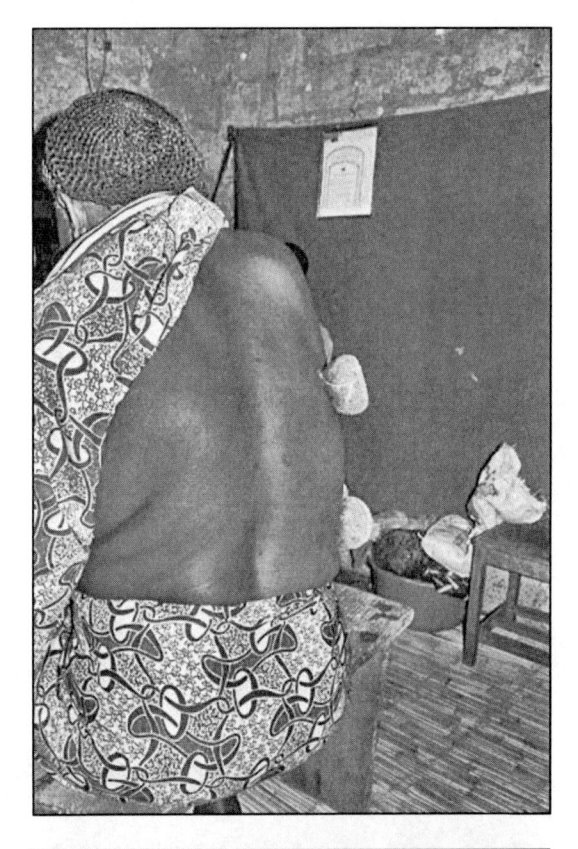

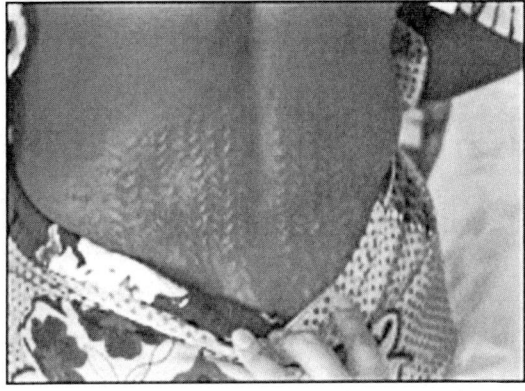

11. Ndembo incisions or "tatoos" – traditional chirurgical method

12. *Mulumiko* cupping horn – traditional chirurgical method
(traditional one – the picture above, modern one – picture below)

13. Prophesying in the Mutumwa Church (Kuku compound, Lusaka)

14. Spiritual healing in the Mutuwa Church
(Kuku compound, Lusaka)

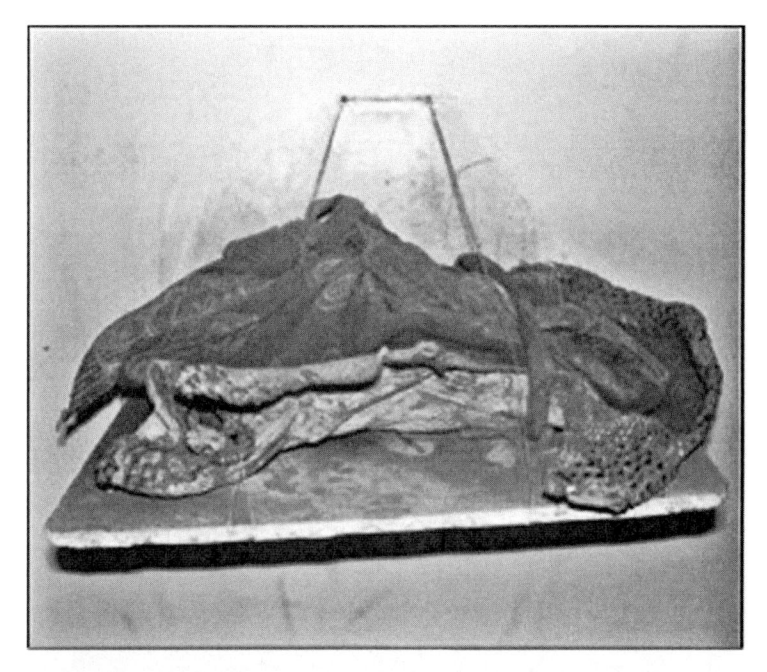

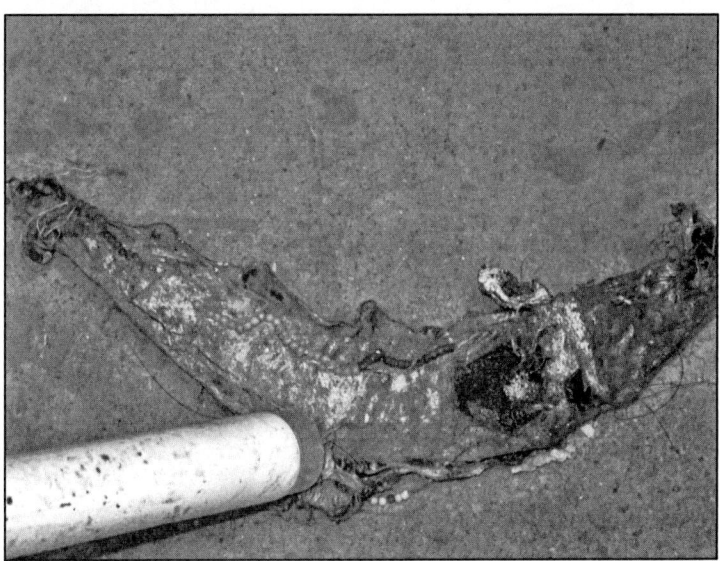

15. Chinyanga, a witchcraft object in the form of chizimba

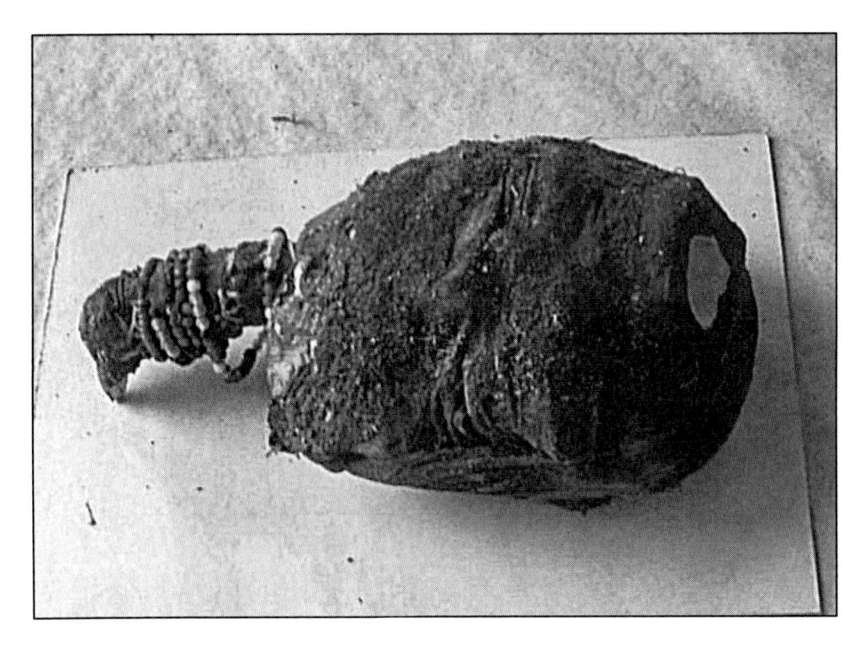

16. *Kalupe* "magical plane" used by witches
(photo from the Livingstone Museum)

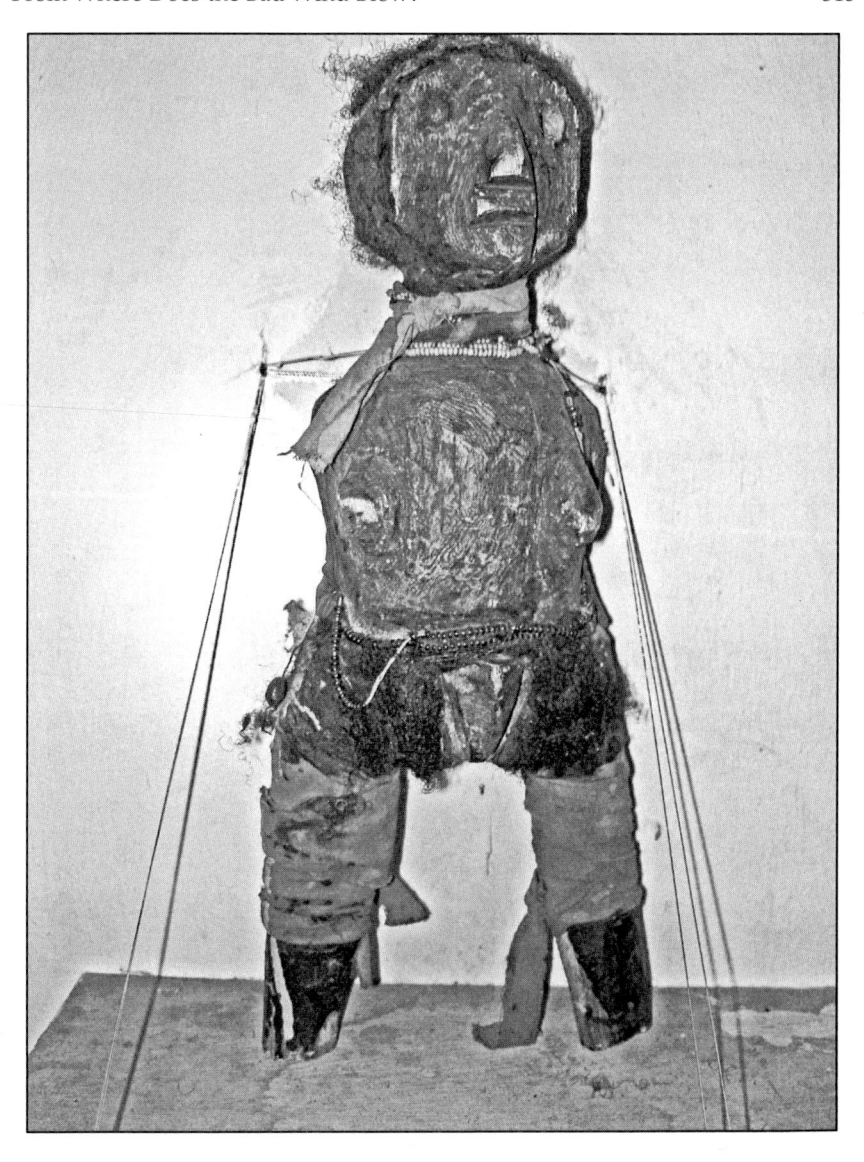

17. *Chilubi,* a magical object representing a victim of witchcraft
(photo from the Lusaka National Museum)